First World War
and Army of Occupation
War Diary
France, Belgium and Germany

40 DIVISION
119 Infantry Brigade
Royal Welsh Fusiliers
19th Battalion
2 June 1916 - 15 February 1918

WO95/2607/3

The Naval & Military Press Ltd
www.nmarchive.com
Published in association with The National Archives

Published by

The Naval & Military Press Ltd

Unit 10 Ridgewood Industrial Park,

Uckfield, East Sussex,

TN22 5QE England

Tel: +44 (0) 1825 749494

www.naval-military-press.com

www.nmarchive.com

This diary has been reprinted in facsimile from the original. Any imperfections are inevitably reproduced and the quality may fall short of modern type and cartographic standards.

© **Crown Copyright**
Images reproduced by permission of The National Archives, London, England, 2015.

Contents

Document type	Place/Title	Date From	Date To
Heading	3		
Heading	40th Division 119th Infy Bde 19th Roy. Welsh Fus. Jun 1916-Feb 1918.		
War Diary	Le Havre	02/06/1916	02/06/1916
War Diary	Lillers	03/06/1916	03/06/1916
War Diary	Bourecq	04/06/1916	08/06/1916
War Diary	Houchin	09/06/1916	09/06/1916
War Diary	Calonne	10/06/1916	10/06/1916
War Diary	Houchin	14/06/1916	17/06/1916
War Diary	Calonne	18/06/1916	20/06/1916
War Diary	Houchin	21/06/1916	21/06/1916
War Diary	Marles	22/06/1916	30/06/1916
Operation(al) Order(s)	3rd Brigade Operation Order No. 89.	13/06/1916	13/06/1916
Operation(al) Order(s)	3rd Brigade Order No. 90.	17/06/1916	17/06/1916
Operation(al) Order(s)	3rd Brigade Order No. 92.	20/06/1916	20/06/1916
Operation(al) Order(s)	3rd Brigade Order No. 93.	20/06/1916	20/06/1916
Miscellaneous			
War Diary	Marles-Les-Mines	01/07/1916	04/07/1916
War Diary	Bully Grenay	07/07/1916	10/07/1916
War Diary	Calonne	11/07/1916	22/07/1916
War Diary	Les Brebis	23/07/1916	31/07/1916
Operation(al) Order(s)	119th Brigade Order No. 3. Appendix-A	02/07/1916	02/07/1916
Operation(al) Order(s)	119th Brigade Order No. 4.	03/07/1916	03/07/1916
Miscellaneous			
Operation(al) Order(s)	119th Brigade Order No. 5.	06/07/1916	06/07/1916
Operation(al) Order(s)	119th Brigade Order No. 6. 10th July, 1916.	10/07/1916	10/07/1916
Operation(al) Order(s)	119th Brigade Order No. 7. 14th July 1916.	14/07/1916	14/07/1916
Operation(al) Order(s)	119th Brigade Order No. 9. 18th July, 1916.	18/07/1916	18/07/1916
Operation(al) Order(s)	119th Brigade Order No. 10. 20th July 1916.	20/07/1916	20/07/1916
Miscellaneous	Amendments To 119th Brigade Order No 10 Dated 20th July 1916	20/07/1916	20/07/1916
Operation(al) Order(s)	119th Brigade Order No 11 28th July 1916	28/07/1916	28/07/1916
Operation(al) Order(s)	Operation Order. No 5. Appendix B	03/07/1916	03/07/1916
Operation(al) Order(s)	Operation Order. No 6.	10/07/1916	10/07/1916
Operation(al) Order(s)	Operation Order No 7.	29/07/1916	29/07/1916
Operation(al) Order(s)	Operation Orders No 5. by Lieut Col. W.C. Newton Cmdg. 13th Bn. East Surrey Regt. Calonne	29/07/1916	29/07/1916
Miscellaneous	Progress Report. No I Appendix C		
Operation(al) Order(s)	Operation Orders No 5. by Lieut Col. W.C. Newton. Cmdg 13th Bn. East Surrey Regt. Calonne	29/07/1916	29/07/1916
Miscellaneous	Progress Report No I Appendix C	05/07/1916	05/07/1916
Miscellaneous	Progress Report No. 2.	06/07/1916	06/07/1916
Miscellaneous	Tactical Progress Report. No. 3.	07/07/1916	07/07/1916
Miscellaneous	Tactical Progress Report No. 4.		
Miscellaneous	Operation Report No. 6.	12/07/1916	12/07/1916
Miscellaneous	Report on Information & Work done. No. 7.	12/07/1916	12/07/1916
Miscellaneous	Operation Report. No. 8.		
Miscellaneous	Information Work done. No. 9.		
Miscellaneous	Operation Report. No. 10.	14/07/1916	14/07/1916
Miscellaneous	Information Work done. No. 11.	14/07/1916	14/07/1916

Miscellaneous	Operation Report No. 12.		
Miscellaneous	Report on Information & Work done. No 13.	15/07/1916	15/07/1916
Miscellaneous	Information & Work done. No 14.	17/07/1916	17/07/1916
Miscellaneous	Information & Work done. No 15.	15/07/1916	15/07/1916
Miscellaneous	Report No 16.	19/07/1916	19/07/1916
Miscellaneous	Daily Progress Report No. 17.	20/06/1916	20/06/1916
Miscellaneous	Daily Progress Report No. 18.	21/07/1916	21/07/1916
Miscellaneous	Daily Progress Report No. 19	22/07/1916	22/07/1916
Miscellaneous	Daily Report Operations		
Miscellaneous	Daily Report Operations Aug. 1st 1916		
War Diary	Calonne	01/08/1916	16/08/1916
War Diary	Petit Sains	16/08/1916	20/08/1916
War Diary	Les Brebis	24/08/1916	28/08/1916
War Diary	Loos	29/08/1916	31/08/1916
Operation(al) Order(s)	119th Brigade Order No 12	06/08/1916	06/08/1916
Operation(al) Order(s)	Operation Orders. No.	06/08/1916	06/08/1916
Miscellaneous	Operation Orders.	09/08/1916	09/08/1916
Operation(al) Order(s)	119th Brigade Order No 15.	17/08/1916	17/08/1916
Miscellaneous	Operation Orders. 12-8-16.	12/08/1916	12/08/1916
Operation(al) Order(s)	119th Brigade Order No 16	14/08/1916	14/08/1916
Miscellaneous	Operation Orders By Lieut Col B.J. Jones. D.S.O. Commanding 19th Battn R.W. Fusrs.	15/08/1916	15/08/1916
Operation(al) Order(s)	119th Brigade Order No 17	23/08/1916	23/08/1916
Miscellaneous	Operation Orders by Lt Col B. J. Jones D.S.O. Commdg. 19th Battn Royal Welsh Fusiliers	27/08/1916	27/08/1916
Miscellaneous	Daily Report Operations	02/08/1916	02/08/1916
Miscellaneous	Daily Report Operations	03/08/1916	03/08/1916
Miscellaneous	Daily Report Operations	04/08/1916	04/08/1916
Miscellaneous	Daily Report Operations	05/08/1916	05/08/1916
Miscellaneous	Daily Operations	06/08/1916	06/08/1916
Miscellaneous	Daily Report Operations	07/08/1916	07/08/1916
Miscellaneous	Daily Report Operations	08/08/1916	08/08/1916
Miscellaneous	Daily Report Operations	09/08/1916	09/08/1916
Miscellaneous	Daily Report Operations	10/08/1916	10/08/1916
Miscellaneous	Operations Aug 14th	14/08/1916	14/08/1916
Miscellaneous	Operation Report Aug 15th	15/08/1916	15/08/1916
Miscellaneous	Daily Operation Report Aug. 29th	29/08/1916	29/08/1916
Miscellaneous	Operation Report	30/08/1916	30/08/1916
Miscellaneous	To:- Adjutant Warrior Report on Enemy Trenches from noon 20/8/16 to noon 30/8/16	30/08/1916	30/08/1916
Miscellaneous	Operation Report date. August 31st.	31/08/1916	31/08/1916
Miscellaneous	Information Aug 1st 1916.	01/08/1916	01/08/1916
Miscellaneous	Daily Report-Information. 2/8/16.	02/08/1916	02/08/1916
Miscellaneous	Information	03/08/1916	03/08/1916
Miscellaneous	Information		
Miscellaneous	Information	05/08/1916	05/08/1916
Miscellaneous	Information	06/08/1916	06/08/1916
Miscellaneous	Information	07/08/1916	07/08/1916
Miscellaneous	Information	08/08/1916	08/08/1916
Miscellaneous	Daily Report-Information	09/08/1916	09/08/1916
Miscellaneous	Information	10/08/1916	10/08/1916
Heading	19 R W F Vol 4 Sep 16		
Miscellaneous	On His Majesty's Service. 53rd Mobile Vehy Section Office To A.Gs Office Base		
War Diary	Loos	01/09/1916	05/09/1916
War Diary	Petit-Sains	11/09/1916	11/09/1916

War Diary	Maroc	19/09/1916	26/09/1916
Operation(al) Order(s)	119th Brigade Order No 19.	31/08/1916	31/08/1916
Miscellaneous	Operation Orders by Lt Col. B. J. Jones D.S.O. Commdg 19th Batt. R.W.F. 22.	31/08/1916	31/08/1916
Miscellaneous	Operation Orders by Lt Col B. J. Jones D.S.O. Commdg. 19 R.W.F. 23		
Operation(al) Order(s)	119th Brigade Order No. 21.	05/09/1916	05/09/1916
Operation(al) Order(s)	119th Brigade Order No 22.	09/09/1916	09/09/1916
Miscellaneous	Table to accompany. 119th Brigade Order No 22		
Miscellaneous	Operation Orders by Lt Col B. J. Jones D.S.O. Commdg. 19 Battn. R.W.F. 24	10/09/1916	10/09/1916
Miscellaneous	A Form. Messages And Signals.		
Operation(al) Order(s)	119th Brigade Order No. 23	17/09/1916	17/09/1916
Miscellaneous	Operation Orders by Lt. Col. B. J. Jones D.S.O. Commdg. 19th Batt. R.W.F.	18/09/1916	18/09/1916
Operation(al) Order(s)	119th Brigade Order No. 24.	22/09/1916	22/09/1916
Operation(al) Order(s)	Operation Orders by Lt. Col. B. J. Jones D.S.O. Commanding 19th. Batt. R.W.F. 26	22/09/1916	22/09/1916
Operation(al) Order(s)	119th Brigade Order No 25	25/09/1916	25/09/1916
Miscellaneous	Operation Orders by Major A.O. Vaughan Commdg 19th Batt. R.W.F. 27	26/09/1916	26/09/1916
Miscellaneous	Operations Report. Sept 7th 1916.	07/09/1916	07/09/1916
Miscellaneous	Report on enemy (Rt Bn. R. Loos Sector), from noon 6/9/16 to noon 7/9/16	07/09/1916	07/09/1916
Miscellaneous	Operations Report. Sept. 8th 1916	08/09/1916	08/09/1916
Miscellaneous		08/09/1916	08/09/1916
Miscellaneous	Report on Enemy Trenches from noon 7/9/16 to noon 8/9/16.	08/09/1916	08/09/1916
Miscellaneous	Operations Report. Sept 9th 1916	09/09/1916	09/09/1916
Miscellaneous		09/09/1916	09/09/1916
Miscellaneous			
Miscellaneous	Report on Enemy trenches Loos 8/9/16 to Noon 9/9/16 Loos (Rt Battr.) Sector		
Miscellaneous	Operation Report	10/09/1916	10/09/1916
Miscellaneous	A Form. Messages And Signals.		
Miscellaneous	Report on enemy trenches noon 9/9/16 to noon 10/9/16 Loos Sector Rt Battn.	10/09/1916	10/09/1916
Miscellaneous	Operations Report Sept 11th 1916.	11/09/1916	11/09/1916
Miscellaneous	Report on Enemy trenches noon 10/9/16 to noon 11/9/16. Loos. Sector Right	11/09/1916	11/09/1916
Miscellaneous	Report on Enemy trenches. noon 19/9/16 to noon 20/9/16 "Maroc."	20/09/1916	20/09/1916
Miscellaneous	Report on Enemy trenches noon 20/9/16 to noon 21/9/16 Maroc.	21/09/1916	21/09/1916
Miscellaneous	Report on Enemy trenches noon 21/9/16 to noon 22/9/16 Maroc.		
Miscellaneous	Report on enemy trenches noon 22/9/16 to noon 23/9/16 'Maroc'	23/09/1916	23/09/1916
Miscellaneous	Report on Enemy trenches noon 23/9/16 to noon 24/9/16 "Maroc."	24/09/1916	24/09/1916
Miscellaneous	Report on Enemy trenches noon 24/9/16 to noon 25/9/16 Maroc.	25/09/1916	25/09/1916
Miscellaneous	Report on Enemy trenches noon 25/9/16 to noon 26/9/16 "Maroc"	26/09/1916	26/09/1916
Miscellaneous	Report on Enemy trenches noon 26/9/16 to noon 27/9/16 "Maroc"	27/09/1916	27/09/1916

Miscellaneous	Operations Report. Sept 28th 1916.	28/09/1916	28/09/1916
Miscellaneous	Report on Enemy trenches noon 27/9/16 to noon 28/9/16 "Maroc"	28/09/1916	28/09/1916
Miscellaneous	Operation Report. Sept 29th 1916	29/09/1916	29/09/1916
Miscellaneous	Report on enemy trenches noon 28/9/16 to noon 29/9/16 "Maroc".	29/09/1916	29/09/1916
Miscellaneous	Operation Report. Sept 30th 1916	30/09/1916	30/09/1916
Miscellaneous		30/09/1916	30/09/1916
Miscellaneous	Report on Enemy trenches noon 29/9/16 to 30/9/16 "Maroc."		
Miscellaneous	On His Majesty's Service. D.A.G.		
Heading	19 R.W.F Vol 5 Oct 16		
Operation(al) Order(s)	119th Brigade Order No 26.	29/09/1916	29/09/1916
Miscellaneous	O.C. 18th Welsh. O.C. 224th Coy. R.E. O.C. Right Group Artillery Brigade Bomb Officer O.C. 40th Division. Artillery O.C. 119th M.G. Coy. "G" 40th Division. O.C. 119th T.M.B. H.Q. 121st Brigade. S.O. for T.Ms. O.C. 19th R.W.F. Office.	29/09/1916	29/09/1916
Operation(al) Order(s)	119th Brigade Order No. 27.	03/10/1916	03/10/1916
Operation(al) Order(s)	119th Brigade Order No. 28.	08/10/1916	08/10/1916
Operation(al) Order(s)	119th Brigade Order No. 29.	09/10/1916	09/10/1916
Miscellaneous			
Operation(al) Order(s)	Supplement to 119th Brigade Order No 29.	10/10/1916	10/10/1916
Operation(al) Order(s)	119th Brigade Order No 30	14/10/1916	14/10/1916
Operation(al) Order(s)	119th Brigade Order No. 31.	18/10/1916	18/10/1916
Operation(al) Order(s)	119th Brigade Order No. 34.	22/10/1916	22/10/1916
Operation(al) Order(s)	119th Brigade Order No 35.	24/10/1916	24/10/1916
Miscellaneous			
Miscellaneous	March Table to Accompany 119th Brigade Order No. 36		
Operation(al) Order(s)	119th Brigade Order No. 36	28/10/1916	28/10/1916
Miscellaneous	Operation Orders by Capt J.H.R. Downes-Powell Commanding 19th Batt R.W. Fus.	01/10/1916	01/10/1916
Miscellaneous	Operation Orders by Capt J.H.R. Downes-Powell Commdg 19th Bn. R.W.F.	08/10/1916	08/10/1916
Miscellaneous	Operation Orders by. Lt. Col B. J. Jones. D.S.O. Commanding 19th Batt. R.W.F. No. 30	11/10/1916	11/10/1916
Miscellaneous	O.C. A Coy.	15/10/1916	15/10/1916
Miscellaneous	Operation Orders by Lt. Col. B.J. Jones. D.S.O. Commanding 19th Battn. Royal Welsh Fusiliers.	19/10/1916	19/10/1916
Miscellaneous	Operation Orders by Capt. J.H.R. Downes. Powell Commdg 19th Bn. R.W.F.	08/10/1916	08/10/1916
Miscellaneous	Operation Orders by Ltd Col B.J. Jones D.S.O. Commdg 19th (S) Bn R.W.F.	24/10/1916	24/10/1916
Miscellaneous	Operation Orders by Lt Colonel B. J. Jones D.S.O. Commanding 19th Bn Royal Welsh Fusiliers	27/10/1916	27/10/1916
Miscellaneous	On His Majesty's Service. A.G's. Office Base		
Heading	19 R W F Vol 6 Nov 16		
Miscellaneous	Operation Report Oct 1st 1916.	01/10/1916	01/10/1916
War Diary	Maroc	01/10/1916	29/10/1916
Miscellaneous	Report on Enemy trenches. noon 30/9/16 to noon 31/10/16 "Maroc"	01/10/1916	01/10/1916
Miscellaneous	Operation Report Oct 2nd 1916	02/10/1916	02/10/1916
Miscellaneous	Report on enemy trenches noon 1/10/16 to noon 2nd/10/16 "Maroc"	02/10/1916	02/10/1916

Miscellaneous	Report on Enemy trenches noon 2/10/16 to noon 3/10/16	03/10/1916	03/10/1916
Miscellaneous	Operation Report Oct 3rd. 1916.	03/10/1916	03/10/1916
Miscellaneous	Operation Report. Oct 4th 1916.	04/10/1916	04/10/1916
Miscellaneous	Report on Enemy trenches noon 3/10/16 to noon 4/10/16 "Maroc".	04/10/1916	04/10/1916
Miscellaneous	Operations Report Oct 5th 1916.	05/10/1916	05/10/1916
Miscellaneous	Report on enemy trenches noon 4/10/16 to noon 5/10/16 Maroc.	05/10/1916	05/10/1916
Miscellaneous	Report on enemy trenches noon 5/10/16 to noon 6/10/16 "Maroc."	06/10/1916	06/10/1916
Miscellaneous	Report on enemy trenches noon 6/10/16 to noon 7/10/16 "Maroc."	08/10/1916	08/10/1916
Miscellaneous	Report on enemy trenches noon 7/10/16 to noon 8/10/16 "Maroc."	07/10/1916	07/10/1916
Miscellaneous	Report on enemy trenches noon 8/10/16 to noon 9/10/16 "Maroc."	09/10/1916	09/10/1916
Miscellaneous	Report on Enemy trenches noon 12/10/16 to noon 13/10/16 Loos.	13/10/1916	13/10/1916
Miscellaneous	Operation Report. Oct 13th 1916.	13/10/1916	13/10/1916
Miscellaneous	Report on enemy trenches noon 13/10/16 to noon 11/10/16 Loos	14/10/1916	14/10/1916
Miscellaneous	Street Label	14/10/1916	14/10/1916
Miscellaneous	Report on enemy trenches noon 14/10/16 to noon 15/10/16 Loos.		
Miscellaneous	Operation Report	14/10/1916	14/10/1916
Miscellaneous		15/10/1916	15/10/1916
Miscellaneous	Operation Report	15/10/1916	15/10/1916
Miscellaneous	Report on enemy trenches noon 15/10/16 to noon 16/10/16 Loos.	16/10/1916	16/10/1916
Miscellaneous	Operation Report Oct 16th 1916.	16/10/1916	16/10/1916
Miscellaneous	Report on enemy trenches noon 16/10/16 to noon 17/10/16 Loos.	17/10/1916	17/10/1916
Miscellaneous	Operation Reports.		
Miscellaneous	Report on Enemy trenches noon 17/10/16 to noon 18/10/16 Loos.	18/10/1916	18/10/1916
Miscellaneous			
Miscellaneous	Report on Enemy trenches noon 18/10/16 to noon 19/10/16 Loos.	19/10/1916	19/10/1916
Miscellaneous	Operation Report		
Miscellaneous	Report on Enemy trenches noon 19/10/16 to noon 20/10/16 Loos.	20/10/1916	20/10/1916
Miscellaneous	Operation Report		
Miscellaneous	Report on enemy trenches noon 22/10/16 to noon 23/10/16 Loos. & Maroc.	23/10/1916	23/10/1916
War Diary	Petit Sains	31/10/1916	30/11/1916
Operation(al) Order(s)	119th Brigade Order No. 36	28/10/1916	28/10/1916
Miscellaneous	March Table to Accompany 119th Brigade Order No. 36		
Miscellaneous	Operation Orders by Lt. Col B.J. Jones Commdg 19th Batt. R.W.F.		
Operation(al) Order(s)	119th Brigade Order No. 37	31/10/1916	31/10/1916
Miscellaneous	Operation Orders By Lt Colonel B. J. Jones D.S.O. Commanding 19th Bn Royal Welsh Fusiliers	31/10/1916	31/10/1916
Operation(al) Order(s)	119th Brigade Order No. 38	01/11/1916	01/11/1916

Miscellaneous	Operation Orders by Lt Col B. J. Jones D.S.O. Commdg 19th Bn. R.W. Fus.	01/11/1916	01/11/1916
Operation(al) Order(s)	119th Brigade Order No 39.	03/11/1916	03/11/1916
Miscellaneous	Operation Orders By Lt. Colonel B.J. Jones D.S.O. Commdg. 19th Battn. Royal Welsh Fus.	03/10/1916	03/10/1916
Operation(al) Order(s)	119th Brigade Order No. 40	04/11/1916	04/11/1916
Miscellaneous	Operation Orders By Lt. Colonel B.J. Jones D.S.O. Commanding 19th Bn Royal Welsh Fus.	04/11/1916	04/11/1916
Operation(al) Order(s)	119th Brigade Order No. 41	14/11/1916	14/11/1916
Miscellaneous	Operation Orders. by Lt. Col. B.J. Jones D.S.O. Commdg. 19th Batt. R.W.F.	15/11/1916	15/11/1916
Operation(al) Order(s)	119th Brigade Order No 42.	16/11/1916	16/11/1916
Miscellaneous	Operation Orders by Lt. Col. B. J. Jones D.S.O. Commanding 19th Batt. R.W.F.	16/11/1916	16/11/1916
Operation(al) Order(s)	119th Brigade Order No 43.	17/11/1916	17/11/1916
Miscellaneous			
Miscellaneous	Operation Orders by Lt. Col. B.J. Jones D.S.O. Commdg. 19th Batt. R.W.F.	17/11/1916	17/11/1916
Miscellaneous	Offence Report (Field Service only).		
Miscellaneous	O.C. 19th R.W.F. 119th T.M.B. 12th S.W.B. No. 2. Coy. A.S.C. 17th Welsh 136th Field Ambulance. 18th Welsh. H.Q. 40th Division (Q) 119th M.G. Coy.	18/11/1916	18/11/1916
Miscellaneous	Operation Orders by Lt Colonel B.J. Jones D.S.O. Commdg. 19th Bn Royal Welsh Fusiliers	18/11/1916	18/11/1916
Operation(al) Order(s)	119th Brigade Order No. 44	21/11/1916	21/11/1916
Miscellaneous	March Table		
Miscellaneous	O.C. 19th R.W.F. 136th Field Ambulance. 12th S.W.B. H.Q. 40th Division. "G" 17th Welsh. H.Q. 40th Division. "Q" 18th Welsh. War Diary. 119th M.G. Coy. Brigade Major. 119th T.M.B. Staff Captain. No. 2. Coy. A.S.C. O.C. Signals.	21/11/1916	21/11/1916
Miscellaneous	Operation Orders by Lt Colonel B.J. Jones D.S.O. Commdg 19th Battn Royal Welsh Fus	21/11/1916	21/11/1916
Operation(al) Order(s)	119th Brigade Order No. 45	22/11/1916	22/11/1916
Miscellaneous	March Table.		
Miscellaneous	Billeting	22/11/1916	22/11/1916
Miscellaneous	Operation Orders by Lt Col B.J. Jones D.S.O. Commdg 19th Battn Royal Welsh Fus		
Operation(al) Order(s)	119th Brigade Order No. 46	23/11/1916	23/11/1916
Miscellaneous	Allotment Of Billets In 119th Brigade Area.	23/11/1916	23/11/1916
Miscellaneous	March Table		
Miscellaneous	Operation Orders by Lt Col. B.J. Jones D.S.O. Commdg 19th Bn Royal Welsh Fus.	23/11/1916	23/11/1916
Operation(al) Order(s)	119th Brigade Order No. 50.	07/12/1916	07/12/1916
Miscellaneous	O.C. 19th R.W.F. O.C. No 2 Coy. A.S.C. O.C. 12th S.W.B. Signals. O.C. 17th Welsh. H.Q. 40th Division (G) O.C. 18th Welsh. H.Q. 40th Division (Q) O.C. 119th M.G. Coy. War Diary. O.C. 119th T.M.B. Brigade Major. O.C. 136th Field Amb. Staff Captain.	07/12/1916	07/12/1916
Operation(al) Order(s)	119th Brigade Order No. 51	09/12/1916	09/12/1916
Miscellaneous	Schedule To Accompany 119th Brigade Order No. 51.		
Operation(al) Order(s)	119th Infantry Brigade Order No. 52	24/12/1916	24/12/1916
Miscellaneous	March Table To Accompany 119th Infantry Brigade Order No. 52		
Miscellaneous	Amendment To 119th Brigade Order No. 52	25/12/1916	25/12/1916
Operation(al) Order(s)	119th Brigade Order No. 53	25/12/1916	25/12/1916

Miscellaneous	Table Of Relief To Accompany 119th Brigade Order No. 53		
Operation(al) Order(s)	119th Brigade Order No. 54.	29/12/1916	29/12/1916
Miscellaneous	1. 25 HR		
Miscellaneous	Operation Orders by Lt Colonel B.J. Jones D.S.O. Commdg. 19th Bn Royal Welsh Fus	07/12/1916	07/12/1916
Miscellaneous	Operation Orders by Lt Colonel B.J. Jones D.S.O. Commdg. 19th Bn Royal Welsh Fus.	09/12/1916	09/12/1916
Miscellaneous	Operation Orders by Lt Colonel B.J. Jones D.S.O. Commdg. 19th Bn Royal Welsh Fusiliers	20/12/1916	20/12/1916
Miscellaneous	Operation Orders by Lt Colonel B.J. Jones D.S.O. Commdg. 19th Bn Royal Welsh Fus	30/12/1916	30/12/1916
War Diary	Bellancourt	01/12/1916	31/12/1916
War Diary	Rancourt	01/01/1917	13/01/1917
War Diary	Boochauesnes North	13/01/1917	19/01/1917
War Diary	Rancourt	22/01/1917	26/01/1917
War Diary	Albany Camp 12.	27/01/1917	29/01/1917
War Diary	Bois Celestines	01/02/1917	13/02/1917
War Diary	Rancourt	13/02/1917	16/02/1917
War Diary	Maurepas	16/02/1917	19/02/1917
War Diary	Rancourt	19/02/1917	23/02/1917
War Diary	Camp. 21.	23/02/1917	23/02/1917
War Diary	Bray	24/02/1917	28/02/1917
Miscellaneous	Headquarters 119th Inf Bde Herewith War Diary.	02/04/1917	02/04/1917
War Diary	Bray	01/03/1917	06/03/1917
War Diary	Camp 19	08/03/1917	08/03/1917
War Diary	Clery	09/03/1917	15/03/1917
War Diary	Curlu	15/03/1917	16/03/1917
War Diary	Suzanne Curlu	16/03/1917	24/03/1917
War Diary	Suzanne	20/03/1917	31/03/1917
War Diary	Road Wood	01/04/1917	06/04/1917
War Diary	Etricourt	07/04/1917	16/04/1917
War Diary	Gouzeaucourt	17/04/1917	30/04/1917
War Diary	R14. Central Gouzeaucourt	30/04/1917	08/05/1917
War Diary	Dessart Wood	08/05/1917	14/05/1917
War Diary	Gouzeaucourt	14/05/1917	31/05/1917
War Diary	Dessart Wood	01/06/1917	30/06/1917
War Diary	Bde Support W 9.d.8.7.	01/07/1917	06/07/1917
War Diary	Bde Reserve	06/07/1917	31/07/1917
Heading	War Diary 19th (S) Btn. Royal Welsh Fusiliers. August 1917.		
War Diary	Connelieu	01/08/1917	06/08/1917
War Diary	Villers Plouich Sector	06/08/1917	31/08/1917
War Diary		11/08/1917	31/08/1917
Heading	War Diary 19th (S) Bn. Royal Welsh Fusiliers. September 1917		
War Diary	Gonnelieu Sector	01/09/1917	07/09/1917
War Diary	Centre Brigade (Rt. Subsector)	07/09/1917	01/10/1917
Heading	War Diary 19th (S) Bn. Royal Welch Fusiliers October 1917		
War Diary	Brigade Reserve	01/10/1917	07/10/1917
War Diary	Heudecourt	07/10/1917	08/10/1917
War Diary	Doingt	08/10/1917	09/10/1917
War Diary	Simencourt	10/10/1917	27/10/1917
War Diary	Couturelle	29/10/1917	31/10/1917

Heading	War Diary 19th (S) Bn. Royal Welsh Fusiliers November 1917		
War Diary	Couturelle	01/11/1917	15/11/1917
War Diary	Simencourt	16/11/1917	16/11/1917
War Diary	Gommiecourt	17/11/1917	17/11/1917
War Diary	Barastre	19/11/1917	19/11/1917
War Diary	Doignies	21/11/1917	21/11/1917
War Diary	Anneux	22/11/1917	23/11/1917
War Diary	Bourlon	23/11/1917	24/11/1917
War Diary	Bourlon Wood	24/11/1917	26/11/1917
War Diary	Lechelle	26/11/1917	26/11/1917
War Diary	Bienvillers	27/11/1917	30/11/1917
Heading	War Diary 19th. (S) Bn. Royal Welsh Fusiliers. Dec 1917		
War Diary	Bienvillers	02/12/1917	02/12/1917
War Diary	Bullecourt Right Sub-Sector	02/12/1917	15/12/1917
War Diary	Right Sub-Sector	15/12/1917	31/12/1917
Heading	War Diary 19th R W Fusiliers January 1918		
War Diary	Bullecourt Sector Right Sub-Sector Left Bde.	01/01/1918	16/01/1918
War Diary	Right Sub-Sector	17/01/1918	30/01/1918
Heading	War Diary February 1918 19th Royal Welsh Fusiliers		
War Diary	Bullecourt Left Bde Rt Sub-Sector	01/02/1918	03/02/1918
War Diary	Mory	06/02/1918	06/02/1918
War Diary	Bailleulval	08/02/1918	15/02/1918

40TH DIVISION
119TH INFY BDE

19TH ROY.WELSH FUS.
JUN 1916-FEB 1918.

Army Form C. 2118

WAR DIARY or INTELLIGENCE SUMMARY

19th Battalion Royal Welsh Fusiliers.

(Erase heading not required.)

Instructions regarding War Diaries and Intelligence Summaries are contained in F.S. Regs., Part II. and the Staff Manual respectively. Title Pages will be prepared in manuscript.

Place	Date June 1916.	Hour	Summary of Events and Information	Remarks and references to Appendices
LE HAVRE	2nd		The Battalion arrived at LE HAVRE about 5.0 and after disembarking marched to No. 5 Rest Camp where it spent the night.	
"	3rd		The Battalion entrained at 5.0. and proceeded to LILLERS, arriving about 3.0. on the 4th. Thence it marched to billets in BOURECQ.	
LILLERS.	4th.			
BOURECQ.	5-8th		In billets at BOURECQ.	
BOURECQ.	9th		The battalion marched to the standing camp at HOUCHIN, 14 miles.	
HOUCHIN.	10th.		In the afternoon the Battalion marched up to the trenches (CALONNE SECTOR) for instruction. The headquarters and A and B companies were attached to the 2nd Royal Munster Fusiliers, and C and D Companies to the 1st Gloucester Regiment. The tour of duty lasted four days, during which time the enemy's artillery was fairly active though there was but little rifle or Machine gun fire. The total casualties were four men killed by shells and one man wounded by rifle or machine gun fire. During the whole four days the weather was cold and wet.	A
CALONNE.				
HOUCHIN.	14th.		The battalion returned to HOUCHIN.	
HOUCHIN	15-17		In rest camp.	
CALONNE	18th		The Battalion marched to the CALONNE trenches, the Headquarters with C and D Companies being attached to the 2nd Welsh Regiment, and A and B Companies to the 1st South Wales Borderers. The tour of duty lasted for three days. The enemy's trench mortars, machine guns and rifle grenades were active. The weather was fine. Five N.C O's and men were killed or died of wounds, nine were wounded.	B
"	19th			
"	20th.			

WAR DIARY
or
INTELLIGENCE SUMMARY

(Erase heading not required.)

Army Form C. 2118

Place	Date	Hour	Summary of Events and Information	Remarks and references to Appendices
	June 1916.			
HOUCHIN.	21st		On the 20th the 2nd Welsh and the 1st S.W.Borderers were relieved by the 2nd Gloucesters and the 2nd R.W. Fusiliers respectively. The Battalion marched to HOUCHIN after relief by the 12th S.W.Borderers.	C D
MARLES	22nd		The Battalion marched to billets in MARLES – LES – MINES.	
MARLES.	23–30		In billets. no incident.	

O.S.Flones Lt.Colonel
Comdg. 19th R. Welsh Fusiliers

SECRET.   A   Copy No. 23

3RD BRIGADE OPERATION ORDER NO. 89.

1.   The 12th Bn. SOUTH WALES BORDERERS, will arrive at BULLY GRENAY at 12 noon, tomorrow, 14th June, for attachment as follows:-
        Headquarters, A and B Companies, with 2 Lewis Guns to 1st Bn. SOUTH WALES BORDERERS.
        C and D Companies with 2 Lewis Guns to 2nd Bn. THE WELCH REGIMENT.

2.   Route will be via NOEUX LES MINES - CROSS ROADS (PETIT SAINS) R.2.b.5.8 - Road Junction L.28.c.2.4. - Road Junction L.35.a.8.0. - Railway Bridge R.5.c.5.6. - BULLY GRENAY R.5.c.9.2. (Reference Sheets 36.b. 1/40,000).
        From cross roads (PETIT SAINS) R.2.b.5.8. the Battalion will proceed by Companies at 200 yards interval.

3.   On arrival at BULLY GRENAY the Battalion will halt for dinners. The Company Cookers will thus accompany the Battalion as far as BULLY GRENAY, where instruction as to their future movement will be given.

4.   At 1.30 p.m. C and D Companies will proceed by platoons at 200 yards interval to GRENAY BRIDGE, H.1.d.8.2, where guides from 2nd Bn. THE WELCH REGIMENT will meet them.
        Headquarters, and A and B Companies will meanwhile join up with 1st Bn. SOUTH WALES BORDERERS in BULLY GRENAY.

5.   Necessary regimental transport should reach L.35.a.28 at 3 p.m., and take over standings vacated by 19th Bn. ROYAL WELSH FUSILIERS.

6.   The 19th Bn. ROYAL WELSH FUSILIERS will be withdrawn from the line tomorrow, 14th June, and will march back to billets at HOUCHIN.
        Headquarters and two Companies attached to 2nd Bn. ROYAL MUNSTER FUSILIERS will move back to BULLY GRENAY via CALONNE SOUTH, which will be reserved for them between the hours of 12 noon, and 1 p.m. Between 1 p.m. and 2 p.m. CALONNE SOUTH will be reserved for the two Companies attached to 1st Bn. GLOUCESTERSHIRE REGIMENT. Near GRENAY BRIDGE, H.1.d.8.2, guides will await them to conduct them to their halting place in BULLY GRENAY, where dinners will be prepared.

7.   At 3 p.m. (30) Officer Commanding 19th Bn. ROYAL WELSH FUSILIERS will arrange for his leading Company to move off from BULLY GRENAY, followed in succession at not less than 200 yards interval by the remaining Companies.
        Billeting parties to be sent on in advance at 1 p.m.

8.   Route will be the reverse of that shewn in para 2.

9.   The Brigade internal relief will take place tomorrow under arrangements to be made between the Commanding Officers concerned, with the exception that relieving units of 1st Bn. SOUTH WALES BORDERERS will not reach GRENAY BRIDGE before 3. p.m.

                                    D Burt Marshall   Captain,
                                    Brigade Major, 3rd Infantry Brigade.

13th June, 1916.

3rd Brigade Operation Order 89   -   Continued.

Copies to -

1. Office.
2. Office.
3. 1st Bn. South Wales Borderers.
4. 1st Bn. Gloucestershire Regt.
5. 2nd Bn. Welch Regiment.
6. 2nd Bn. Royal Munster Fusiliers.
7. Staff Captain.
8. Brigade Transport Officer.
9. Brigade Scout Officer.
10. Signals.
11. Right Group Artillery.
12. 1st Division.
13. Supply Officer 3rd Brigade.
14. 255th Company, R.E.
15. 141st Field Ambulance
16. Q.Mr. 1st South Wales Borderers.
17. Q.Mr. 1st Gloucester Regt.
18. Q.Mr. 2nd Bn. Welch Regt.
19. Q.Mr. 2nd Royal Munster Fusiliers.
20. 23rd Field Company R.E.
21. 119th Infantry Brigade.
22. 12th South Wales Borderers.
23. 19th Royal Welsh Fusiliers.
24. 141st Infantry Brigade.

B

3RD BRIGADE ORDER NO. 90.

17th June, 1916.

1. The 19th Bn. Royal Welch Fusiliers will arrive tomorrow the 18th June, and be attached as follows :-
A and B Companies, with 2 Lewis Guns to 1st Bn. South Wales Borderers.
C and D Companies with 2 Lewis Guns to 2nd Bn. The Welch Regiment.

2. Route will be via NOEUX LES MINES - cross roads R.2.b.4.8, - road junction L.28.c.2.4, - road junction L.35.a.8.0 - railway bridge R.5.c.5.6 (Reference sheet 36.b. 1/40,000.). From cross roads R.2.b.4.8, the Battalion will proceed by Companies at 200 yards intervals.

3. The Battalion will reach the ABATTOIR, R.5.a.5.7, at 1.0 p.m, when a halt will be made for dinners. The Company cookers will here receive instructions as to their future movements.

4. At 2.30 p.m. Headquarters, C and D Companies, followed in succession by A and B Companies, will proceed by platoons at 200 yards intervals to GRENAY BRIDGE, M.1.d.8.2, where guides from 2nd Bn. The Welch Regiment and 1st Bn. South Wales Borderers will meet them.

5. Necessary Regimental Transport should reach L.35.a.2.2 at 3.0 p.m., and take over standings vacated by 12th Bn. South Wales Borderers.

6. The 12th Bn. South Wales Borderers will be withdrawn from the line, tomorrow, 18th June, and will march back to billets at HOUCHIN.
The two Companies attached to the 2nd Bn. Welch Regiment, will move back to BULLY GRENAY via CALONNE SOUTH, which will be reserved for them between the hours of 12.0 noon, and 1.0 p.m. Between 1.0 p.m. and 2.p.m. CALONNE SOUTH will be reserved for Headquarters, and the two Companies attached to 1st Bn. South Wales Borderers. Near GRENAY BRIDGE, M.1.d.8.2, guides will await them to conduct them to their halting place in BULLY GRENAY, where dinners will be prepared.

7. At 3.30 p.m. O.C.,12th South Wales Borderers will arrange for his leading Company to move off from BULLY GRENAY, followed in succession at not less than 200 yards intervals by the remaining Companies.
Billeting parties to be sent in advance at 1.0 p.m.

8. Route will be the reverse of that shewn in par. 2.

D.Burt Marshall, Captain,
Brigade Major, 3rd Infantry Bde.

3rd Brigade Order No. 90.   Continued.

Issued to -

1. Office.
2. Office.
3. 1st Bn. South Wales Borderers.
4. 1st Bn. Gloucestershire Regt.
5. 2nd Bn. Welch Regiment.
6. 2nd Bn. Royal Munster Fusiliers.
7. Staff Captain.
8. Brigade Transport Officer.
9. Brigade Scout Officer.
10. Signals.
11. Right Group Artillery.
12. 1st Division.
13. Supply Officer, 3rd Brigade.
14. 255th Company, R.E.
15. 141st Field Ambulance.
16. Qr.Mr. 1st South Wales Borderers.
17.   ,,   1st Gloucester Regt.
18.   ,,   2nd Welch Regt.
19.   ,,   2nd Royal Munster Fusiliers.
20. 23rd Field Company, R.E.
21. 119th Infantry Brigade.
22. 12th South Wales Borderers.
23. 19th Royal Welch Fusiliers.
24. 141st Infantry Brigade.
25. 2nd Brigade.

SECRET.   3RD BRIGADE ORDER NO. 92.   C   Copy No. 23

(Reference Sheet 36.b. 1/40,000).

1. The 12th Bn. South Wales Borderers will relieve 19th Bn. Royal Welsh Fusiliers in the CALONNE SECTION tomorrow, 21st June, 1916. They will arrive at the ABATTOIR, R.5.a.5.7, from HOUCHIN, at 12.0 noon, tomorrow, where a halt will be made for dinners. Company Cookers will here receive orders for their further movement.

2. Route will be via NOEUX LES MINES — cross roads R.2.b.4.8 — road junction L.28.c.2.4 — road junction L.35.a.8.0 — railway bridge R.5.c.5.6. From cross roads R.2.b.4.8, the Battalion will proceed by Companies at 200 yards interval.

3. At 1.0 p.m. Headquarters, C and D Companies, will proceed by platoons at 200 yards interval, to GRENAY BRIDGE M.1.d.8.2, where guides from Headquarters, C and D Companies, 19th Bn. Royal Welsh Fusiliers, will meet them.
Similarly A and B Companies will follow D Company, and be met by guides from A and B Companies, 19th Bn. Royal Welsh Fusiliers.

4. Necessary Regimental Transport will reach L.35.a.2.2, at 3.0 p.m. and take over standing vacated by 19th Bn. Royal Welsh Fusiliers.

5. On relief, platoons of 19th Bn. Royal Welsh Fusiliers will move back via CALONNE SOUTH, to GRANDE PLACE, BULLY GRENAY, R.5.c.8.2, where they will come under orders of 119th Brigade.

6. Relief to be reported to 3rd Brigade Headquarters.

D. Burt-Marshall, Captain,
Brigade Major, 3rd Infantry Brigade.

20th June, 1916.

Copies to —
1. Office.
2. ,,
3. 1st South Wales Borderers.
4. 1st Bn. Gloucester Regt.
5. 2nd Bn. Welch Regt.
6. 2nd Bn. R. Munster Fusiliers.
7. Staff Captain.
8. Brigade Transport Officer.
9. Brigade Scout Officer.
10. Signals.
11. Right Group.
12. 1st Division.
13. Supply Officer 3rd Brigade.
14. 255th Tunnelling Coy. R.E.
15. 141st Field Ambulance.
16. Qr.Mr. 1st South Wales Bords.
17. ,,   1st Gloucester Regt.
18. 2nd Bn. Welch Regt. Qr.Mr.
19. Qr.Mr. 2nd R. Munster Fus.
20. 23rd Field Coy. R.E.
21. 119th Infantry Brigade.
22. 12th South Wales Bords.
23. 19th Royal Welsh Fus.
24. 141st Infantry Brigade.
25. 2nd Infantry Brigade.
26. 1st Infantry Brigade.
27. 3rd Company M.G. Corps.
28. 3/1 Trench Mortar Bty.

Copy No. 28

D

3RD BRIGADE ORDER NO. 93.

1. The 3rd Infantry Brigade, less 12th Bn. South Wales Borderers, will be relieved by 1st Infantry Brigade in the CALONNE SECTION on 22nd June, 1916, in accordance with table overleaf., details to be arranged between Commanding Officers concerned.

   On relief, the 3rd Infantry Brigade will come into Divisional Reserve. Battalions at LES BREBIS will be at 1 hour's notice, and the Battalion at PETIT SAINS at 2 hours' notice.

2. The 12th Battalion, South Wales Borderers will remain in the line, and come under the orders of G.O.C, 1st Infantry Brigade.

3. No. 3 Company, Machine Gun Corps will be relieved by No. 1 Company, Machine Gun Corps on 23rd June, 1916, under arrangements to be made between Commanding Officers concerned.

4. The 3/1 Trench Mortar Battery will be relieved by the 1/1 Trench Mortar Battery on 22nd June, 1916, under arrangements to be made between Commanding Officers concerned.

   Z/1 Trench Mortar Battery, and 4 French Mortars will remain in the line, and come under the orders of G.O.C, 1st Infantry Brigade.

5. Completion of relief to be reported to 3rd Infantry Brigade Headquarters.

20th June, 1916.

S Burt-Marshall Captain,
Brigade Major, 3rd Infantry Brigade.

Issued to-
1. 1st Bn. South Wales Borderers.
2. 1st Bn. Gloucestershire Regt.
3. 2nd Welch Regt.
4. 2nd Bn. Royal Munster Fusiliers.
5. Staff Captain.
6. Brigade M.G. Company.
7. Brigade Transport Officer.
8. Brigade Scout Officer.
9. Signals.
10. Left Group Artillery.
11. Right ,, ,,
12. 1st Division G Branch.
13. 1st Division Q Branch.
14. 1st Infantry Brigade.
15. 2nd Infantry Brigade.
16. 142nd Infantry Brigade.
17. 3rd Brigade Supply Officer
18. 3/1 Trench Mortar Battery.
19. 155th Tunneling Coy. R.E.
20. 141st Field Ambulance.
21. Qr.Mr. 1st South Wales Bor
22. ,, 1st Gloucesters.
23. ,, 2nd Welch Regt.
24. ,, 2nd R. Munster Fus.
25. 23rd Field Company, R.E.
26. Captain Sparrow.
27. 119th Infantry Brigade.
28. 19th Bn. Royal Welsh Fus.
29. 12th Bn. South Wales Bord
30. Office.

Unit of 3rd Brigade.	Will be relieved by unit of 1st Brigade.	4 Guides per Company 3rd Brigade will be at	Route of 1st Bde.	Route of 3rd Bde.	Billeting parties of 1st Bde.	Billeting parties of 3rd Bde. 11.0 a.m. at
1st Gloucester Regt.	Black Watch	Railway Crossing R.6.c.7.8. near Railway Station 600 yards N.W. of GRENAY BRIDGE. M.1.d.7.3. at 3.0 p.m.	Along Railway Cutting to GRENAY BRIDGE M.1.d.7.3. thence along CALONNE NORTH (1st Bde to have free use of all BOYAUX leading out N. and E from CALONNE NORTH.	CALONNE SOUTH as far as entrance to BULLY GRENAY R.6.c.9.5 thence via Railway Bridge R.5.c.4.6 to LES BREBIS.		Headquarters Black Watch. Area. B and C LES BREBIS.
2nd Royal Munster Fusiliers.	8th Royal Berks.	ditto 4 p.m.				Headquarters 10th Glouc Regt Area. D. LES BREBIS.
1st Bn. South Wales Bords.	1st Cameron Highlanders.	ditto 5 p.m.	Road leading out N. and E from CALONNE PETIT SAINS.	Road junction R.5.a.0.0 PETIT SAINS.	Headquarters 1st South.W. Borderers CALONNE 3 p.m.	Headquarters. 8th Royal Berks Regt. PETIT SAINS.
2nd Welch Regt.	10th Gloucester Regt.	GRANDE PLACE BULLY GRENAY 5.30 p.m.	Railway Bridge. R.5.c.4.6.R.5.c.4.6.	Railway Bridge R.5.c.4.6. LES BREBIS	Hd Qrs. 2nd Welch Regt. BULLY GRENAY 3 p.m.	Headquarters 1st Camerons. Area. A. LES BREBIS. Fosse 2

Army Form C.2118

WAR DIARY
or
INTELLIGENCE SUMMARY

19th Battalion Royal Welsh Fusiliers.

(Erase heading not required.)

Instructions regarding War Diaries and Intelligence Summaries are contained in F.S. Regs., Part II. and the Staff Manual respectively. Title Pages will be prepared in manuscript.

Place	Date	Hour	Summary of Events and Information	Remarks and references to Appendices
	July 1916.			
BILLES-EN-GOHELLE	1-2.		In Billets, no incident of importance.	
	3.	4pm.	The Battalion marched to CITE LIAUTEY near BARLIN.	
	4.		The Battalion marched up to the trenches and took over the right half of the CALONNE subsector from the 1st Cameron Highlanders, having then the 22nd London Regt on the right and the 12th S.W.B. on the left. The tour lasted three days during which time much rain fell. The enemy's trench mortars were extremely active and the damage which they caused were so extensive that it was almost impossible to cope with the necessary repairs. The casualties amounted to 1 officer (Captain E Glyn Davies) 'killed and two officers (Captain E.B.Jones and 2nd Lieut T.Roberts) 'wounded; other ranks 1 'killed and 3 wounded.	
BULLY GRENAY	7.		The Battalion marched to billets after handing over to the 17th Welsh Regt.	
"	8.	2-2.7am.	The Battalion stood to arms in consequence of a reported attack but was dismissed before any other action could be taken.	
	9-10.		In billets, no incident.	
CALONNE	11th		The Battalion relieved the 17th Welsh Regt in the right half of CALONNE subsector.	
	12-15.		The enemy's trench mortars were fairly active during the tour. On the 12th he shelled the neighborhood of the Battalion headquarters in TEMPLE STREET with 5.9" guns destroying several houses. Only one man was hit. The weather during the tour was generally fine but cool. Total casualties 1 officer (Lieut Hargraves F.) 'Killed and 1 'private died of wounds.	

Army Form C. 2118

WAR DIARY
OR
INTELLIGENCE SUMMARY
(Erase heading not required.)

Instructions regarding War Diaries and Intelligence Summaries are contained in F.S. Regs., Part II. and the Staff Manual respectively. Title Pages will be prepared in manuscript.

Place	Date	Hour	Summary of Events and Information	Remarks and references to Appendices
CALONNE 15th	16-18		In the afternoon the Battalion was relieved by the 17th Welsh Regt and went into close support in CALONNE. In billets furnishing numerous working parties for the front line. No casualties.	
	19		Took over right subsector from 17th Welsh Regt.	
	20-21		On the whole a quiet tour, the enemy's trench mortars being less active than usual. Casualties 1 man slightly wounded.	
	22		Relieved by 120th Brigade. To billets in LES BREBIS.	
L'S BREBIS 23-28			In billets at LES BREBIS.	
	29	8a.m.	Relieved 120th Brigade at CALONNE.	
	30-31st		Enemy's snipers and trench mortars active. He shelled TEMPLE STREET BOYAU THOMAS, and neighborhood of MARBLE ARCH with 4.2" and 5.9" shells about 9-15 p.m. on the 31st but little damage. Casualties 2 men slightly wounded.	

Appendix A. - Brigade Operation Orders
" B - Battalion Operation Orders
" C - Daily Tactical Progress Reports.

Appendix - A.

119TH BRIGADE ORDER NO. 3.

Copy No ...4...

1. The brigade, less 17th Bn Welsh Regt, will leave its present billets at MARLES LES MINES and DIVION tomorrow and will march to billets at BARLIN in two columns as under; and in the order shown :-

    Right column (Commander, Lt. Col. R.Grant Thorold, 18th Bn Welsh Regt)
        18th Welsh Regt.
        ~~119th Trench Mortar Battery.~~ 119th. Bde. M. G. Coy.

    Left column (Commander, Major C.B.Hore, 12th Bn S.Wales Borderers)
        19th Bn R.Welsh Fusiliers.
        Brigade Band.
        12th Bn S.Wales Borderers.
        119th Trench Mortar Battery.
        Brigade Bomb School.
        Brigade Headquarters.

2. Routes will be as follows ;
    Right column ;- HOUDAIN   MAISNIL LES RUITZ.   Starting point,
        Cross roads I.24.d.9.9,   4.30 p.m.

    Left Column :- HAILLICOURT   RUITZ.   STARTING point, railway
        crossing D.25.D.   4.p.m.

3. Units will take over billets as follows :-
    Brigade Headquarters   from   H.Q. 121st Bde   at K.31.d.2.2.
    19th Bn R.W.F.   from   21st Middlesex Regt   at K.31.d.
    12th Bn S.W.B.   from   Suffolk Regt   at K.33.c.
    18th Welsh Regt   from   13th Yorks   at MAISNIL and K.31.c.
    119th B.M.G.Coy)   -----   (at BOIS DOLHAIN (cross
    Bomb School   )   roads in Q.14.b.)
    119th T.M.B.   from   -----   at 1st in OBSERVATOIRE Q.15.a.

4. Billetting parties from above 3 Battalions and 119th Brigade Machine Coy will report to the Staff Captain at Headquarters 121st Brigade (K.31.d.2.2.) at 11 a.m.

5. The 17th Bn Welsh Regt proceeded to BARLIN today. They will reach the Grand Place, BULLY GRENAY at 4 p.m. tomorrow. Their billiting parties will be at the Grand Place at 2 p.m.

6. Officers Commanding Battalions and Companies [less 17th Welsh Regt] who have not yet visited the 1st Brigade trenches today will do so tomorrow, reporting at Headquarters, 1st Brigade MINE BUILDINGS, at 2 p.m.

                        (Sgd)   A.G.Soames, Captain,
                                Brigade Major,
2-7-16.   119th Infantry Brigade.

Copy.	No.1.	War Diary.
"	No.2.	Brigade Major.
"	No.3.	Staff Captain.
"	No.4.	19th. Bn. R.W.F.
"	No.5.	12th. Bn.S.W.B.
"	No.6.	17th. Welsh Rgmt.
"	No.7.	18th. Welsh Regmt.
"	No.8.	119th. M.G. Coy.
"	No.9.	119th. T.M.Battery.
"	No.10.	Bomb School.
"	No.11.	40th Division.
"	No.12.	Camp Commandant.

SECRET.

119th Brigade Order No. 4.

Copy No ...4......

1. The 17th BN Welsh Regt came under the orders of G.O.C. 1st Brigade today.

2. The Brigade will relieve the 1st Infantry Brigade in the CALLONE Section tomorrow, in accordance with table overleaf.

3. The 119th Brigade M.G.Coy and 119th Trench Mortar Battery will relieve 1st Brigade M.G.Coy and 1st Trench Mortar Battery under mutual arrangements. These reliefs will be completed by 1 p.m. tomorrow.

4. Route will be as follows :- BARLIN - HERSIN - PETIT SAINS - road junction at L.28.c.2.5. (control posts found by 1st Infantry Bde) road junction at L.35.a.8.9.

5. All movement of troops from PETIT SAINS eastward will be by platoons at 5 minutes interval. If hostile observation balloons are up, this march formation will be adopted from HERSIN eastwards.

6. Dinners will be issued under Battalion arrangements before reaching PETIT SAINS. Teas will be issued after the relief is completed.

7. O's C units will take over fatigues and working parties from their opposite numbers.

8. Units will take over Transport lines, Quarter Master's Stores, billets etc., vacated by the units which they relieve.

9. Completion of relief to be reported to Brigade Headquarters, which will be at MINE BUILDINGS, LES BREBIS (35.a.5.3.) (Headquarters, 1st Brigade). This report will consist of the word SAUSAGE.

10. Until completion of the Brigade relief, tactical reports will be rendered to the 1st Brigade.

11. 1 Officer (preferably a Signal Officer) and 17 Battalion Signallers per Battalion will report to the Brigade Signal Officer at the MINE BUILDINGS, LES BREBIS at 10.30.a.m. to reconnoitre communications.
4 Company Signallers per Battalion will also report at the same time and place. These latter will be permanently attached to the Brigade Signal Section from tomorrow for instruction.

(Sgd) A. G. SOAMES. CAPTAIN.
BRIGADE MAJOR.
119TH INFANTRY BRIGADE.

5.7.16.

Copy No.1. War Diary.
" 2. Brigade Major.
3. Staff Captain.
4. 19th. R.W.F.
5. 12th S.W.B.
6. 17th Welsh Rgt.
7. 18th Welsh Rgt.
8. 119th Bde M.G.Coy.
9. 119th T.M.Battery.
10. Signals.
11. Intelligence.
12. 40th. Division.
13. 120th Brigade.
14. 121st Brigade.
15. 1st Brigade.
16. Bomb School.

Date	119th Brigade unit.	Will relieve 1st Bde unit.	Guides, 1st Brigade.	Billeting Parties, 119th Brigade.	Remarks.
July 2nd	17th Welsh Regt. (less M.G.Section)	Blackwatch (Reserve) BULLY GRENAY.			Came under orders of G.O.C. 1st Bde 2/6/16 until completion of relief.
4th	19th R.W.Fusiliers. (less M.G.Section)	1/Cameron Highrs (Front line)	GRAND PLACE BULLY GRENAY. 2-30 p.m.		
4th	12th S.W.Borderers. (less M.G.Section)	10th Gloucester Regt (Front line)	GRAND PLACE BULLY GRENAY. 4 p.m.		"
4th	18th Welsh Regt. (less M.G.Section)	2/Berks Regt (Support)	GRAND PLACE BULLY GRENAY. 3-30 p.m.	GRAND PLACE BULLY GRENAY. 2-30 p.m.	Billetting party will march with rear platoon, 19/R.W.F.
4th	M.G.Sections, 4 Battalions.	M.G.Sections in Front & support line.	GRENAY BRIDGE M.1.d.7.2.(Sheet 36c.) 12 noon		Will take over emplacements in trenches occupied by their own units as far as possible.

119th BRIGADE ORDER NO. 5.

6th July 1916.

1. The following Internal Reliefs will take place tomorrow, July 7th, in the CALONNE Section.

    (a) 17th Welsh Will relieve 19th R.W.F. in the right subsection.
    (b) 18th Welsh   "   "   12th S.W.B.   "   left   "
    (c) 12th S.W.B. will move into support in CALONNE.
    (d) 19th R.W.F. will move into reserve in BULLY GRENAY.

2. Reliefs will be carried out under arrangements made direct between Commanding Officers concerned, and will be completed by 7 p.m.

3. Bombing and Snipers posts will be relieved by 12 noon.

4. Completion of relief to be reported to these Headquarters.

5. All Lewis Guns will remain in the line. Personnel to man them will be found by the Officer Commanding the particular subsection, who will take over the guns and appliances from the units to which they may belong.

                                      (Sgd) A.G. Soames,   Captain,
                                              Brigade Major,
                                                 119th Brigade.

Copy No. 1. War Diary.   11. Bde T.M. Battery.
         2. Brigade Major.   12. 40th Division.
         3. Staff Captain.   13. 120th Brigade.
         4. Transport Officer.   14th 121st Brigade.
         5. Intelligence Officer.   15. Supply Officer.
         6. 19th R.W.F.   16. Bomb Officer.
         7. 12th S.W.B.   17. Signals.
         8. 17th Welsh.   18. 231st Coy R.E.
         9. 18th Welsh.   19. Right Group Artillery.
       10. Bde M.G. Coy.

119TH BRIGADE ORDER NO. 6.

10th July, 1916.

No. 1......

1. The following internal relief will take place tomorrow, July 11th, in the CALONNE Section :-

   (a) 19th R.W.F. will relieve 17th Welsh in the right subsection.
   (b) 12th S.W.B.   "   " 18th Welsh   " left   "
   (c) 17th Welsh will move into support in CALONNE.
   (d) 18th Welsh will move into reserve in BULLY GRENAY.

2. Reliefs will be carried out under arrangements made direct between Commanding Officers concerned, and will be completed by 7 p.m.

3. Bombing and Snipers posts will be relieved by 12 noon.

4. Completion of relief to be reported to these Headquarters.

5. All Lewis Guns will remain in the line. Personnel to man them will be found by the Officer Commanding the particular subsection, who will take over the guns and appliances from the units to which they may belong.

                                 (sgd) A.G.Soames, Captain,
                                      Brigade Major,
                                        119th Brigade.

Copy No. 1. O.C. 19th R.W.F.
        2. O.C. 12th S.W.B.
        3. O.C. 17th Welsh.
        4. O.C. 18th Welsh.
        5. Q.M. 19th R.W.F.
        6. Q.M. 12th S.W.B.
        7. Q.M. 17th Welsh.
        8. Q.M. 18th Welsh.
        9. 119th Bde M.G.Coy.
       10. Bde Transport Officer.
       11. " Intelligence Officer.
       12. " Supply Officer.
       13. " Signals.
       14. Bde Bomb Officer.
       15. O.C. 231st Field Coy R.E.
       16. "G" 40th Division.
       17. "Q" 40th Division.
       18. 120th Brigade.
       19. 121st Brigade.
       20. War Diary.
       21. Brigade Major.
       22. Staff Captain.
       23. O.C. Right Group Artillery
       24. 47th Division(for left Bde)
       25. 119th T.M.Battery.
       26. Divl. T.M.Officer.

119th BRIGADE ORDER NO. 7

14th July 1916.
---------------   No../.....

1. The following internal relief will take place tomorrow, July 15th in CALONNE Section.

    (a) 17th Welsh will relieve the 19th R.W.F. in the right subsection
    (b) 18th Welsh   "   "   " 12th S.W.B.   "   left   "
    (c) 19th R.W.F. will move into support in CALONNE.
    (d) 12th S.W.B. will move into reserve in BULLY GRENAY.

2. Reliefs will be carried out under arrangements made direct between Commanding Officers concerned, and will be completed by 7 p.m.

3. Bombing and Snipers posts will be relieved by 12 noon.

4. Completion of relief will be reported to these Headquarters.

5. Lewis Guns will remain in the line as required.

                        (Sgd) A.G.SOAMES. Captain
                            Brigade Major
                            119th Brigade.

Copy No.1 O.C. 19th R.W.F.   14. Bde Bomb Officer.
     2. O.C. 12th S.W.B.   15. O.C. 231st Field Coy R.E.
     3 O.C. 17th Welsh.   16. "G" 40th Division.
     4 O.C. 18th Welsh.   17. "Q" 40th Division.
     5 Q.M. 19th R.W.F.   18. 120th Brigade.
     6 Q.M. 12th S.W.B.   19. 121st Brigade.
     7 Q.M. 17th Welsh.   20. War Diary.
     8 Q.M. 18th Welsh.   21. Brigade Major.
     9 119th Bde M.G.Coy.   22. Staff Captain.
    10 Bde Transport Officer   23. O.C. Right Group Artillery.
    11   " Intelligence Officer   24. 47th Division (for left Bde.)
    12   " Supply Officer   25. 119th T.M.Battery.
    13   " Signals.   26. Divl. T.M.Battery.

S E C R E T.   COPY NO. 1

119TH BRIGADE ORDER NO. 9.

18th July, 1916.

1.   The following internal reliefs will take place tomorrow, July 19th, in the CALONNE section :-

   (a) 19th Bn R.W.F. will relievé 17th Welsh in the right subsection.
   (b) 12th Bn S.W.B.   "   18th Welsh in the left subsection.
   (c) 18th Bn Welsh. will move into support in Calonne.
   (d) 17th Bn Welsh. will move into reserve in BULLY GRENAY.

2.   Reliefs will be carried out under arrangements to be made between Commanding Officers concerned, and will be completed by 7 p.m.

3.   Bombing and Snipers Posts and Lewis Guns will be relieved by 12 noon.

4.   Completion of relief will be reported to these Headquarters.

                               (Sgd) A.G.Soames, Captain,
                                         Brigade Major,
                                           119th Brigade.
   18-7-16.

Copy No. 1 O.C. 19th R.W.F.   Copy No 14 Bde Bomb Officer
         2 O.C. 12th S.W.B.   15 O.C. 231st Field Coy R.E.
         3 O.C. 17th Welsh.   16 "G" 40th Division.
         4 O.C. 18th Welsh.   17 "Q" 40th Division.
         5 Q.M. 19th R.W.F.   18 120th Brigade.
         6 Q.M. 12th S.W.B.   19 121st Brigade.
         7 Q.M. 17th Welsh.   20 War Diary.
         8 Q.M. 18th Welsh.   21 Brigade Major.
         9 119th Bde M.G.Coy.   22 Staff Captain.
        10 Bde Transport Officer.   23 O.C.Right Group Artillery.
        11 " Intelligence Officer.   24 47th Division (for left Bde)
        12 " Supply Officer.   25 119th T.M.Battery.
        13 " Signals.   26 Divl. T.M.Battery.

S E C R E T.   COPY NO... 1.....

119TH BRIGADE ORDER NO. 10

20th July 1916.

1. The 119th Brigade will be relieved by the 120th Brigade in CALONNE Section on the 21st and 22nd July.

2. Guides will be supplied by Units of 119th Brigade in accordance with table overleaf.
   All other arrangements will be made by Os C. Units direct.

3. The following will be handed over:-

   a. Trench Stores. 1 officer per Battalion and 1 N.C.O per Company from each of 3 Battalions of 120th Brigade will be met by a guide from each of 3 Battalions of 119th Brigade at GRENAY BRIDGE (M.1.d.7.2.) at 6 a.m. on 22nd. July and Guided to Headquarters of Battalions.

   13th Bn E.Surrey Regt. will take over from 19th Bn.R.W.F.
   11th Bn R.Lanc Regt.   "   "   12th Bn.S.W.B.
   14th Bn H.L.I.   "   "   18th Bn.Welsh Regt.

   b. Brigade S.A.A. And Bomb Stores, on the 22nd July under arrangements to be made by Staff Captains direct.
   Receipts will be taken for all trench stores, and a list sent to these Headquarters by 12 noon on the 23rd July.

4. Units on relief will proceed to billets as under:-

Unit	Billets	Now occupied by
19th Bn R.W.F.	PETIT SAINS	11th Bn R.Lanc Rgt
12th Bn S.W.B.	LES BREBIS, Area A	14th Bn H.L.I.
17th Bn Welsh Rgt.	LES BREBIS, Area B & C	14th Bn A & S Highrs
18th Bn Welsh Rgt.	LES BREBIS, Area D	13th Bn E.Surrey Regt.

   Billetting parties of Units of 119th Brigade will report to the Staff Captain, 120th Brigade, at Mine Buildings, LES BREBIS, at 12 noon on the 22nd July when guides will meet them.
   Brigade Headquarters, 119th Brigade Machine Gun Coy. and 119th Trench Mortar Battery, and Transport and Quartermaster's Stores of Battalions, will remain in their present billets.

5. The fatigue party found three times daily by the Battalion in Support for the 255th Tunnelling Coy. R.E. will be found on the 22nd July as follows,

   8.0 a.m.   Support Battalion 119th Brigade
   4.0 p.m. and onwards   "   "   120th Brigade

6. Signallers will be relieved by 8 p.m. on the 21st July under arrangements to be made by Signal Officers direct. One signaller of the 119th Brigade will remain at each station till relief is complete on the 22nd.

7. Brigade Snipers and Observers will be relieved on the 22nd July under arrangements to be made by Brigade Intelligence Officers direct.

8. Completion of relief will be reported to Brigade Headquarters, G.O.C. 119th Brigade will hand over the command of the CALONNE Section to G.O.C. 120th Brigade on completion of relief.

9. The personnel attached to the 231st Coy R.E. for dug-out construction will remain in the line. Os C. Units may make any changes in the personnel if they wish to do so.

(Sgd) A.G. SOAMES. Captain
Brigade Major
119th Brigade.

Date.	Unit to be Relieved 119th Brigade.	Relieving Unit 120th Brigade	Guides Place	Time	
July 21	119th.Bde.M.G. Coy.	120th Bde M.G. Coy.	GRENAY CHURCH M.1.d.3.9½.	5.0 p.m.	1 guide per gun
"	Lewis Guns:- 19th R.W.F. 12th S.W.B. 18th Welsh.	Lewis Guns:- 13th E.Surrey 11th R.Lancs. 14th H.L.I.	Do	6.30.p.m.	1 guide per gun
"	119th Trench Mortar Battery	120th Trench Mortar Battery	Do	6.0 p.m.	1 guide per Mortar
July 22	19th R.W.F. (less M.G.Sctn)	13th E.Surreys (less M.G.Sectn)	Do	2.0 p.m.	1 guide per platoon & 1 for Bde H.Q.
"	12th S.W.B. (less M.G.Sctn)	11th R.Lancs (less M.G.Sectn)	GRANDE PLACE BULLY GRENAY	3.30 p.m.	Do
"	18th Welsh (less M.G.Sctn)	14th H.L.I. (less M.G.Sectn)	GRENAY CHURCH	5.0 p.m.	Do
"	17th Welsh	14th A & S Highs	GRANDE PLACE BULLY GRENAY	5.0 p.m.	Billetting parties will be at same place at 2.30 p.m.

NOTE:- All movements will be by platoons in the case of Infantry, and by detachments in the case of Machine Gunners and Trench Mortar Battery at 200 yards interval.

```
Copy No 1 O.C.19th R.W.F.              Copy No 14 Bde Bomb Officer
        2 O.C.12th S.W.B.                      15 O.C.231st Field Coy.R.E.
        3 O.C.17th Welsh                       16 "G" 40th Division
        4 O.C.18th Welsh                       17 "Q" 40th Division
        5 Q.M.19th R.W.F                       18 120th Brigade
        6 Q.M 12th S.W.B.                      19 121st Brigade
        7 Q.M.17th Welsh                       20 War Diary
        8 Q.M.18th Welsh                       21 Brigade Major
        9 119th Bde M.G.Coy                    22 Staff Captain
       10 Bde Transport Officer                23 O.C.Right Group Artillery
       11.  "  Intelligence Officer            24 R.N.D.(for left Bde)
       12.  "  Supply Officer                  25 119th T.M.Battery
       13.  "  Signals                         26 Divl.T.M.Battery.
```

SECRET   COPY NO...(...

AMENDMENTS TO 119TH BRIGADE ORDER NO 10
DATED 20TH JULY 1916

1. Owing to the readjustment of the 1st Corps front whereby the 40th Division takes over additionally the LOOS Section from the 16th Division, the CALONNE Section is extended to M.4.c.5.6.

2. The following amendments will therefore be made in 119th Brigade Order No 10 of yesterday's date:-

   (a) <u>Para.4</u>. The table will be amended as follows:-

Unit	Billets	Now occupied by
19th Bn R.W.F.	LES BREBIS.Area B & C	14th Bn A & S.Highrs
12th Bn S.W.B.	LES BREBIS,Area A	14th Bn H.L.I.
18th Bn Welsh Rgt.	N.E.MAROC	12th Suffolks Rgt.

   17th Bn Welsh Rgt. will remain in their present billets in BULLY GRENAY.
   The Billeting party 18th Bn Welsh Regt, will report to the Staff Captain 121st Brigade, and not to the Staff Captain,120th Brigade.

   (b) <u>Insert new paras</u>.
   4a. On completion of the relief, the 17th Bn Welsh Regt will form the Brigade Reserve, at call, for tactical purposes, of G.O.C 120th Brigade.
   The 18th Bn Welsh Regt will form the Brigade Reserve, at call, for tactical purposes, of G.O.C.121st Brigade.
   4b. O.C.119th Brigade Machine Gun company will detail 2 Vickers Guns with trains to report to O.C.Pioneers,16th Division, at LOOS by 10 a.m. 23rd July for LOOS DEFENCES.

   (c) The last line of table on page 2 (commencing July 22,17th Welsh) will be deleted.

                                              (Sgd) A.G.SOAMES.Captain
                                                    Brigade Major
                                                    119th Brigade.

Copy No				
1	O.C.19th R.W.F.		14	Bde Bomb Officer
2	O.C.12th S.W.B.		15	O.C.231st Field Coy R.E.
3	O.C.17th Welsh		16	"G" 40th Division
4	O.C.18th Welsh		17	"Q" 40th Division
5	Q.M.19th R.W.F.		18	120th Brigade
6	Q.M. 12th S.W.B.		19	121st Brigade
7	Q.M.17th Welsh		20	War Diary
8	Q.M.18th Welsh.		21	Brigade Major
9	119th Bde M.G.Coy.		22	Staff Captain
10	Bde Transport Officer		23	O.C.Right Group Artillery
11	" Intelligence Officer		24	1st Bde R.N.D.(for left Bde)
12	" Supply Officer		25	119th T.M.Battery
13	" Signals.		26	Divl T.M.Battery

SECRET.   COPY NO. 1.

119TH BRIGADE ORDER NO 11

28th July 1916

1. **RELIEF.** The 119th Brigade will relieve the 120th Brigade in the CALONNE Section (new) on 29th and 30th insts, in accordance with the table overleaf.

2. **GUIDES.** These will be provided by units of the 120th Brigade in accordance with the table.

3. **STORES.**
   (a) <u>Trench Stores</u> 1 Officer per Battalion and 1 N.C.O per Company will meet guides of the 120th Brigade at GRENAY BRIDGE (M.l.d.7.2) at 10 a.m. on the 30th, and proceed to Battalion Headquarters, to take over Trench Stores.
   Certificates of Stores taken over (on A.F.W 3405) will be rendered to this office by noon on the 31st.
   (b) <u>Brigade S.A.A. and Bomb Stores</u>, will be taken over on the 30th under arrangements to be made by Staff Captains direct.

4. **BILLETING.** 1 N.C.O per platoon and 1 from Battalion Headquarters of each of the 19th R.W.F. and 12th S.W.B. will report to the Staff Captain at Brigade Headquarters at 12 noon on the 30th instant to guide billetting parties of 120th Brigade units to their areas.
   Billetting arrangements between 17th and 18th Bns Welsh Regiment and their relieving units will be made by Os C direct.

5. **SIGNALLERS** will complete relief by 8 p.m. on the 29th under arrangements to be made by Signal Officers direct.

6. **BRIGADE SNIPERS & OBSERVERS** will relieve on 30th under arrangements to be made by Brigade Intelligence Officers direct.

7. **MACHINE & LEWIS GUNS & T.M.B.** These will relieve on the 29th in accordance with the table overleaf.

8. **MOVEMENT.** All movement will be by platoons or detachments at 200 yards distance.

9. **COMPLETION OF RELIEF** will be reported to Brigade Headquarters by telephone.

10. **DISPOSITIONS.** The dispositions in the CALONNE Section will be as follows:

    <u>Right Subsection</u> (19th R.W.F.)
        2 Coys Front Line
        1 Coy   ALGIERS TRENCH (in billets)
        1 Coy   CHARCOAL TRENCH.

    <u>Right Centre Subsection.</u> (17th Welsh)
        1 Coy   Front Line
        2 Coys CALONNE
        2 Ptns BAJOLLE LINE
        2 "   at disposal of O.C. Battalion.

Left Centre Subsection (12th S.W.B)
    3 Coys Front Line
    1 Coy   Support.

Left Subsection. (18th Welsh)
    2 Coys Front Line
    2 Coys Support.

11. The "Programme of Reliefs (Amendment)" circulated on the 26th instant is cancelled.

12. Acknowledge.

Date	Relieving Unit 119th Bde.	Unit Relieved 120th Bde.	Guides Place	Time	No to be met
29 July	119th Bde M.G.Coy.	120th Bde. M.G.Coy	GRENAY CHURCH M.1.d.3.9½	5 p.m.	1 guide per gun
"	LEWIS GUNS. 19th R.W.F. 12th S.W.B. 17th Welsh 18th Welsh	13th E.Surrey R 11th K.O.R.L. 14th H.L.I. 14th A.&.S.H.	do	6.30 p.m.	1 guide per gun
"	119th T.M.B.	120th T.M.B.	do	6 p.m.	1 guide per mortar
30 July	19th R.W.F. less Lewis Gun Section	13th E.Surrey Rgt. less Lewis Gun Section	do	8 a.m. ~~2 p.m.~~	1 guide per platoon and 1 for H.Q. Bn
"	12th S.W.B. less Lewis Gun Section	11th K.O.R.L less Lewis Gun Section	do	4 p.m.	do
"	17th Welsh less Lewis Gun Section	14th H.L.I less Lewis Gun Section	GRANDE PLACE BULLY GRENAY	✗ 6 p.m.	do
"	18th Welsh less Lewis Gun Section	14th A.&.S.H. less Lewis Gun Section	HOLE IN THE WALL M.2.d.3.8.	3 p.m.	do

✗ The Company in the front line may be relieved at a later hour if desired by C.Os.

                                            (Sgd) A.G.SOAMES.Captain
                                                Brigade Major
                                                119th Brigade.

```
Copy No 1. O.C.19th R.W.F.        Copy No 14. Bde Bomb Officer
        2. O.C.12th S.W.B.                15. O.C.231st Field Coy. R.E.
        3. O.C.17th Welsh                 16. "G" 40th Division
        4. O.C.18th Welsh                 17. "Q" 40th Division
        5. Q.M.19th R.W.F.                18. 120th Brigade
        6. Q.M.12th S.W.B.                19. 121st Brigade
        7. Q.M.17th Welsh                 20. War Diary
        8. Q.M.18th Welsh                 21. Brigade Major
        9. 119th Bde M.G.Coy.             22. Staff Captain
       10. Bde Transport Officer          23. O.C.Right Group Artillery
       11.  "  Intelligence Officer       24. 1st Bde R.N.D. (for left Brigade)
       12.  "  Supply Officer             25. 119th T.M.Battery
       13.  "  Signals                    26. Div1 T.M.Battery
```

Copy No. 1. C.Flt. H.Q.R.   Copy No. 14. Bde Bomb Officer
2. " S.M.R.   15. O.C.Stat Flt Coy. R.E.
3. " C.O. 1st Wg   16. "C" Coln Division
4. " O.C.1st Wg Motor   17. "G" Coln Division
5. " H.W.1st Wg   18. 13oth Brigade
6. " S.W.1st Wg   19. 131st Brigade
7. " O.W.1st Wg Motor   20. Wg Diary
8. " M.1st Wg M.O.B.   21. Brigade Major
9. "1st Bde M.G.Coy.   22. Staff Captain
10. Bde Transport Officer   23. O.C.Staff Group Artillery
11. " Intelligence Officer   24. 1st Bde M.M.D. (for 1st Brigade)
12. " Supply Officer   25. 11th T.M.Battery
15. " Signals   26. D1v1s.M.Battery

x
The company in the front line may be relieved
at a later hour if desired by C.O's.

Appendix B

OPERATION ORDER.   NO 5.

1. The Battalion will march at 10-30 tomorrow via HERSIN, PETIT SAINS to BULLY GRENAY. Starting point "A" Company's Headquarters; order of march, Snipers, D,A,B,C, Headquarters.

2. Signallers and Machine Gunners and Bombing Officer will march at 8-30 and 9-0 respectively under special orders. The Machine Gun, Sniping and bombing Officers will proceed in advance reaching GRENAY Bridge by 11-30.

3. The Field Kitchens will accompany the Battalion and dinners will be served at 12 noon. Tea and bread for the evening meal will be carried on the man. Water bottles will be filled at.

4. Guides will meet the Battalion on BULLY GRENAY square at 14-30.

5. Companies will take over trenches from the 1st Cameron Highlanders as follows.

19th R.W.F.	1st C.H.
D	B (Right Coy)
A	A (Centre)
B	C (Left)
C	D (Support)

6. Companies will telephone the word "ADSUM" to Battn Headquarters on completion of relief.

7. The Commanding Officer will see Company Commanders and Transport Officer at the Orderly Room at 9-00.

3/7/16

OPERATION ORDER.   No 6.

1. The Battalion will relieve the 17th Welsh in the Right sub section tomorrow, the 11th.

2. (a) Scouts and Snipers will move into the trenches at 8 o'c night of the 10th.

   (b) Signallers, Machine Gunners and Battalion Bombers will leave BULLY Bridge at 10 a.m. on the 11th.

3. Each man will carry on him his tea ration for the 11th, men will leave BULLY with full water bottles.

4. Companies will take over trenches from the 17th Welsh as follows:-,

19th R.W.F.	17th Welsh.
"C" Coy (Right)	"D" Coy.
"D" Coy (Centre)	"A" Coy.
"A" Coy (Left)	"B" Coy
"B" Coy (Support)	"C" Coy.

5. Company Commanders and Company Sergeant Major's will leave leave BULLY Bridge at 11 o'clock.

6. No 9 Platoon will leave BULLY Bridge at 2-30 p.m. Platoons will follow at 5 minutes interval. Order of Companies. C, D, A, B. and Headquarters.

7. Completion of relief will be notified by Runner.

(Snd) ......P.E.Williams.
Captain & Adjutant.
19th Battalion R.W.F.

OPERATION ORDER NO. 7   No. 7.

1. The Battalion will relieve the 13th East Surreys in the Right Sub Section Calonne tomorrow the 30th.

2. Signallers and Lewis Gun Detachments will be relieved on the 29th inst as per Brigade Order No 11.

3. Guides will be at Grenay Church at 8 a.m. men will move by platoons at 20 yards distance.

4. Companies will move and will relieve the 13th Est Surreys in the following order:-

19th R.W.F.	13th East Surreys.
A	D.
C.	C.
D.	B.
B.	A.

   The platoons of "A" Coy will not proceed beyond MARBLE ARCH until the platoon relieved has moved North of MARBLE ARCH. "C" Coy will use CHAPTAL ALLEY. The first detachment of D Coy will relieve the Tunnel Guards and point duty men. 1 N.C.O and 27% men.

5. The C.S.M. of each Coy and 1 N.C.O. from Headquarters will meet Guides at GRENAY BRIDGE at 5 a.m. on the 30th. They will take over Trench Stores for their respective Companies. Copies are to be forwarded to Battalion Orderly Room CALONNE as soon as possible.

6. BILLETTING. 1 N.C.O. per platoon and 1 N.C.O. from Batt Headquarters will report at Brigade Headquarters at 12 noon on the 30th to Guide billetting parties of 120th Brigade to their areas.

7. Completion of relief will be notified by runner.

                                        (Snd) ......P.E.Williams.
                                              Captain & Adjutant.
29/7/16   19th Battn. R.W.F.

OPERATION ORDERS   NO 5.

by

Lieut Col. W.C. Newton Cmdg 13th Bn. East Surrey Regt.   CALONNE

29.7.16.

1. WARRIOR will relieve ALBATROSS in Front Line Trenches in RIGHT SUB-SECTOR CALONNE to-morrow.

2. ALBATROSS will move into Billets at LES BREBIS on relief.

3. GUIDES from each platoon and one from Battalion Headquarters will be at GRENAY CHURCH at 8 hours to-morrow 30th inst., Coys. will be relieved in the following order:-

ALBATROSS		WARRIOR	In Trench	Out Trench
"D" Coy	relieved by	"A" Coy	BIRDCAGE WALK	BIRDCAGE WALK
"C" "	do	"C" "	CHAPTEL ALLEY	BOVRIL ALLEY AND ALGIERS TRENCH
"B" "	do	"D" "		
"A" "	do	"B" "		

4. In the case of "D" Co ALBATROSS, each platoon when relieved must be clear of MARBLE ARCH before next platoon of WARRIOR enter BIRDCAGE WALK

In the case of "C" Coy ALBATROSS, platoons must not leave ALGIERS TRENCH until CHAPTEL ALLEY is clear of last platoon of WARRIOR.

5. All Coys. will proceed via CALONNE SOUTH and thence to LES BREBIS at 200 yds distance

6. Headquarters WARRIOR will arrive ALBATROSS 9.30 hours

7. An advance party consisting of Bombing Officer, R.S.M. and one N.C.O. per Coy of WARRIOR for the purpose of taking over stores will be at GRENAY BRIDGE at 5 hours.
Guides for this party will be found by Headquarters ALBATROSS. Usual lists will be prepared.

8. Guides will be at GRENAY CHURCH at 18.30 hours 29th inst., to direct relieving Lewis Gun Teams.

9. Snipers will be relieved on July 30th under arrangements to be made direct through Brigade Intelligence Officer.

10. Signallers will be relieved by 20 hours on July 29th under arrangements to be made by Signalling Officers direct

11. Bombing Platoon will proceed to Billets in LES BREBIS 200 yards distance from last platoon of "A" Coy.

Lieut.
a/Adjutant 13th Bn. East Surrey Regt.

Appendix C
Progress Report. NO I

WARRIOR.

1. Operations: Relief of 1st THISTLE
completed about K.15.
 + Enemy's Rum
jar was very active at M.20.b.5.9

2. Information:
                Nil.

3. Work done. Two gaps made by
enemy Trench Mortars at 20.C.4.6 were
repaired & the wire in front of gaps C
& D still could. At 20.b.2.7/, the
disused trench beyond the mine to
PICK AXE TRENCH was filled with
busted trench-wire.
            Short wire bales
were made & the front from 20.b.3,6
to 20.b.4.3, rewired. At the pit
20.b.1½ the barricade was filled
with wire.
            at 20.b.3.9, some

OPERATION ORDERS   NO 5.

by

Lieut.Col. W.C. Newton Cmdg. 13th Bn. East Surrey Regt.   CALONNE
                                                                 29.7.16.

1.   WARRIOR will relieve ALBATROSS in Front Line Trenches in
      RIGHT SUB-SECTOR CALONNE to-morrow.

2.   ALBATROSS will move into Billets at LES BREBIS on relief.

3.   GUIDES from each platoon and one from Battalion Headquarters
      will be at GRENAY CHURCH at 8 hours to-morrow 30th inst.,
      Coys. will be relieved in the following order:-

      ALBATROSS   WARRIOR   In Trench   Out Trench

      "D" Coy relieved "A" Coy   BIRDCAGE WALK   BIRDCAGE WALK
               by
      "C" "   do   "C" "   CHAPTEL ALLEY   BOVRIL ALLEY
                                                       AND
                                                       ALGIERS TRENCH

      "B" "   do   "D" "
      "A" "   do   "B" "

4   In the case of "D" Coy ALBATROSS, each platoon when
      relieved must be clear of MARBLE ARCH before next platoon of
      WARRIOR enter BIRDCAGE WALK
            In the case of "C" Coy ALBATROSS, platoons must
      not leave ALGIERS TRENCH until CHAPTEL ALLEY is clear of
      last platoon of WARRIOR.

5   All Coys. will proceed via CALONNE SOUTH and thence
      to LES BREBIS at 200 yds distance.

6   Headquarters WARRIOR will arrive ALBATROSS 9.30 hours

7   An advance party consisting of Bombing Officer,
      R.S.M. and one N.C.O. per Coy of WARRIOR for the purpose of
      taking over stores will be at GRENAY BRIDGE at 5 hours.
            Guides for this party will be found by Headquarters
      ALBATROSS. Usual lists will be prepared.
                                                          29th inst.,
8   Guides will be at GRENAY CHURCH at 18.30 hours to
      direct relieving Lewis Gun Teams.

9   Snipers will be relieved on July 30th under
      arrangements to be made direct through Brigade Intelligence
      Officer.

10   Signallers will be relieved by 20 hours on July
      29th under arrangements to be made by Signalling Officers direct

11   Bombing Platoon will proceed to Billets in
      LES BREBIS 200 yards distance from last platoon of "A" Coy.

                                                Lieut.
                                    a/Adjutant 13th Bn. East Surrey Regt.

Appendix C
Progress Report. No I

WARRIOR.

1. Operations: Relief of 1st THISTLE completed about 13.15.
   + Enemy's Buen gave us a very nature at M.20.b.5.9

2. Information:
                Nil.

3. Work done. Gaps gaps made by enemy Trench Mortar at 20 C.4.6. were repaired & the ground in front of gaps C & D settled would at 20 b [struck] 7/. the disused trench beyond the mine in PICK AXE TRENCH was filled with barbed concertina wire.
            Shirts wire balls were made & the front from 20 b 3½, 5½ to 20.b.3½.7½ wired. At the pt. 20.b 1½ 2 the barricade was filled with wire.
            at 20 b 38 Some

slight cover was wrecked while the
parapet had been reduced.

P L Williams
Capt & Adjt
NARRR.

5.11.16.
13.15

Progress Report. No. 2.

1. <u>Operations</u>: R.E exploded a mine about 11.30pm. on the 5th at M.20.b.5.8. The front ~~was~~ line was shelled about 10pm. with "Rum Jars" + the trenches badly damaged at the following points. M.21.a.1.9½ - 15 yards
M.20. b. 8.9½ - 20 yards.
M.20. b. 3½.8½ - 10 yards.

Trench about M.20.b.2.8. ~~trench~~ blocked by some debris from the house + by 'rum jars', making communication down that trench impossible.

2. <u>Information</u>: Nil.

3. <u>Work done</u>: 15 yds. of new wire laid in front of trenches about M.20.b.2.3 + the barricade on this section was completed. About 280 wire balls were made. The trenches were drained + new trench boards laid down at M.20.c.5.9.
M.20. c. 6.9

Wiring was also commenced at a point 30 yards to right of Boyeau 209 but heavy Machine Gun fire was brought to bear on the party

P E Williams Capt Adj
19th R.W.F.

6. VII. 16.

No. 2   Tactical Progress Report.

1. Operations.   About 6 a.m. on the
6th the enemy dropped a rum jar
at the pt. M.20.b.37 + completely
stopped all passage down the trench.
A large amount of damage was
done, but the trench is now passable.
During the day of the 6th, the enemy
continued his activity with Rum
Jars, shelling the School at M.14.a.9.4
possibly having located a F.O.O observing
post which is the other side of the
road. Our retaliation however
was effective. M.G. fire was
brought to bear on the road about
M.14.a.55 while the transport
brought up rations about 10.45
p.m. Our artillery were very
active throughout the night.

                    P.E.Williams.
                    Capt & Adj
7.vii.16.   19th R.W.F.

Tactical Progress Report
No. 4.

Information:- Enemy wiring party observed at M.21.a.2,7 about 11.30pm. It is reported that enemy are using dummy figures about M.21.a.4,3½.

Work done:- Cleaning of fire trench & opening out of 15 yards of trench at M.20.C.7,7 & revetting the same. In Sap D which has been badly damaged by Rum Jars, work of deepening & building up of the same was carried out. In this part of the line from M.19.D.5,8 - 19.D.8,8 wiring parties were out and 93 wire balls put out; the filling of the disused trench at M.19.d.8,9 with concertina wire was continued. Ten yards of trench at M.20.b.3,5. were built up &

revetted. The new Trench which is being proceeded with for a distance of about 5 yards & to a depth of 3 feet. The work had to be abandoned owing to the heavy bombardment by Trench Mortars. Fifty wire balls were made under the supervision of the R.E.s attached.
The fire Steps & parapet at M 20.b. 6.9 - 20.b 7.9 were repaired a working party from the Support Coy. assisting. Work was delayed owing to the heavy bombardment by "Rum Jars".

P E Williams
Capt & Adj.
19th R.W.F.

Operation Report No. 6.

1. Our own troops: A number of Grenades were sent over during the night; no retaliation of any kind was made.

An Officer's patrol left about 12.30 (midnight) towards the truck on the embankment at 21.A.2.10. It was suspected that a sniper occupied this during the night time, returning to the German lines before dawn. The truck however was found to be unoccupied.

Enemy's troops. Very quiet.

Six whiz-bangs were sent over on to MARBLE ARCH about 2.15 a.m.

P.E. Williams Capt & Adj
19th Regt.

12.VII.16.

Report on Information
& Work done.   No. 7.

Information:- Periscope seen at
M.20.b.0,6½: also large loophole
with iron plate at side at M20.b.8¾,6.

Loophole.   Iron plate.

At 3pm on the 11th Snipers Post observed at
M.20.b.7½,5½ in a ruined house, bricks
were at this pt. being very thin. About 11pm.
red light observed in the direction about
M.27. central for about 10 minutes:
this same light was seen again about
midnight. About 2 a.m. a red light
was seen at M.21.7.5: this light
remained in the air for about 8 minutes
& when it was extinguished about
20 whizz-bangs were distributed
along the line.
    About 4.30 a.m. sniper observed

German officer wearing blue peaked cap & gold braid at a pt. M.20.b.3.3. sniper claims a hit. About 5.a.m. head seen over parapet wearing blue cap & a bright badge similar to a grenade. Trench rail observed at M.20.b.4.4.

A light gun evidently movable in the vicinity of the cross roads M.26.b.7½.6¾.

Work done. Nine new trench boards put down in Algeria Trench about M.20.a.3.4. New trench proceeded with from M.20.b.4.7½ to M.20.b.6.5½ in rear of old trench. Two wiring parties out at M.20.a.4.5. Portable entanglements put out & about 60 wire balls to fill gaps. Clearing of small obstructions in the hedges from M.20.b.10.0 — M.20. b 5.6.

P.E.Williams.
Capt & Adj 19th R.W.F.

12.VII.16.

Operation Report. No. 8.

1. Operations ⓒ. A patrol went out at M 20 b. 5½.3 about 11 pm. & came in about 12.30 (midnight) There was no movement in the haunted house & no enemy's patrol was encountered.

An enemy wiring party came out about 10 pm at the point M.20.b.7.5. fire was opened & they immediately retired.

Ⓑ From about 5·45 pm. to 9·45 pm a very heavy bombardment of MARBLE ARCH took place. Shells used were chiefly Rum Jars with some 3·9 shells. Retaliation by our Trench Mortars was not very effective. one of our Trench Mortars was put out of action, a "Rum Jar" falling on a box of ammunition. Retaliation by the Artillery was very slow.

P. E. Williams Capt
Adjt 19th R.W.F.

Information & Work done. No. 9.

a. A new loophole was observed in enemy's front trench position about M.20.b.3½,3½. About 5.30 p.m. a party of men was observed at M.27.A.8.1. carrying discs of some description; this party stopped at M.27.a.8,3½. fresh wire appeared at M.20.b.4.2½. About 10 am (18th) a number of our shells were seen dropping in enemy's reserve line at M.27.a.7.1. causing much damage. New enemy wire was observed at M.20.b.9.5½; evidently placed there last night.

At 12.0 midnight a patrol of 1 Officer, 1 NCO & 1 man emerged from our trench at M.20.b.1.1. for inspection of enemy's wire. A gap was discovered in the wire about 4 yds. wide at M.20.c.4.3. There was also a gap in the wire about M.20.d.2,4½. The enemy was heard working at his parapet, the noise resembling a long wire being drawn some distance; a large amount of trenching noise this work. The obstacles appeared as a rule of a rigid type with stakes, there were no knife rests. Flashes observed on the firing of a machine gun indicate the gun to be about M.20.C.4.3.

The probable position of the Trench Mortars which bombarded our lines last night -
   Minitar Gun - M.20.b.5½.3½.
                 M.20.b.6.4.

Work done : At 20.C.4.5, the earth was removed from the trench & forward slope revetted for about 2 yds.
At 20.C.4½.5 : 6 yds of revetting
   20.C.4.5 . 5 yds of trench at corner
                          rounded off
20.C.6½.7 . Sand bags filled with
            loose earth in trenches
         4 yds of trench revetted.
20.C.6.6   30 yards of wire put out
         (continued).
Trench between 209 & 210 improved by making new fire steps

The new fire trench to join up
with Royan 10 was continued
Wiring parties placed about
110 W'd balls + about 8' x 2'
of portable entanglements at
M.20.b.6.9.

J Trench boards were
placed down at M.20.a.3.6 to
M.20.b.7.2.

Slates from roofs shelled
last night cleared: M.20.b.9.10,
- M.20.b.10.10

P. Ewell ... Capt
Adj 19th R.W.F.

Operation Report.   No 10.

1. A number of Newton Pippins were sent over during the night. Machine Gun fire overhead was active.

A working party of the enemy was fired on by Machine Guns & beat a hasty retreat

About 2.15 p.m. of the 13th a heavy bombardment of the Marble Arch & Temple Ct. tok place. Shells used were 5.9's. Retaliation by the artillery was effective & for the rest of the day the enemy was very quiet.

Operations on the part of the enemy during the night confined themselves to Machine Gun fire & some sniping.

P. Llewellyn Capt.
A/of 19th Reg.

Information & Work done. No 11.

Information

Machine Gun in the crater at M.20.l. was fairly active. At M.20.d.4.5 a dummy fire was seen showing from the hips to the helmet. Shots were fired at the figure fell & was quite stationary until it fell. The light however (time 6.45 am) was very deceptive. Three enemy wiring parties were out at M.20.4.5 apparently repairing gaps in the wire.

Snipers unable to locate position of T. Mortar which Bombarded TEMPLE St about 3.15 pm. (13th)

At M.20.b.4.4 a man was seen to jump from front line trench into communication trench, apparently clearing some obstacle. At 10 am new stock of sandbags seen at M.20.b.2.4.

Work done.

At 20.C.5.4 a new traverse & the fire step raised by the use of 11 sandbags

At 20.C.5.4½ the old revetment was removed & new put in its place for a length of 2 yds.

At 20.C.5.6. old revetment was removed & new placed there for a length of 3 yds. 45 sandbays being used

In Boyau 204 pits for drainage purposes were dug to a length of about 15 yards. relaid with trench boards.

At 20.C.9.7½ fire step was constructed & the fire bay widened for a length of 4 yds.

At 20.C.9.7½ buried trench boards were taken up for a length of 7 yds. the trench was deepened further by about 9"

The making of Boyau 207 to Fire Trench was started. Trench was cleared to a depth of about 5'.

A dozen trench boards placed in support line & Burdock Walk & new sump holes dug.

Ten iron stakes, 2 coils of barbed wire + 30 wire balls fixed up at M.20.b.5.6. Ten stakes, 2 coils + 30 wire balls fixed at about M.20.b.3.4. Two chevaux-de-frise, 10 iron stakes + 15 wire balls fixed at 20.b.2.3.

For a distance of 10 yds to left pt M.20.b.4.6, the trench was deepened by 1½ ft. To the right of M.20.d.9.1 two new loop-holes were made. At pt M.20.b.7.9½ the parapet was thickened by the use of 30 sandbags. A large amount of debris was cleared from Morgan Trench.

General. Heavy bombardment of TEMPLE ST. at about 3.15 p.m. on 13th april 25-30, 5.9 shells entering. Bombardment was evidently methodical; starting at West end & ending at East end. Retaliation by Artillery very effective. Conditions very quiet.

P.C. William, Capt.
Adjt. 19th R.W.F.

14.VII.16

Operation Report No 12

About 7.45 p.m. an enemy aeroplane was seen over our lines. At about 8 p.m. it was seen making off over the enemy's lines.

About 11.35 p.m. the enemy fired a number of red rockets from SP. given M.20.c.8.9. & M.20.d.3.4. At 11.40 p.m. a very heavy bombardment began by enemy, using light field guns, trench mortars & aerial torpedoes. After about 5 minutes they were silenced by our artillery.

At about 2.15 a.m. the enemy sent over a number of N.am? bombs. The parkas of trench left of 20.9 for a length of 5 yards has been partly knocked in.

H. Borellium Capt
Aus 11th Regt

Report on Information
+ Work done.   No 13.

Information: An enemy aeroplane was sighted at 7.45 p.m. over our lines. At 8 p.m. it was seen making it was over the enemy's lines. About 11.10 p.m. 13 red lights were seen to go up from the enemy's trenches, followed by 7 or 8 green lights. This was followed by 12 minutes' heavy bombardment, the enemy using light field guns, trench mortars & rifle grenades, the shells for the most part falling about M.20. C.3.5. Our Artillery soon retaliated and at about 11.35 things resumed their normal state.

No enemy patrols or wiring party appeared to be out.

At 6.50 p.m. a large working party was seen at M.26. b.3,2 apparently digging trenches.

Considerable work reported at M.20 b. 4.4. behind the front line trench.

Work done

M.20.C. 5.4½ ⎫ Removing sand bags
& Boyau 206 ⎬ stacked & blocking
⎭ Boyau 206. These sandbags
emptied into ~~Boyau 206~~ shelter at
M.20.C.5.4½.

M.20.C. 4¾.5¼ : Constructing new bay
& filling of sandbags.

M.20 C 5½.6¼ : Revetting slope of trench
& filling sandbags

Boyau 206. Constructing 3 new fire
bays.

Support Trench at about M.20 C. 5.8
cleared and about 30 pieces (slats)
nailed on trench boards. Obstacles
removed at 20.C.7.9¾.

Boyau 207 : Cleaning & making of
four fire bays each to hold
four men.

Between Boyau 207 & 210 two fire
steps have been raised. Five yards
of revetting done in Boyau 210.

Work on new trench joining left of
firing line with Boyau 210 was
carried on & a traverse has been

dug round to a depth of 3 feet. Eight new trench boards were put down at about M.20.b.3.4.

Three wiring parties went out at midnight. One party at M.20.b.5.6 put out 2 coils of barbed concertina wire & dozen stakes.

The other party at M.20.b.3.5 put out 3 coils of wire, 20 wire balls & 1 concertina.

The third party at M.20.b.2.4 put out 3 coils, 1 concertina & 30 wire balls.

New fire bays at about M.20.b.5.9 completed & 150 sandbags used. Fire bay near mouth of Stafford Trench was completed, 80 sandbags being used. On left of the Burning Bing, parapet repaired & 50 sandbags used.

Boyau 210 was cleared for a distance of about 10 yds. & a depth of 2 feet.

15.VII.16.

P.E. Williams, Capt.
Adjt. 19th HPWR.

Information & Work done. No 14.

Information: Nil.

Work done. Nearly the whole of the men of the support Battalion were at work in the various Coys & Sections of the 231st Field Coy R.E. & 255 Tunnelling Coy.

In case of necessity the number of men to man the village lines would be wholly inadequate to offer even the most meagre resistance.

a. 2 NCO's & 24 men Carrying sandbags from 225 Starlight to New Shaft. Time 7.30pm to 8AM.

b. 4 NCOs & 25 men Unloading & loading ammunition from Bomb Store. Three Transport loads of 30 boxes each. 10 pm – 1.30 pm

c. 1 NCO & 30 men. Digging emplace for T.M.B. from 8 am to 12 noon

d. 1 NCO & 14 men Brigade Bombing

stokes from 9.30am to 4.30pm.

e. 1 NCO + 30 men Trench Mortar
Battery Fatigue from 7.45pm
- 10.30pm

f. 1 NCO + 16 men RE Stores 231st F Co
Carrying pit props for mining.

g. 1 NCO + 30 men RE Stores for
work constructing a part of the
new Support Trench.

h. 1 NCO + 15 men RE Stores at
11.15 for trench digging at
Boyau 210.

j. 1 NCO + 40 men reported to 255th
Tunnelling Coy. for carrying
sandbags from Sap W dump.

1 NCO + 11 men assisting RE's
to clear out Sap entrance

1 NCO + 40 men carrying
sandbags from Rim for
Little Welle & Theofa Minso
in Boyaux 206 & 207.

17.7.16.

P.E. Williams. Capt.
A/Sgt 19th R.W.F.

Information & Work done. No 15.

Information: Nil.

Work done:- 1 N.C.O + 30 men under
supervision of R.E. these were
divided into three sections.
    a. Deepening trench on left of
    Amptheatre Tunnel Morval trench.
    b. Deepening trench in new support
    trench left of Marble Arch.
    c Sapping in R.E. store.
1 N.C.O + 40 men " 258th Tunnelling Coy

1 officer + 30 men completing bays + fire
steps in Chenevil trench - N of Laurel
Wood 250.

1 N.C.O. + 10 men carrying bags from
dumps to Lucas Mill Mine.
1 N.C.O + 9 men assisting R.E. to mix
concrete for foundation of Water Tank.

Leipport trench from Calonne Nord to
Railway. 105 picquets made +
collected. 250 sandbags filled
+ placed in position on 75 bays. the

bays extending over a frontage of 40 yards.

The sink under the water tap was found to be out of working order. This has been reported to the R.E.'s

In addition fatigue parties were found for Bomb Stores & Trench Mortar Battery.

15.VII.16.

P.E. Williams Capt.
Adjt. 19th R.W.F.

April   8.5.16.

[Hon?]   Enemy shelled ? village
      ? Afrett? in the afternoon
      About one ???   ?? to burn
      of ? ? ?? ? pm. Our artillery
      ?? off ?

?? ??   ?

1 NCO + 30 men
repaired of R.E. store the party
was divided into 4 sections, two
parties were hard digging at
new support trench & Bridge
walk. ?? of the Pioneers
first ? ? ?? on a day out.
            1 NCO + 30 men employed
by the 255th R.E. carrying our ???
from pit mouth.
            NCO + 25 men assisting
R.E's at Starlight ?? Carrying
250 sandbags.
            1 NCO + 40 men assisting
R.E's in removing sandbags from
Russian Sap Chic? Miner.
            1 NCO + ? men carrying
timber from R.E. yard to N.T. O.P.

1 NCO & 30 men Trench Mortar Fatigue
carrying ammunition & digging
T.M. emplacement.

73 trench boards were laid &
cleaned & sump holes dug
under road in trench (Reserve
Line) between Colne Ave. &
Railway.

NCO & 30 men fatigue party at
Brick stores, transferring ammunition
& unroofing R.E. wood & new cellar
for storage of Brigade Ammunition

B.C. Williams, Capt
Adjt 19th Regt

14.7.16

Daily Progress Report No 17.

Operations. a. Our own men.

Patrols: 1. An officer Lt Lt ap I Shaulbans 1 NCO & 2 men emerged from the bombing post at M.20.d.1.9 at 11pm, & returned at 12.40 having as object the determination of any work done by the enemy & the close examination of gaps in the wire.

A gap in the wire was discovered opposite D sap, this gap was kept under constant observation but no repairing party of the enemy put in an appearance. The gap measured 3'. A red rocket was observed being sent up at 12 midnight followed by 3 green rockets.

2. Another patrol went out, consisting of 2nd Lt J. S. Evans, 1 NCO & 4 men, at 10.30 pm from M.20.b.2.3½. & a third patrol consisting of Lt. H Langford 1 Sergt. & 4 men at 1 a.m from M.20.b.3.7. Both patrols were out for 2 hrs. each, from 10.30-12.30 & from 1-3 am. The enemy's wire does not appear to be damaged on this particular front up from M.20.d.3.8. – M.20.b.4.3.

No enemy left the trench, but hard work repairing was in progress, shovels apparently being used.

b. The enemy: Enemy's machine guns & snipers were fairly busy throughout the night; otherwise a normal night.

Information. A working party of 4 men was observed at M.20.b.4½.2 between the hours of 12 noon & 3 pm.

At M.20.b.7 & 5 fresh chalk & sand-bags have been used on the trench.

About 9.15 pm two Germans were seen at M.20.b.2½.1¼. One appeared to be an officer. He had a map & was pointing towards our lines taking notes.

Work done
Sap A. 1 Sapper & 3 men revetting slopes & building fire steps. 60 sandbags were used.
Boyau 204. (M.20.C.8½.6¾)
1 NCO. & 2 men removing obstruction caused by projecting wire frame & deepening trench for a length of about 5 yds by a depth of 2'.

Boyau 207. Reopening with a view to
converting it to a fire trench. 1 Sapper
+ 4 men. Amount excavated 4' x 2' x 7'.

Boyau 206. Constructing fire steps in the
three bays already commenced.
60 sandbags were placed in each
bay. Four men were employed in
distributing sandbags filled from the
mines amongst the parties in the front
line.

Boyau 207. This trench was cleared
ready for revetting with sandbags -
amount cleared 18' x 1' x 2'.

Between Boyau 207 + 208. Making of a
new fire bay. This has been cut
out + revetting is in progress.

Between Boyaux 209 + 210. 6 yds of trench
were blown in. This has since been
cleared + the trench newly revetted.
The new trench from Boyau 213 was begun.

Byou 211. Party of 1 NCO + 10 men partially deepened 40 yds of trench by a depth of about 1 foot.

Byous 211 & 212 Joined up by a trench of about 5 yards in length.

Entrance to Byau 211 revetted - about 4 yards in length.

Approach to Buoning Biug deepened by about 1 foot & for a length of about 10 yards.

<u>Wiring</u> About 90 yards of wire put out at the point M.20.C.4½.7.

At M.20.b.1½.3 two posts were out and 5 rolls of wire were put out on a front of about 9 yards.

At M.20.b.4.9¾ about 18 screw stakes were put up & joined with 7 rolls of barbed wire.

P. E. Williams. Capt
Adjt 19th RWF

20.VI.16

Daily Progress Report No 18.

Operations: a. Our artillery opened a heavy fire on the enemy's trenches at 10.30 pm. 20th. This bombardment lasted continuously for ½ an hour. Our Trench Mortars seemed particularly effective several good shots being recorded on the nearest row of houses in Cité des Cornailles.

b. The enemy replied to our bombardment with shrapnel which burst well in rear of the front line. Snipers + machine guns were firing at intervals through the night.

A patrol of 1 officer (2nd Lt J.S. Evans) 1 NCO + 3 men went out as far as the enemy's wire about the point M.20.b.3.6. No gaps were reported in the wire + although out for 1hr 50 mins, no sign of the enemy was heard in their front trenches.

Information.
At M 20. b 2½.½ four green sandbags with a loophole between were observed: this is thought to be an enemy O.P.

Two men appeared in sight at M.20.b.3.1. wearing grey cloth dress + round black hat with metallic badge or number. Two men were also observed at M.20.b.5½.6 wearing similar uniforms.

Also at M.20.b.3.1 signalling by means of flag was observed, possibly signalling results of observation by periscope at this point

A party of Germans was observed at M.26.d.7.4½ rolling coats. between hours of 3 + 6 p.m.

At M.20.b.4.3. officer observed wearing blue hat with red band.

An enemy aeroplane was observed flying over our lines between 4.40 + 5 p.m.

A Sniper + M.G. emplacement was located from two different sources to be at M.20.d.2.8½.

Machine gun also located at M.20.d.
8½.4. This gun was very active up to
11 o'clock; but about that time three
shells fired dropped at this point &
the firing immediately ceased. It has
not been repeated since.

    Tappings & suspicious noises were
heard at M.20.c.6.6½ from a dug out.
Tappings were distinctly heard from
6 - 6.10 pm 20th.

<u>Work done</u>. 1 Officer, 1 NCO & 20
men working on Alger's Trench. The
bottom part of 8 bays & 5 fire steps were
put in order. 20 yds of trench were
deepened to a depth of 1 foot at
about M.20.a.1.3.

    1 NCO & 20 men opening
out & deepening Bryaux 21 & 21c;
about 20 yds. to a depth to a depth
of 9-12 inches.

    6 men under R.E. instruction
constructing new Traverse in approach
to Burning Bny - about 3½ yds completed.

    The support trench was
cleared of & deepened to a depth of

1 foot + for a length of 15 yds at M.20
b. 9. 9½.

The new trench from Boyau 210 was continued for a length of 5 yds.

New fire bays were constructed one in Boyau 207 & one between Boyau 208 & 209.

At M.20. C. 10, 9¾ 1 NCO + 8 men removed the old traverse: sand bags were filled with the soil thus removed preparatory to building a loop-holed traverse to command the old fire trench

~~M 20 c. 9½~~ + M. 20. a. 9¼. 1 3 men + 1 R.E. constructing new trench to join Boyau 207: quantity excavated 4' x 2' x 7'

Boyau 204. 17 men + 1 N.C.O. ~~raising~~ trench boards + deepening trench to a depth of 2' also digging sump holes beneath the boards. 21 boards were raised + 50 yds. from M.20.C. 8½,7 - M 20.C. 7.7½.

Wiring: 25 yards of barbed
  concertina wire + 4 coils of
barbed loosely entwined in it
was put out by two wiring parties.
The concertina was firmly staked
to the ground. Position M.20.b.
2.3.
       1 N.C.O. + 8 men protected
by covering party put out 90 yds
of concertina wire between
M.20.C.6¾.7 + M.20.C.7.5½.

21.VII.16.

P E Williams Capt
Adjt 19th Regt.

Daily Progress Report. No. 19

Operations. a. Our own men: Machine guns & Trench Mortars opened fire on working parties observed at M.20.c.4.3. & M.20.c.8.4. Much new soil is seen at these points.

A patrol of 1 officer (Lt. J. Williams), 1 NCO & 3 men went out at 11 p.m. returned at 1.10 a.m. from pt. M.20.b.1..3, the object of the patrol being to inspect the enemy's s.p. in front of Boyau 210 & also the enemy's wire about this point. The sap was found to be disused from the "head" about half way down. While the patrol was out one of the enemy came halfway up the s.p. fired a very light & immediately returned to the firing line.

The enemy's wire is not badly damaged about this point but as it is it can be easily penetrated: no attempt at repair has been made since 19th inst.

A patrol of 1 officer (See. Lt. E. J. Jones) 1 Corp & 9 men left our trenches at M.20.b.7½,9½ at midnight & returned at same spot at 2.20 a.m. A gap was found in our wire at M.20.b.7½.9

the side of the road was followed as soon as all the men were through. Having followed the road for about 40 yds the patrol made for M.20.b.10,8½. following this direction a number of large shell holes was passed; they were quite empty. The road was again reached & the patrol was halted for listening purposes about 50 yards from the enemy's wire. Two men were sent forward from here to enemy sap at M.21.a.1,6½. Reaching the sap the enemy's wire was followed towards the road. The sap is very narrow & has a T head with the earth piled high in the middle. the earth is cut away giving a low parapet. A sniper was located firing in the right corner of the sap head, without cover or loophole. Wire in this locality thick & in good condition. Three gaps each about a yard wide were seen in front of sap & the right at M.21.a.1,7.

Information: The enemy was seen to send up 1 red & 1 green light at 1.30 am & 3.45 am respectively. The shock of a mine explosion was felt about 1.15 am.

The enemy was reported repairing their front trench at M.20.c.8.5. This party was seen by a wiring party who reported that some of the enemy wore steel helmets & others Caps. On the return of the wiring party our Machine Gunners opened fire on the position indicated. The enemy were at work on their front line at M.20.c.8.4 & much new soil is seen at this spot.

A new loophole is observed at M.20.b.3½.3.

P.E.Williams. Capt.
Adjt. 19th R.W.F.

22.VII.16.

Daily Report Operations

	Own	Enemy
Artillery	18 9dnr active between 9.45 + 10.20 pm. Fire at M.20.d.77. silenced for a time the T.M. of enemy.	
Trench Mortars	Our T.M's very active between 10.20 + 11 pm. and dropped Trench Mortars in neighbourhood of M.20.c.54. This was very effective & states were seen in the air.	T.M's active between 9.45 + 10.20 pm. & also about 3.30 am. drops & chiefly about Boyau 210 & the muddy Arch about T.M. about the neighborhood of M.20.C.7.5.
Machine Guns	Burst of fire between 2 + 2.30 a.m. on line at huns M.20 B 6.3 where enemy snipers were active.	Active at intervals between 1 & 3 am. Emplacement seems to be in support line in front of M.20 B 3.0 Bursts at regular intervals.
Bombing	Rifle grenade active about M.20 b. 1½. 4½.	Fairly active throughout the day about M.20.b.5.3½ result on our trenches nil
Sniping Rifle Fire	Occasional shots fired throughout the night	Enemy rifle fire throughout the night chiefly from M.20.b.3.1. Snipers located at M.20.b.6.3. verified by sentry at 11 am.
Patrols	Patrol under Cpl Williams (C Coy) left D Sap at 11.35 pm. object - examination of enemy's wire. the patrol consisted of Cpl + 2 men & enemy party of 5 men & broken up by 2 men discovered turning wildly were kept under observation for a time. Patrol then returned & reported the party to the known been who opened fire at spot M.20 d. 1½. 9. Patrol under Capt G & Andrews about 1.30 am opened the enemy's wire badly damaged at M.20.b.3.3½	Nil

P Russellbourn. Capt
A/C.O. 15 RIF
31.7.16

Daily Report – Operations   Aug. 1st 1916.

	Own Troops	Enemy Troops
Artillery	Retaliation on Boche lines about M.20.b.53. at 10pm to 2's High Explosive. 11.15pm Shrapnel fire about M.20.c.27 where enemy two made attempts to repair the gap.	Intermittent shells 7"mm between Support Trench & COAL ST. also about M.20.c.9¾.9. 7mm 5.45–10pm Shrapnel & whizz bangs about Bryan 210 + Bryan 212
Trench Mortars	12.35 + 1.15pm Rumjars fell at M.20.b.6.4. 5m number 7.30 + 8pm Rumjars fell in enemy's line opposite Bryan 206. Strong fire brought between on M.20.d.7.8 at 12.30 (midnight) caught a working party about M.20.d.1.6	12.45 + 2pm raygun between 1pm + 8.30pm Rumjars fire between Marble Arch + Bryan 210. Direction of Rumjars about M.20.b.3.4 8pm Trench Mortar blew in shelter & traverse in front line at M.20.c.5½.6½ This Mortar came from M.20.d.2.9
Machine Guns	about 2.45 No. 3 Gun caught an enemy wiring party & dispersed them	No great activity
Snipins & Rifle Fire	Quiet	Quiet
Patrols	Lt Powell + 3 men went out at 12.15pm to inspect enemy's wire. Corporal Williams + 2 men went out at 12.10pm to reconnoitre of wire opposite D Sap.	Nil

P. E. Williams Capt
Capt. 19th R.W.F.

WAR DIARY
INTELLIGENCE SUMMARY

Army Form C. 2118

1/19th R.W.F.

August 1916

Vol 3

Place	Date	Hour	Summary of Events and Information	Remarks and references to Appendices
CALONNE	1-10		The Battalion held a Coy supporting front in the extension of the	A.C.G. 12
			CALONNE sector having two companies in front line in ordinary lines	
			Artillery fairly active on both sides	
			[illegible lines]	
			occasional minor operations	
			24 wounded and one man missing	
	10th		The Battalion was relieved by the 17th Welsh Regt in the	15.
	15th		support in CALONNE village & have the line on...	
			the Battalion moved to...	16.
	16th		Casualties in men wounded 3	

Army Form C. 2118

WAR DIARY
or
INTELLIGENCE SUMMARY

(Erase heading not required.)

19 F B W 3 August 1916

Place	Date	Hour	Summary of Events and Information	Remarks and references to Appendices
PETIT SAINT	16-23		In billets	
LES BREBIS	24th		Moved to LES BREBIS	
	28th		The Battalion took over the right subsector of LOOS subsector from the 17th	17.
			Welsh Regiment in the afternoon.	
ZOO S	29-31		During this time the enemy shelled us heavily in the whole sub	
			sector, he attempted to the line matter damaging his trenches and	
			casualties which were mainly all due to trench mortars fire amounted	
			to 3 killed and 5 wounded.	

J.H.S.Holand
Comdg. 19 F B W 3

S E C R E T.   COPY NO. 1.

119TH BRIGADE ORDER NO 12

1. The 40th Division front is to be readjusted to its original line, consisting of CALONNE and MAROC Sections, during the period August 9th to 11th.

2. The 120th Infantry Brigade in the present LOOS Section will "sidestep" to its right on the dates mentioned above.

3. The 120th Infantry Brigade will take over the present left subsection, CALONNE Section, the 14th Bn H.L.I. relieving the 18th Bn Welsh Regt. on the 10th instant.
The 18th Bn Welsh Regt will on relief move into Section Reserve at BULLY GRENAY, taking over the billets occupied by the 20th Bn Middlesex Regt. 121st Infantry Brigade.
Arrangements regarding both these reliefs will be made by O.C. 18th Bn Welsh Regt direct with the Os.C. 2 Battalions mentioned.

4. Elements of 119th Machine Gun Company, 119th Trench Mortar Battery, and Signallers in the present left subsection, CALONNE Section, will be relieved by corresponding elements of the 120th Brigade on the 10th instant, under arrangements to be made direct by Os.C. Units concerned.

5. Two Companies 17th Bn Welsh Regt will relieve the two front Companies, 19th Royal Welsh Fusiliers in the present right subsection, CALONNE Section, on the 10th instant, under arrangements to be made direct between Os.C. concerned.

6. On the completion of the relief mentioned in 5, O.C. 17th Bn Welsh Regt, will assume command of the (original) right subsection, CALONNE Section, O.C. 19th Bn R.W.Fusiliers (Support Battalion CALONNE) assuming the command of the CALONNE Defences.
The necessary adjustment of billets in CALONNE will be made under arrangements to be made between the Officers Commanding two Battalions concerned direct.

7. On the completion of the reliefs mentioned in 3, 4, 5, and 6, the Brigade will be disposed in accordance with the 119th Brigade Defence Scheme dated 14th July 1916, the various units being situated as follows :-

    CALONNE. Right Subsection.   17th Bn Welsh Regt.
    "   Left Subsection.   12th Bn S.W.Borderers
    Support and CALONNE Defences.   19th Bn R.W.Fusiliers
    BULLY GRENAY, Section Reserve. 18th Bn Welsh Regt.

8. Completion of the reliefs will be wired to these Headquarters, the usual code word being used.

                                            Captain
                                            Brigade Major
                                            119th Infantry Brigade.

6th August 1916.

P.T.O.

COPY NO 1. O.C. 19th R.W.F.	COPY NO. 15. O.C. 231st Field Coy. R.E.
2. O.C. 12th S.W.B.	16. "G" 20th Division
3. O.C. 17th Welsh.	17. "Q" 40th Division.
4. O.C. 18th Welsh.	18. 120th Brigade.
5. Q.M. 19th R.W.F.	19. 121st Brigade.
6. Q.M. 12th S.W.B.	20. War Diary.
7. Q.M. 17th Welsh.	21. Brigade Major.
8. Q.M. 18th Welsh.	22. Staff Captain
9. 119th Machine Gun Coy.	23. O.C. Right Group Artillery.
10. Bde. Transport Officer	24. 1st Bde. R.N.D.
11. " Intelligence Officer	25. 119th T.M. Battery.
12. " Supply Officer	26. Divisional T.M. Officer.
13. " Signals.	27. O.C. No 2 Company A.S.C.
14. " Bomb Officer.	

OPERATION ORDERS.

1. "A" & "C" Coys will relieve "D" & "B" Coys respectively in the RIGHT subsection CALLIER tomorrow 7th inst.

2. Coy Commanders will visit their portion of the line to be taken over on the morning of the 7th. They will be accompanied by their O.C.'s who will take over all trench stores. Lists to be forwarded to Bn Hqrs by 5 p.m.

3. "B" & "C" Coys will use CHAPEL ALLEY.
   "A" & "D" Coys will use MARBLE ARCH & BIRDCAGE WALK.
   Movement by platoons at 5 min. distance.

4. 1 Guide per platoon "B" Coy will report at "C" Coy's Hqrs at 2 p.m.
   1 Guide per platoon "D" Coy will report at Bn Hqrs at 2 p.m.

5. "A" & "C" Coys will leave their billets scrupulously clean.
   1 N.C.O. per platoon will be left behind as a guide to billets for the incoming company.

6. "B" & "D" Coys will take over Fatigue Parties. Strength to be pass on the 7th.

7. Written certificates regarding the cleanliness of billets taken over will be handed to the O.C. outgoing companies.

8. "A" Coy will leave billets at 2 p.m.
   "C" Coy will leave billets at 2-30 p.m.

9. Completion of relief will be notified by runner.

                                        (Sgd)... F.L. Williams.
                                        Captain & Adjutant.
                                        19th Battn. C.E.F.

6 Aug. 1916

OPERATION ORDERS.   9-8-16.

1. The 19th R.W.F. will be relived by 17th Welsh tomorrow the
   10th inst.
   Coys will be relieved in the following manner.

R.W.F.	Welsh.
Right Coy. "C" Coy	"D" Coy.
Centre Coy. "A" Coy.	"A" Coy.
Support Coy "D" Coy.	"C" Coy.

   "B" Coy will not move.

2. The Right Coy will use CHAPTEL ALLEY.
   The Centre Coy will use BIRDCAGE WALK.
   1 guide per platoon "A" Coy will be at Bn Hqrs at 3 p.m.
   1 guide per platoon "C" Coy will be at Barricade BERTHOLET
   St (M.14.c.8.7.) at 3 p.m.

3. Billeting officer and 1 N.C.O. per Coy and HQ's will report
   at Battn Hdqrs Orderly Room at 11-30.

4. Lewis Gunners, Snipers & Signallers will be relieved at
   10 p.m.
   1 guide per Lewis Gun will be at Bn Hdqrs at 10 am.

5. R.S.M.& C.S.M.'s 17th Welsh will take over stores at 11 a.m.
   C.S.M. "D" Coy 19th R.W.F. will take over stores from "C"
   Coy 17th Welsh. Bn Hdqrs at 11 a.m.

9-8-16.   (Snd)'...P.E.Williams.
                                     Captain & Adjutant.
                                        19th Battn R.W.Fus.

SECRET   COPY NO. 1

                        119TH BRIGADE ORDER NO 15.
                        ----

1. The following internal reliefs will take place tomorrow, August
    13th in the CALONNE SECTION.-

    (a) 19th Bn Royal Welsh Fusiliers will relieve 17th Bn
        Welsh Regiment in the right subsection.

    (b) 18th Bn Welsh Regiment will relieve 12th Bn South
        Wales Borderers in the left subsection.

    (c) 12th Bn South Wales Borderers will move into Support
        in CALONNE.

    (d) 17th Bn Welsh Regiment will move into Reserve in
        BULLY GRENAY.

2. Reliefs will be carried out under arrangements to be made between
    Commanding Officers concerned, and will be completed by 7 p.m.

3. Bombing and Snipers Posts and Lewis Guns will be relieved by 12
    noon.

4. Completion of relief will be reported by the usual code to these
    Headquarters.

                                                  Captain
                                                  Brigade Major
12-8-16.   119th Brigade.

COPY NO. 1. O.C. 19th R.W.F.   COPY NO. 12. Bde Signals.
         2. O.C. 12th S.W.B.   13. " Bomb Officer.
         3. O.C. 17th Welsh   14. O.C.231st Field Coy.R.E.
         4. O.C. 18th Welsh   15. 121st Brigade.
         5. Q.M. 19th R.W.B.F   16. War Diary
         6. Q.M. 12th S.W.B.   17. Brigade Major
         7. Q.M. 17th Welsh   18. Staff Captain
         8. Q.M. 18th Welsh   19. O.C.Right Group Artillery
         9. 119th Bde M.G.Coy.   20. 188th Brigade.
        10. Bde Transport Officer   21. 119th T.M.Battery
        11. " Intelligence Officer   22. S.O. for T.Ms.

OPERATION ORDERS.   12-8-16.

1. The 19th R.W.F. will relieve the 17th Welsh in the right subsection tomorrow 13th.

2. Coys will relieve in the following manner.

17th Welsh.	19th R.W.F.
"D" Coy. Right.	"B" Coy.
"A" Coy. Centre.	"D" Coy.
"C" Coy. Left.	"A" Coy.
"B" Coy. Support.	"C" Coy.

3. No guides will be necessary. Coys will use the following communication Trenches.

   Right "B" Coy.   CHAPTAL ALLEY.

   Centre "D" Coy.   BIRDCAGE WALK.

   Left. "A" Coy.   BOYAU THOMES.

4. "B" & "A" Coys will commence the relief at 1-30 p.m. "C" & "D" coys at 1-30 p.m. Dignallers, Snipers and Lewis Gunners will reliefe at 11 a.m.

5. 1 N.C.O. per coy & 1 N.C.O. from Headquarters will remain as Billeting N.C.O's for he incoming Battalion, 12th S.W.B. Billets will be left clean by all parties. Billeting N.C.O. from "C" Coy will take over Support Coy billets at 12 noon.

6. Company Commanders will reconnoitre the line at 10 a.m. R.S.M. & C.S.M's will take over stores at 10 a.m.
   Lists handed in to Battn Orderly Room will have signatures of C.S.M's of relieving unit and relieved unit.

12-8-16.

(Snd)...P.E.Williams.
Captain & Adjutant.
19th Battn. R.W.Fus.

SECRET   COPY NO. ....

119TH BRIGADE ORDER NO 16

1. **RELIEF.** The 119th Brigade will be relieved by the 120th Brigade in CALONNE Section on the 15th and 16th August in accordance with the table overleaf.
   All other arrangements will be made by Os. C. Units direct.

2. **STORES.**
   a. Trench Stores will be taken over by the usual parties of the 120th Brigade, which will be at GRENAY BRIDGE at 5.30 a.m. in the case of the 13th E.Surrey Regt., and at 2 p.m in the case of the 11th K.O.R.Lancs., on the 16th instant in both cases. Guides from the 19th Bn R.W.Fusiliers and 18th Bn Welsh Regt., will meet at above times and place.
   b. Brigade S.A.A. and Bomb Stores will be taken over on the 16th instant under arrangements to be made by Staff Captains direct.

3. **FATIGUES.** The fatigue party of 1 N.C.O. and 20 men found thrice daily for the Tunnelling Company will be found by the 12th Bn South Wales Borderers up to 8 a.m. on the 16th inclusive.
   The working party of 2 Officers, 4 N.C.Os and 100 men found by the 17th Bn Welsh Regt., for burying cable in CALONNE will be relieved by a corresponding party of the 14th A & S.Highrs, at 4 p.m. on the 16th.
   Arrangements with regard to the handing over of billets etc., will be made between Officers in charge of parties direct.

4. Completion of relief will be reported to these Headquarters in the usual code.
   G.O.C. 119th Brigade will hand over command of the CALONNE Section to G.O.C. 120th Brigade on completion of relief.

5. The personnel attached to the 231st Company R.E. for dug-out construction will remain in the line. Os.C. Units may make any changes in the personnel if they wish to do so.

6. Billeting parties of Units will report to the Staff Captain, at these Headquarters on the 16th instant as under :-
   19th R.W.F. 8 a.m.   17th Welsh Rgt. 8 a.m.
   12th S.W.B. 12 noon.   18th Welsh Rgt. 12 noon.

                                              Captain
                                              Brigade Major.
                                              119th Brigade.

14-8-1916.

Date	Unit of 119th Bde to be relieved	Unit of 120th Bde to relieve	Guides Time	Guides Place	Unit of 119th Bde to billet in	Billets vacated by
August 15.	119th M.G.Coy	120th M.G.Coy	4 p.m.	GRENAY CHURCH	-	-
do	Lewis Guns 19th R.W.F. 18th Welsh 12th S.W.B.	Lewis Guns 13th E.Surreys 11th K.O.R.Lancs 14th H.L.I.	5 p.m.	do	-	-
do	119th T.M.B.	120th T.M.B.	6 p.m.	do	-	-
August 16	19th R.W.F.	13th E.Surreys.	8 a.m.	GRANDE PLACE BULLY GRENAY	PETIT SAINS	13th E.Surrey Regt.
do	17th Welsh.	14th A & S.H.	9 a.m.	do	LES BREBIS Areas B & C	14th A & S. Highrs.
do	12th S.W.B.	14th H.L.I.	3.30p.m	GRENAY CHURCH	LES BREBIS Area: D	14th H.L.I.
do	18th Welsh	11th K.O.R.Lancs	6 p.m.	do	LES BREBIS Area A and Fosse 2.	11th K.O.R.Lancs.

Note. 1. The usual number of guides will be found by units of 119th Brigade.
2. The usual distances will be observed between parties of all units on the road.

COPY NO.
1. O.C.19th R.W.F.
2. O.C.12th S.W.B.
3. O.C.17th Welsh.
4. O.C.18th Welsh.
5. Q.M.19th R.W.F.
6. Q.M.12th S.W.B.
7. Q.M.17th Welsh
8. Q.M.18th Welsh
9. 119th M.G.Coy.
10. Bde Transport Officer
11. " Intelligence Officer
12. " Supply Officer
13. " Signals
14. " Bomb Officer
15. O.C.231st Field Coy R.E.
16. "G" 40th Division
17. "Q" 40th Division
18. 120th Brigade
19. 121st. Brigade.
20. War Diary
21. Brigade Major.
22. Staff Officer
23. O.C.Right Group Artillery
24. 188th Brigade.
25. 119th T.M.B.
26. Divisional T.M.B.
27. O.C.No 2 Company A.S.C.
28. 12th Bn York Rgt.

OPERATION ORDERS BY LIEUT: COL B.J.JONES. D.S.O.
COMMANDING 19TH BATTN R. W. FUSRS.

1. The 19th Battn R.W.F. will be relieved by the 13th East Surreys on the 16th inst and will move into billets at PETIT SAINS.

2. Companies will be relieved in the following manner.

R.W.F.	E.Surreys.	Route in for Surreys.	Exit for R.W.F.
B Coy.	B Coy.	CHAPTAL ALLEY.	NEW TRENCH, BOX TUNNEL, to COAL STREET.
D Coy.	D Coy.	BIRDCAGE WALK.	BIRDCAGE WALK.
A Coy.	C Coy.	H Q STREET & BOYAU THOMAS.	2 Platoons AMPTHILL TUNNEL. 2 platoons BOYAU THOMAS.
C Coy.	A Coy.	------- --	--------

3. Coys will be relieved in the following order.

	East Surreys.	R.W.F.	
1.	"C" Coy.	"A" Coy.	Left.
2.	"B" Coy.	"B" Coy.	Right.
3.	"D" Coy.	"D" Coy.	Centre.
4.	"A" Coy.	"C" Coy.	Support.

Headquarters.

4. 1 N.C.O. per Coy & 1 N.C.O. for Headquarters will report at Battn Orderly Room at 6-30 a.m. prompt. for billetting purposes.
1 Guide per platoon will report at Battn H.Q. at 5 a.m. without fail.
1 Guide for signallers will report at Battn H.Q. at 6 a.m.

5. Trench stores will be taken over at 6-30 a.m. Care will be taken that all items are entered & the lists signed by both Units.

6. Movements will be by platoons any stragglers will be absorbed into the nearest platoon or unit.

7. Completion of relief to be notified by runner.

15-8-16.

(Snd)...P.E.Williams.
Captain & Adjutant.
19th Battn. R.W.F.

S E C R E T. COPY NO....... 1

119TH BRIGADE ORDER NO 17

1. **RELIEF.**   The 119th Brigade will relieve the 47th Brigade in the LOOS Section on the 23rd and 24th instant, in accordance with the table overleaf.

2. **GUIDES.**   Guides will be provided by units of the 47th Brigade.

3. **STORES.**
   (a) Trench Stores. 1 Officer per Battalion and 1 N.C.O per Company will take over Trench Stores, meeting guides of the 47th Brigade at the places shewn in the table two hours before the time at which the unit commences to reach the rendezvous.

   (b) Brigade S.A.A. and Bomb Stores will be taken over under arrangements to be made by Staff Captains direct.

4. **BRIGADE SNIPERS AND OBSERVERS** will relieve under arrangements to be made by Brigade Intelligence Officers direct.

5. **MOVEMENT.**   All movement will be by platoons or detachments at 200 yards interval.

6. **DISPOSITIONS.** On completion of the relief, dispositions will be as follows :-

   Right Subsection. 17th Bn Welsh. 3 Coys in front line.
                                          1 Coy in ENCLOSURE.
   The front of this subsection is from HAYMARKET inclusive to PICCADILLY inclusive.

   Left Subsection. 12th Bn S.W.B. 3 Coys in front line.
                                        1 Coy in PIP STREET.
   The front of this subsection is from PICCADILLY exclusive to CAMERON ALLEY. inclusive.

   Support Battalion. 18th Bn Welsh 1 Coy LENS ROAD REDOUBT
                                               1 Coy DUKE STREET.
                                               2 Coy ENCLOSURE.

   Reserve Battalion. 19th Bn R.W.F. (less 5 Lewis Guns and teams) move into billets in LES BREBIS, Area D, on the 24th instant under arrangements to be made between Os.C.Units direct.

   Brigade Headquarters will remain at MINE BUILDINGS, LES BREBIS.

   Headquarters of Battalions will be as follows :-

            Right Subsection.   HATCHETTS
            Left   do   PIP STREET.
            Support   PRIVATE PASSAGE.

7. MAPS.

Os C. Units will take over all Maps, Sketches, Plans, Air Photographs and such defence orders as are available from the Unit which they relieve.
Units will return to this Office all Maps, Plans and Air Photographs of CALONNE Section which they have in their possession for safe custody.

8. BILLETS.

The billets in LES BREBIS permanently occupied by Units of the Brigade will be retained. Transport will remain as at present.

9. WORKING PARTIES.

Carrying parties for 173rd and 258th Tunnelling Companies R.E. will be found by the 18th Bn Welsh Regiment in accordance with instructions issued to O.C. that Unit direct.

                                                Captain.
                                                Brigade Major.
                                                119th Infantry Brigade.

23-8-1916.

Copy No 1. O.C. 19th R.W.F.
2. O.C. 12th S.W.B.
3. O.C. 17th Welsh.
4. O.C. 18th Welsh.
5. Q.M. 19th R.W.F.
6. Q.M. 12th S.W.B.
7. Q.M. 17th Welsh.
8. Q.M. 18th Welsh.
9. 119th M.G.Coy.
10. 119th T.M.B.
11. Bde Transport Officer.
12. Bde Intelligence Officer
13. Bde Supply Officer.
14. Bde Signals.

Copy No. 15. Bde Bomb Officer.
16. "G" 40th Division.
17. "Q" 40th Division.
18. 120th Brigade.
19. 121st Brigade.
20. 47th Brigade.
21. War Diary.
22. Brigade Major.
23. Staff Captain.
24. 173rd Tunnelling Coy.
25. 258th   do
26. O.C. LOOS.
27. "G" 16th Division.
28. Left Group Artillery.

Date.	Unit of 119th Brigade relieving.	Unit of 47th Brigade to be relieved	Destination of Unit 119th Brigade	Guides Place	Guides Time	Guides Number	Remarks.
23rd.	Lewis Guns. 17th Welsh.	Lewis Guns. 6th Conn.Rangers	Right Subsection	HATCHETTS	5 p.m.	1 per gun	5 guns only Remaining Gun will
"	Lewis Guns 19th R.W.F.	Lewis Guns 6th R.I.R.		G.35.d.55.55			move with
"	Lewis Guns. 12th S.W.B.	Lewis Guns. 8th R.M.F.	Left Subsection	do	6 p.m	do	Battalion.
"	Lewis Guns. 18th Welsh.	Lewis Guns. 7th Leinsters.					
"	119th M.G.Coy	47th M.G.Coy.	—				Arrangements to be made between Os.C. units direct.
"	119th T.M.B.	47th T.M.B.	—	do	4 p.m.	1 per mortar	
24th	1 Coy. 18th Welsh	1 Coy. 6th R.I.R.	LENS ROAD REDOUBT	47th Bde H.Q. MAZINGARBE L.29.a.70.95	8 a.m.	1 per platoon	Route via PHILOSOPHE and NORTHERN UP.
"	do	do	DUKE STREET	do	8-30a.m.	do	do
"	2 Coys. 18th Welsh.	2 Coys 6th R.I.R.	ENCLOSURE	HATCHETTS	9 a.m.	do	
"	12th S.W.B.	8th R.M.F.	Left subsection	do	11a.m.	do	
"	17th Welsh.	6th Conn Rangers	Right Subsection	do	6 p.m.	do	Centre Company will not be relieved till after dark.

NOTE :- Except where otherwise stated in Remarks Column, the route for units of 119th Brigade will be MAROC and PICCADILLY.

Operations Orders by Lt Col
B. J. Jones. DSO Commdg. 19th Battn
Royal Welsh Fusiliers

1. The 19th R.W.F will relieve the 14th Welsh Regt in the Right sub-Sector LOOS. on the 28th inst.

2. Snipers & Bombers will relieve by 6 AM they will march off at 3.30 A.M.

3. Coys will march off in the following order starting at 3.30 P.M. D.B.A. Headqrs. ALL movements will be by platoons at 5 mins interval. "C" Coy. will march off at 6 P.M.

4. Route for all parties will be LONDON ROAD, NORTH STREET, PICCADILLY.

5. Guides will be at HATCHETTS at 6 P.M. Mens & Officers valises will be handed in at Q.M Stores by 12 noon

6. Completion of relief to be notified by Runner

(Sd) P.E Williams Capt
Adjt 19th Bn R.W.F

Field
27/8/16.

Aug 2nd

Daily Report Operations

Type	Own Troops		Enemy Troops	
Artillery	7.30-8 pm	1Shrap & Strontium fell in enemy's support line about M.20.f.30. These were effective as enemy activity ceased about 7.30 pm.	5.45 pm	Aerial whizzbang, aerial torpedoes fell in rear of Support line about M.20.b.3.6.1
	10 am	Retaliation with Howitzers on CITÉ de CARENCIÈRES	6.30 & 7.30	Shrapnel burst above Peak-ac corner & about 40 were counted about Marble Arch & West of it. These were 4.7's & 5.9. They appeared to come from about M.21.a.i.3. No damage was done.
			6 am	4 + 77mm shells burst above Bogan 20.3.204. Succeeded in removing 20 and traps. Appeared to come from a point immediately in rear of Bogan 204.
			9.30 am	No. of 4·2 + shrapnel dropped on MARBLE ARCH + BOX TUNNEL
			6 & 7 pm	No. of Rum jars dropped on Right Support line near M.20.C.37
				No. of aerial torpedoes dropped
			10 & 11 am	No. of Rum jars about 10 fell on left of Bogan 210.
Trench Mortars	4 pm & 7 pm	T.M. bombarded enemy's front line with effect altho' falling into own front line & support line about M.20.c.2.5		
	10.30 & 11.30 am	T.M. extra effective many falling into enemy's line opposite Pick Axe Corner.		

	Own Troops	Enemy Troops
Bombing	4.30 & 7 pm. 30 Rifle Grenades fired falling into enemy's front line about M.20.b.3.3	Submitted Rifle grenade intofunction between Bayrum W & our trenches 3.am. at Vicker's emplacement at M.20.c.5ż.6ż wounding one man. 11½ 11.30 am. Small grenade burst near M 20.b.2.5. Slight muffled explosion not so destructive as Rifle Grenade.
Machine Guns	10.30 pm. Fires no of rounds on enemy working party at M 20.c.5.5. The proved effective & party withdrew. Working party fired at at point M20.b.5.4 party dispersed	No great activity
Sniping Rifle Fire	Midnight - 3.am 30 rounds fired at supposed position of sniper M.20.c.7.4	Snipers active throughout the night ‑ sniping from point M.20.c.2.8.

2/8/16

P. Williams Capt
Adjt 19th R.W.F.

Aug 3rd

Daily Report: Operations

Type	Own Troops		Enemy Troops
Artillery	12 noon 1 pm (2nd Div) Our Artillery bombarded enemy's blind in front of D11 & Bryan heard my destruction of houses in enemy's line	12.30-1 pm	12.30 pm to 1.42 shrapnel & shrapnel burst in F.555 which killed a senior officer of the enemy
	10.30-11 pm Our Artillery effectively silenced enemy M.G.'s near Bryan	10.30 pm	Enemy firing heavy from near Elephant house (Square) M20 b 1-27 No answer damage done
		6 am	100 rds Shrapnel near Zone 5
		11.30 am	rds of High Explosive Shrapnel between PAPPLE ARCH & GATE STREET
Trench Mortars	10 to 10.30 Violent bombardment of enemy's line in retaliation several effective hits on front line	3-3.5 pm	T.M is active fire between front line & about Bryan 20.3 Effectively silenced by our howitzers
			T.M fire kept up Bryan 204 & Bryan 101
		11 am	Sun T.M fire between front lines (stopped about M20 b 11 6
Bombing	9.8 to 10 pm fired about 20 R.L.G grenades onto enemy's line in Bryan 210	9.30-10.30 pm	Enemy kept firing Trench and Rifle Grenades fell in front of our line about M20 b - 13.4
		5 am	One fell near Bryan 207 wounding 2 men of Bryan	2 Sgts D
Sniping/Rifle fire	Enemy MGN constantly active as previous. Given by our enemy's flash	7.30 pm	One gun & one trench M.G of Bryan Sap D open Enemy firing a few rd Rifles & rapid hard Sol C to So L A also occasional shots. Enemy night snipers active shots coming from direction of M.20 3 6

Type	Own Troops	Enemy Troops
Machine Gun	11.30pm Fire directed on Enemy's wiring party who were dispersed. Enemy's wiring party fired on - Direction about N20.d.1.8½	Not active.

6th Fusiliers
31/5/16

"Aug 4th 1916."

DAILY REPORT - OPERATIONS -

TYPE	OUR TROOPS	ENEMY TROOPS
Artillery	At 2.30 am. our Artillery fired a short 6 gun salvo. The fire was normal. Attack normal & disposed of.	1am 1.2 High explosive shells were fired in small numbers at intervals throughout the night. Rifle + M.G. fire on our front 207½ 211. 1.15. 6 rounds heavy phosphor - 40 & 6 inch cannon in FO Sch. No 5.
Trench Mortars	12.30 am to 1.15 am Our Stokes discharged 50 rounds - objective M 20. 6. 4. 7. Much damage was apparently done.	11am to 12pm three Russian fell about trenches - Boyan 210+211. Apparently came from late enemy battle. Engaged Torpedoes fell along our front 207½ 211. Supposed trench damage appeared M 20 C 1½ × 8.
Bombing	7.30 am to 8.15. Fired about 16 Grenades into line M 20 6. 2. 4. + 3 4.	Very quiet.
Machine Guns	No 2. fired 47 rounds in bursts at snipers to his trench.	
Sniping + Rifle Fire	Several very th whole front	Generally very active along front, concentrating mostly Hill 60 others fire was most accurate.

Daily Report - Observations.

Type.	Our Troops.		Enemy Troops.	
Artillery	12 noon	Mills white Art[illery] [?] [?] 1 [?] dropped in enemy trench. About 25 rounds from front trenches had fire	12 noon	Artillery very active about 30 pres dropped between support line & the lines to the W of MARBLE ARCH.
			1-3 pm	Twenty rounds "whizz bangs" came over at the same target. German anti-tank fire at M.20.d.4.9
			3.15 am	2 salvoes of 6 in burst over M.20.b.12.6
French Mortars	3 pm	French mortars fired 5 rounds into CITÉ du CORNEILLES much damage was done	8 + 8.30 pm	Fair enemy fair active throughout the 24 hrs the only effective retaliation
	8 pm	Stokes gun fired about 15 rounds on enemy trenches about M.20.C.7.4.		being artillery. Extremely active at times mentioned.
Bombing		15 Italia Rifle Grenades were all put to dropped 20.35 directly in enemy's trench about M.20.A.	8 & 8.2 pm	Enemy response very active about 210 + 209 Rifle grenades active at the time. Damage thus of Mills bombs
			8.15 am - 9	German dealings. Continuation of heavy bombardment by aerial torpedoes with grenades
Machine Guns	12.30 pm	Burst most of the night on fork Cap. had working parties out in front gun fire at enemy, for ideas or snipers at M.20.b.33. Also burst effort at enemy working party at M.20.C.53		Intermittent firing throughout the night.

DAILY REPORT.
OPERATIONS.

TYPE	OWN TROOPS.		ENEMY TROOPS.	
Snipers Rifle fire	Rifle fire fairly general during the night after the return of patrols		3pm 5pm	Working party in Borgan 2.10 sniped at.

G. Russellaine Capt
1st Rnf
Aug 19
5/8/11

Aug 6th

Daily Operations

Type		Own Troops		Enemy Troops
Artillery	1.15-3.15	Artillery active especially on trenches about M.20.b.5.4	4.40	General artillery activity
	4.55	Two salvos of 18pdr shells into CITÉ de CORNEILLES	4.40	TMs gave very active on BIRD CAGE WALK + Stag Krap
	11.30pm	Six rounds of Howitzers into Enemy's front line about M.20.b.3.3. Main body damaged	5.45	12 Rifle grenade men front support line near Boyau 208, 209
			9.30	Repetition of Operation at 5.45: the Stag front appearing to be their objective
	12.30	3 Howitzer shells enemy position about M.20.d.2.5. damage appears to be great	11.30	30 (4.2") fired at support trenches near Boyau 209, 210
			1.0	Boyau 206 shelled + wandering fairly absurdly. Safety.
Trench Mortars		R.T.M's active throughout the day		Throughout the day Rum farm active especially at 210
	3.55pm	Two 17 Heavy howitzers burst in CITÉ de CORNEILLES about M.20.d.6.5. Causing great deal of damage		Aerial Torpedoes fell on almost every part of the line from 207-211
	4.45	34 rounds fired in retaliation at enemy's trench opposite Sap A	9.30-10pm	Rum farm + Aerial Torpedoes near Boyau 201 + 202
Bombs		During the day 15 Hale's Rifle Grenades fired into enemy's front line near M.20.b.33		One 110 Rifle Grenades fired into Support line near Boyaux 209, 210

CONTINUED.

Type	Own Troops	Enemy Troops
Machine Guns	No great activity	Active during day against aeroplanes
Snipers + Rifle fire	Few bursts of rapid occasionally during the night at supposed German working parties.	Not as heavy as usual.
Patrol	Patrol of 1 Cpl (Cpl Rochnell) + 2 men left Sap C at 12.45 (m'night) to reconnoitre left of Sap C + ascertain whether enemy are working a sap in this direction. When about 25 yds from Sap C patrol saw an enemy patrol of 10 men who tried to intercept them. Our patrol returned at 1.50 having neither seen nor heard any enemy groups.	

Aug 7

Daily Report - Operations

Type	Own Troops		Enemy Troops
Artillery	6-11 pm	20 19 shells fired into enemy's trench opposite Bryan 210 d 8.11. General activity throughout the day. No wheels being fired in all. Spurheds is where thought to be Howitzer	12.30 - 2.30] Shells Fired from (w.f) times at LITTLE WILLIE MINE. Constant shelling of front & its Bring throughout the day.
T.M's	5.30 pt.	5 T.M's hit its enemy's firing line about M 20 d 2.8	Not so active as yesterday
	10.35 pm	8 T.M's dropped on CITE-du-CORNAILLES causing great damage	
	0 - 1.30	Stokes Gun fired 50 rounds opposite PICK AXE CORNER & SAP A	
GRENADES		Rifle grenades active during the day	12.30 - 2.30 Aerial Torpedoes very thick about Bryan 210
			4.30 - 6.30 Aerial Torpedoes about BIRDCAGE WALK & LITTLE WILLIE MINE
M.G's	12.30	No 3 Gun fired burst at enemy working party about M 20 d 3.4. Party dispersed	12.2 am Large no. of Aerial Torpedoes on Bryan 20.6 & 20.5 causing damage to Trenches
		Continual overhead fire from Saphead. rocon fires throughout the night	Firing at Aeroplanes from M 20 d 15.35.
	12.30	Burst fired at enemy partial opposite PICK AXE CORNER	
Snipery + Rifle Fire		Steady fire throughout the night	Desultory firing

P Ewbleum Capt
A/g 19th A.I.F

Daily Report - Operations. Aug 5th

Type	Own Troops	Enemy Troops
Artillery	3-4 p.m. Shallow pattern about 60 yds in rear of front line about M.20.b.5.3. Remainder of day quiet. 10.30 a.m. Artillery reply to enemy's shelling of TENTH St.	6.30–7.30 p.m. Fired 15 rounds of 3" about line between Bayonets 209 & 10. 10.15–10.30 Enemy shelled junction of TENTH & FIFTH Sts. with 4.2's. about 18 rounds. (SHRAPNEL).
TRENCH MORTARS	6.30–8.30 p.m. Active dropping along enemy's front line about M.20.b.4.3. Increased enemy casualties as indicated by retaliation. 1.30 am – 2 am T.M. again active dropping in rear of enemy's line in front of Bayonets 209 & 210.	7.15–7.30 pm Active two pudding closets to ours about M.20.b.3.5. Replies to our bombardment. 2 am about Bayonet 210. 3.15 am No. of aerial torpedoes dropped into mouth of Sap C.
Bombing	8 p.m. & 8.30 p.m. No. of Rifle Grenades fired from Bayonet 207. Our fires in addition at portion of trench M.20.d.05.50	7.07 p.m. Two of fifth grenades (enemy) M.20.b.4.3.
Machine Guns	Intermittent bursts during the night from Reserve trenches. 12.30 Enemy working party fired at M.14.d.2.7	Very few shots (enemy)
Infantry + Rifle fire	Not very active	Occasionally quiet

PATROLS

OWN TROOPS

Lt. E. C. Powell + 3 men patrolled to the front of M.20.b.3.4. No enemy encountered two working parties seen. Enemy could be heard working in the front line about M.20.b.a.5.

Lt. I. Cpt Strickland + 2nd Lt Mullins with 2 N.C.O's + 5 men left Ash D. which the Upper Jumpy laying enemy patrol. Points have been reported here frequently of late. After energy 1st patrol struck a suddenly direction until enemy's wire was encountered between Sap. C + Sap. D. Enemy's wire was very thick about 40 yds to left of Post Picx A x B. Our enemy party (3 a.n.o.s and 2 inns) were there were (A Party was also O/b....) in rear of Post have enemy's buildings + working at a minutes.

No enemy report encountered. Machine guns were seen offensive in return of patrol from no trees patrol.

General

Owing to the slackening in activity in all areas the general impression is that a relief of the enemy has taken place.

R. Ewsillraus Capt
A/T 19th R of F
8/8/16

Daily Report - Operations 9/5/16

Type	Own Troops	Enemy Troops
Artillery	5.45 & 3 pm. Our Artillery active on enemy front & back Pick Axe corner. Our trench trap feeling in trench & did a great deal of damage.	12 noon - 2 pm. Several whizz bangs fell in rear of Southern lines. Enemy replied but feebly to our fire
	4-10-10 pm. Rest of enemy V/L fire, especially on junction trench M.30 & 30 h.5.	
T Mortars	5.10 - 5.30 pm. T.M's active, drawing enormous damage to the front line trenches about M.30.f 40.40	9.30-10.30 pm. Enemy replies vigorously with "Sausages" & Aerial Torpedoes. No damage was done. Sap C + D received attention from the enemy
	3 am. Round of 3 shells fired by No.1 gun & received no reply from the enemy.	
Bombing	12.30 & 2 pm two V/L Rifle Grenades fires at enemy's front line	2.30 & 3.30 pm V/L Rifle Grenade activity, all 5 - 7 pm. Still in rear of Southern line
Machine Gun	12.15 a.m. Machine gun fire at enemy party about 40ft	General absence of activity
	M 30 f 30.35	
Sniping & Rifle fire	No great activity	11.30 pm Sniper opposite Pick Axe corner reported enemy party between 20 & 30 T 9.30 am Rifle shots heard about M 30 f 70. but no reply needed was necessary
Patrols	11.15-1.am Patrol by Lt E C Powell for examination of enemy's wire	
	11 pm Patrol by Lt W & Lt T Shackleton (2 bombers from Bombing men. For results see information)	

P Rivendeux Capt
& Adjt
9/5/16

10.8.16

Daily Report - Operations

Type	Own Troops	Enemy Troops
Artillery	4-6 pm Heavy shelling of enemy's *[trench]* lines by our 18 pdrs. Intermittent shelling throughout the day.	3.30 pm Heavy shelling of MARKLOFKOPF St. & of TRENCH ST. Enemy replied to our bombardment. Minor Trench Mortars caused direct effect on Trenches.
T.M's	9.30 pm About 15 Stokes fired at enemy's trenches in front of D Sap. Shun was no reply. Concentrated damage done to house abt M.20.b.30.35 by T.M's	T.M's very quiet throughout, especially the evening, the enemy not replying to us at all.
Machine Guns	11.15 pm No of rounds fired at working party near Sap D. Enemy was not seen afterwards. No of rounds also fired at House M.20.b.05.50.	Very little activity of M.G. except at aeroplanes. 7.30 pm Reported that more of our aeroplanes were brought down in Enemy lines by M. Gun fire.
Bombing	No of Rifle Grenades fired into Trench & Support line from both Company fronts.	10-1 No of areas hurts fire between 5.15-5.45 pm Hedges Bayeux 210 & 208 otherwise very quiet.
Sniping & Rifle fire	Rifle fire more active than previous days, especially during night attending snipers.	11.30 pm - Started Sniping in area about D Sap throughout between 206 oils fire trench.
Patrols	Officer (2nd Lt M Robinson) 1 N.C.O. 2 men went up from Sap D at 11.30 pm to determine enemy activity. Enemy hostility by trench about to the enemy information who from H. & L. M. Guns were observed firing.	Nil

ARcCartie Capt
10.8.16

Operations - Aug 14/15

Type	Own Troops	Enemy Troops
Artillery	3.15 pm Enemy 15 shells fired on the enemy's lines about A.20.d.7.5	10.15pm Hostile artillery fire on Running Ring and a pt A.20.d. M.G.S. shell came from direction Abost. sw 75
	11 am. Artillery A.20.d. 5 + 4.3 strand+c. K.4	11.15 to 3 pm enemy active fire on 2'S line near MARBLE ARCH
Trench Mortars	4.40 pm Stokes fired return on enemy Running Ring in front line about M.20.d.6	2.15 to 3.30 am about 2 x 9 Rum Jars sent into enemy line in the Netherlands (Region 2?)
	11 pm Stokes again active in retaly to enemy L.T.M. in Bownum Ring	11 am Enemy TM active between 20.11 & 10 Bognum
Grenades / Bombs	During night Stokes Rifle Grenades fires at intervals from Cliffy at M.20.b. 3.3 Just two fell short + afterwards range & no found +	8 + 10 am enemy's aerial darts fell between front & support lines near M20.b. 6+9 Remainder unnoticed
		11 am 30 + 50 aerial darts + grenades fell in line Bognum Ring & 1st trench Unnoticed somewhat
M.G's	During the night intermittent fire on trench on east pt of front at Bownum Ring	No activity of any note except occasional delivery fire between fire
	Here Vickers firing indirect near A.21 & 3.3 two bursts of fire in wire at M.20.b. 44	
Rifle + Sniping	Occasional Shots fired at Flanders Area	Graham @Bushbarn Capt Cap? 14

14.8.16

Operation Report   Aug 15th

Type	Own Troops	Enemy Troops
Artillery.	3.30pm. About 12 shells (4.2) fell in enemy's front line about 4.10pm. M.20.b.8.6. with good effect.	1pm. Left of coy. (R) enemy being observed by 3pm. Whizz-bangs damaging M.G. Emplacement on left of Bay. Intermittent shelling of the Bay.
T.M's.	4pm-5pm. T.M's (Stokes) well distributed along front line about M.20.b.8.6. damaging front line considerably. 5pm. About 5 rum shells from Stokes dropping near M.20.c.5.2. 3-6pm. Medium T.M's active on Minendo Zfranch near M.20.b.3½.3. 6.20pm. 12 T.M's on trench in front of Haunted House.	3pm-6pm. Rum Jars active mainly between Boyaux 208 & 210 near support line. Damage done to Boyau 213 by T.M's.
Grenades.	5-7.30pm. No. 4 Grenade fires at enemy line about M.20.b.50.45.	2-3pm. Aerial darts & Rifle rens active especially near Boyaux 214 rus & Bayaux 204 & 205. 11.0pm. About 15 Rifle rens dropped near party in new trench from 206 near Rehnae Corner.
M.G.	11pm. Magazine fired at working party near M.20.b.3.3. 1.am. Burst fired at rifle lying in the open near M.20.b.7.6. no firing came from that direction afterwards.	General inactivity except for burst at 12.30am. near Boyau 201.
Rifle fire Sniping		Sniping especially at Boyau 206. Some Sniping started near M.20 b.21.2½ M.20f. 4;4.
Patrols.	10.45pm. Lieut. & 3 Patrols & 4 men reconnoitred portion of new minenwerfer M.20.b.3½.3 throws fresh return, working parties being very busy. Returned at 10.30pm.	

P. Swellsam Capt.
19th Kings
Aug 15.16
15.8.16

Daily Operation Report

Aug 29th

Type	Own Troops	Enemy Troops
Artillery	11.30pm Opened fire on enemy's trenches near CITÉ S¹ EDOUARD	11pm No. of trench mortar bombs fell behind support trenches.
T.M's	6pm Occasional shots fired by Stokes Gun 11.30pm Stokes T.M's fired simultaneously with the artillery	6pm Six Rum-jars fell between support line & front line near Bogau 36. Portion of trench blown in at a portion of trench blown in near M.6.C.47.50
Grenades	2.30am No. of Rifle Grenades were fired at enemy's trench near M.6.d 0.8	11-12 pm 2 intermittent Rifle Grenades 12-1 (midnight) About 20 feet near Bogau 34 watching during any noticeable damage.
Machine Gun	9pm Our M.G's opened fire at working party near M.6.c 4.52 who were standing. Several bogans from a trench steadifying them 11pm Burst fired at enemy patrol near M.6.b 2.2	10pm During the night little M.G fire bursts fired at Green Mound
Rifle fire & Sniping	Desultory firing through the night no special sniping post used	not very active
Patrols	— Nil —	Enemy patrol fired on near M.6.t-2.2

P. Ewhana Capt.
Aug 19th Regt.

29/6/16

Operation Report — August 30th 1916

Type	Own Troops	Enemy Troops
Artillery	12.2 pm. A no of 18 pdrs fired over Hart's Crater	12 4 3 pm Began 3' shells about 77mm Recently
	1.15 pm (fired line with shrapnel of enemy's front line between HARRON CRATER & MANNING'S MOUND	7.30 pm Shrapnel burst over the ENCLOSURE - 1st shell 1 came from direction of FOSSE 12 de LENS 77mm fired Bay H.Q. about 13 in salvos
		11.30 am
Trench Mortars	2.50 pm Stokes from Bryan 33 fell into enemy's trench at M.6.C. 25.30. 20 minutes also caused damage at some pt much debris was seen 15 yards in the air	12.45 pm Aerial Torpedo fires from about M.6.C.0.5 fell into (Bryan 34 Aerial Torpedoes were fragment from the front (about 3) Few T.M's (Rurgans) very quiet
Machine Guns	9.45 pm fling burst at working party in the wire near M.6.b. 35 25	occasional bursts during night from north of M.11 B. 20.30
Grenades	No fires from between Hart's CRATER & PICCADILLY	
Rifle fire & Sniping	Very Quiet	Almost complete absence of Sniping
	2 new	Party of are were seen patrolling near
Patrols	Patrol under Lce Cpl Clifford left trench at M.6.a. 50 & worked h Rd light of HART'S CRATER worked their way toward the Brick MOUND, finding a footprint of the enemy from the Shallow Sap Before reaching the Brick MOUND & suddenly running into Germans, who challenged & coursed with German others who were in shaw of the Mound. Hostilities muche to the Enemies some fight	the CRASSIER. they were fired on by MGs. P. Eno Adams Capt Capt 19th R.W.F.

3/9/16

30th Aug 1916

To:- Adjutant
    Warwicks

Report on enemy trenches from noon 29/8/16 to noon 30/8/16

I. Operations — (a) Our T.M. retaliated between for enemy T.M. bombardment between 4 and 5 a.m.
(b) Enemy bombarded our lines between 4 and 5 with T.M.
At 11.30 a.m. the enemy put out a large number of illuminated shells doing no damage.

II. Intelligence — (a) Nil
(b) Nil
(c) (i) Nil
    (ii) O.P. dropped 16 M5 D6 3/4 4/4 from artillery O.P.
    (iii)(iv) Nil
(d) Nil
(e) (i) Enemy wire seems to have been advanced a little at M6 C 3.5½.

H. Wood-Jones 2/Lt
C/o. Warwicks

OPERATION REPORT DATE 8/17/16

TYPE	OWN TROOPS	ENEMY TROOPS
Artillery	11-1 pm 5 shells dropped near Burtha line near HART'S crater. 4-6 am About 14 shells (4·5) fired in the direction between HART'S & HARRISON'S crater. Noon Exchange of shots between batteries	2·45-5·15 am Shelling with shrapnel #17 mm just behind support line near Junction (Bergan 53 & Regent St. 4·30 am 1 mun about 30 in number, breaking from trap of our front line between Manning's mound & HARRISON'S CRATER. Shelling ceased about 5·15 am
T.M's.	1-3 pm. T.M's active effective on enemy's line between CRASSIER & HART'S CRATER 5.15 am. Three heavy T.M's fell into enemy's line at M.6.6.to 30. About 50 rounds fired from Stokes firing slightly tough of HARRISON'S CRATER 10-11 am. Stokes at Bergan 36 retaliated the enemy's RUMT ARS	4 pm. Two heavy trench mortars fire in drug in REGENT ST left of Bergan 34, knocking in entrance. Three burst injuring 5 men. 9.30 pm. Two heavy mortars from MAGGIE FELL Shout of Coy. HQrs in Regent St. 9-45 am. Enemy retaliated to our STOKES with 10 round trap ones which fell behind support line but above K Coy HQrs in Regent St
Grenades	5-7 pm. Rifle Grenades sent over from Bergan 39 Also Allied over Rifle Grenades on to Sap head at M.5. D.50.60.	5-7 pm. No of Rifle grenades dropped near Bergan 52. Between front & support line. Grenadiers were active than previously
Machine Guns	10-11 Burst fired at working party from Shusta Sap near M.6.6.71. 1-1 Burst fired at working party near left of HART'S CRATER	Reading firing from HART'S CRATER on to whole front

Operation Report   date. August 31st

TYPE	OWN TROOPS.	ENEMY TROOPS.
Sniping Rifle fire.	Very quiet throughout the day	no marked activity
PATROL.	1 am Lee Cp C/T Jones again patrolled the green mound, met two under Bhoy Wood came in touch with a strong enemy covering party (8 men) Action resulted: a working party (5 men being the patrol returned to learn & was twice met with party stopped at the more enemy were sent at the front. Sent under Lce Cp/ C.J. Jones 2c/f Lt 11 pm Patrol under Lce C/ Report attached	nil

31/8/16

R. E. Williams Cap
Aug 19th R.W.F.

Information Aug 1st 1916.

Patrol. Patrol consisting of Corporal Williams, L/Cpl Knight + Pte. Wilson emerged from extreme of C Coy line (Boyau 206) about 12.10 p.m. Reexamined enemy sap opposite D Sap. Round the sap-head were numerous tins resembling Salmon tins split at one end to form a fan & distributed apparently with the intention of giving an alarm — composition of the one brought in is thought to be paraffin & sulphur. There were also among the tins several packets resembling our smoke bombs.

    A spiked helmet rested on the parapet but this was not touched fearing an alarm. The enemy's wire at this point is weak.

Trench Mortar observed firing from house M.20.b.4½.4.

New M.G. emplacement is suspected in house M.21.c.1.8½, & a new loophole observed at M.20.b.9.6.

Two Aerial Torpedoes picked up had

the dates clearly marked - one was 5/7/16
& the other 7/7/16.

P E Williams. Capt
Adjt. 19th Regt.

Daily Report - Information. 2/8/16.

1 pm. Man observed looking through periscope at M.20.b. 6½.5. He was fired at + the periscope at once disappeared.

3.35 pm. Man observed behind loophole at at M.20.b.9.6. Two rounds of armour piercing ammunition fired + loophole was immediately closed.

Between 8 + 11 pm. T.M. was observed to fire from point M.20.b. 5.2.

Enemy O.P. seen at M.20.b.5.1. This was reported to the T.M. B + the O.P. was hit.

Flash observed at M.20.D. 1.5 about midnight: this is thought to be a Trench Mortar Emplacement.

Patrol.
Patrol led by Sec. Lt. Swadam comprised of 2 men emerged from sap C + patrolled our wire in direction of Sap D. German working party was discovered, strength 6 men. They were busily wiring. Patrol returned at 12.30 am. + the wiring party was dealt with by our Machine Guns.

Our wire remains thin at Sap D.

P.E.Williams. Capt.
Adj. 19th R.W.F.

2/8/16

Information.   3/8/16.

Between 12 (noon) + 1 'o'clock three men were seen looking over the parapet at pt. M.20.b.5.1. This occurred every time a T.M. was fired into our lines. One man wore a dark round cap with a glossy peak.

About 8 p.m. smoke was seen coming from a cellar about M.20.b.5.2½.

Between 8 + 11 a.m. a man was seen above the parapet at M.20.b.45.40. He was wearing a bluish grey hat with two white buttons on the front. He was fired at and a hit is claimed.

P.E. Williams.

3.VIII.16.

— Information —

12–15 o.c. Very quiet. Nothing of importance was observed in enemy's lines.

15–18 o.c. Sniper's loop hole was observed at M20B 2.1.

4–7 o.c. A periscope was seen in enemy's front line at M20B 5.4. 2 Germans appeared close by, but their movement was too rapid for them to be fired at.

7–11 o.c. German Officers & men were seen looking over parapet at M 20. B. 4. 2.

General —

No 20.P. on the Slag Heap at M 20A 0.6½ was yesterday struck by a shell which was most probably intended for a T.M. which is that vicinity. We have however vacated this post for the time being.

O. Lloyd Roberts
Lieut.
19th R.W.F.

Information.   5/8/16

What is thought to be a store of some description was seen at M.26.B.8.8. Three men were seen coming out of this place carrying what appeared to be a large box. Entered the trench at M.26.B.7.8. Place is being carefully watched.

Working party about M.20.C.5.3 fired on by our M.G. about 22 o'clock.

About 4.30 a.m. three Germans, 2 in Grey uniform with round caps seen trying to get some object into their trenches. One man states he thinks a wounded man was dragged in.

11 a.m. on the 5th a pigeon was observed flying over from direction of LENS towa BULLY GRENAY.

Patrol 1. Under Cpl Seale (total 3) left vicinity of Sap D at 23.30 to examine & report on stake fence wire towards Sap C. This patrol has not been seen since & nothing has been heard of them since.

Patrol II. 2nd Lt E.J.Jones. + 2 men
left Sap C. objective being to
examine enemy's wire opposite Sap
C. They report that enemy's wire
in front of Sap C is in good condition
but not very heavy.

P. E. Williams. Capt
Adjt 19th Regt.

5/8/16.

Information.   6.VIII.16.

M.G. emplacement observed at M.20.b.35.35. Smoke was seen rising in short puffs from this point when one of our aeroplanes was over the enemy's lines.

Gap in enemy's wire at M.20.b.30.28. apparently done by a shell as there is a shell hole quite close.

Enemy's lines badly damaged between M.20.b.40.30 & M.20.b.20.50

Smoke seen issuing from chimneys in CITE-DE-ROLLENCOURT.

P.E.Williams.

6.VIII.16

Information. 7/8/16.

M.G. emplacement at M.20.b.35.35 mentioned in yesterday's report has been destroyed by shells.

Loophole observed at M.20.b.40.30.

In front of M.20.b.40.30 there is a break in enemy's wire.

Large clouds of smoke were seen rising from behind Bois de Rollencourt about M.27.d.3.20. It continued for about ½ an hour.

An Aerial Torpedo which did not explode bears marks R/H M.F. 5/7/16

7/8/16.

p. Evremanio Capt.
Adjt. 19th Regt.

Information.   Aug. 8th

Enemy has been repairing trench during night at M.20.b.35.18. No. of white stones & chalk thrown up from same at the point M.20.d.25.95

New S.P. suspected at the point M.20.d.45.45.

Another M.G. emplacement fixed at M.20.b.35.0. It was observed firing at British Aeroplane during the day.

Red flag observed flying in enemy's front line at point M.20.b.3.1.

At M.20.b.35.25 a loophole plate observed with movement behind it. Plate was fired at & no further movement was observed.

                    8/8/16

Daily Report - Information 9.8.16.

Enemy was seen waving a white flag at M.20.b.5.1. about 3.15 pm. This lasted for about 10 mins & was apparently some form of signalling.

M.G. still exists at M.20.b.35.35. Our T.M's have fired at this point but have only caused damage to the trench. Enemy may have brought up another M.G. as a gun was reported to be causing damage at this point.

Enemy Anti-air Craft gun was seen firing at one of our aeroplanes. It must have been brought up during the night as it sounded quite close & was in the direction of CITE DE ROLLANCOURT.

WIRE Patrol in charge of Lt E.C. Powell reports that the wire in front at M.20.b.30.35 had been cut but there were no actual gaps.

Patrol in charge of Lt. H. of T. Shrubland discovered gap in wire at M.20.c.60.40, length of gap 8.10. also gap 6 to the right.

Also visited two snipers & gaps at M.20.c.80.45 + M.20.d.20.70.

9.8.16.

P Curwen Capt
Adjt 19th R.W.F.

Information – 10/8/16.

Sentry at M.20.b.3.5 reports seeing six of the enemy in neighbourhood of demolished house at at M.20.b.65.50. They seemed to be carrying a heavy object on a stretcher arrangement. There seems to be a passage under this house & boxes can be seen. The position has been indicated to the Division Office.

Fresh soil has been seen at M.20.b.35.40. There seems to be a new sap head as it is only 20 yds from our front line. The enemy has not attempted to disguise the existence of this sap.

A red flag can be observed on enemy's parapet at M.20.b.30.15.

General absence of enemy Machine Gun fire is noteworthy. The only time when their such fire is used is against our air craft. One of our aeroplanes is reported to have been brought down about 5 pm, landing in enemy's lines.

M.G. emplacements observed at M.20.b.8.6.

H. Williams. Capt
Adjt 19th Regt

10/8/16.

19 RWF
Vol 4
Sept

H.H.
63

On His Majesty's Service.

(Secret)

53rd Mobile Veh Section

Officer i/c
J.B. Office
Base

WAR DIARY
or
INTELLIGENCE SUMMARY

(Erase heading not required.)

Army Form C. 2118

19 RWF

Place	Date	Hour	Summary of Events and Information	Remarks and references to Appendices
LOOS	Sept 2nd	6.p.m.	The Battalion was relieved by the 17th Welch in the Regt out sector LOOS limits 17th Welch. The Battalion moved into Dugouts in the Regt out etc. occupied on arrival. Dugouts were brushed up in the Companies lines & occupied before the Battalion's arrival on the 2nd Sept 1915. There were many signs that the battle was on & also to no to indicate that Companies were billeted at the ENCLOSURE & buildings for casualties. The first few days were quiet	Bde O Inst D. No 19 int
LOOS	Sept 5th	5.p.m.	The Battalion moved back to the Right out sector LOOS. The first few days were quite uneventful. On the 9th inst the enemy blew a small CAMOUFLET under that CRater, as a result fire from RE's were passed. Two NCO's from D.Coy (Lieut Wright + Cpl Battersby) gallantly relieved an officer + 2 men from the mine - as a result they were both slightly gassed. This gallant action gained for both of them the Military Medal. Several Officers were very frequent on the night of the 9th inst. Lee R. WD Phillips (A Coy) was killed. Officers were his first night on duty in the trenches this also was most unfortunate. Our total Casualties were 19 other ranks 5 were killed & 9 slightly gassed. We were relieved on the 11th inst by the 21st Middlesex.	21. 23 22. 24
PETIT-SAINS	Sept 11th	9.p.m.	The Battalion reached PETIT SAINS at a very late hour some of the men not reaching the village until midnight. Eight days were spent here in making up deficiencies in kit etc. was no equipping the men: a large no of fatigues had to be found.	
MAROC	Sept 19th 6.p.m.		Brigade took over the MAROC sector the Battalion moved into Reserve taking over the billets vacated by the 14 KHLI. The billets here are the best	23. 25

Army Form C. 2118

WAR DIARY
or
INTELLIGENCE SUMMARY

(Erase heading not required.)

Instructions regarding War Diaries and Intelligence Summaries are contained in F. S. Regs., Part II. and the Staff Manual respectively. Title Pages will be prepared in manuscript.

Place	Date	Hour	Summary of Events and Information	Remarks and references to Appendices
MAROC	23rd	5 p.m.	The Battalion has had & they were still further improves especially as regards drainage & proping of cellars. Lt Col B Jones takes K/Kopha - Major Vaughan 2nd in Command Battalion moved into Support in MAROC, taking over the huts at creeping by the 18th Batt. Welch Regt.	24 26
MAROC	26	4 p.m.	Battalion moved into Right Sub section MAROC. At 6 6 p.o in front line. Enemy very quiet throughout. Casualties up to date 1 man killed, 2 wounded. Battalion was very much strengthened by the influx of a new draft of 80 men: many of them from the 2nd Batt. R.W.F. + a number from the Welsh Horse.	25 27

A Vaughan Major
O.C. 17 Batt. R.W.F.

SECRET.   COPY NO..1.....

119TH BRIGADE ORDER NO 19.

1. The following internal relief will take place on Friday, September 1st, in the LOOS Section.

   (a)   17th Bn Welsh Regt will relieve 19th Bn R.Welsh Fusiliers in the Right Subsection.

   (b)   12th Bn S.Wales Borderers will relieve 18th Bn Welsh Regt in the Left Subsection.

   (c)   19th Bn R.Welsh Fusiliers will move into Support taking over the various trenches, redoubts, keeps and billets vacated by the 17th Bn Welsh Regt.

   (d)   18th Bn Welsh Regt will move into Brigade Reserve in N. MAROC.

2. (a)   Route for 12th Bn S.Wales Borderers and 18th Bn Welsh Regt will be NORTH STREET. The main body of the 12th Bn S.Wales Borderers will be clear of the junction of DUKE STREET and NORTH STREET (on the N.W. outskirts of LOOS) by 3-30 p.m., after which hour NORTH STREET East of G.34.c.57.75. will be used by the 18th Bn Welsh Regt and a Battalion of the 112th Brigade both going Westward.
   This latter Battalion will use DUKE STREET, NORTH STREET and LONDON ROAD after 3-30 p.m.

   (b)   All other details will be made between Os C. concerned.

   (c)   Bombing and Snipers Posts and Lewis Guns will be relieved by 10 a.m. Remainder of the relief will be complete by 10 p.m.

3. Completion of relief will be reported by the usual code to these Headquarters. The hour at which the various reliefs are completed will be included in the wire in future.

                                                    Captain.
                                                    Brigade Major.
31st August 1916.   119th Brigade.

Copy No. 1. O.C. 19th R.W.F.   Copy No. 13. 121st Brigade.
         2. O.C. 12th S.W.B.   14. 112th Brigade.
         3. O.C. 17th Welsh.   15. Bde Transport Officer
         4. O.C. 18th Welsh.   16. " Intelligence Officer.
         5. Q.M. 19th R.W.F.   17. " Signals.
         6. Q.M. 12th S.W.B.   18. " Bomb Officer
         7. Q.M. 17th Welsh.   19. War Diary.
         8. Q.M. 18th Welsh.   20. Brigade Major.
         9. 119th M.G.Coy.   21. Staff Captain.
        10. 119th T.M.B.   22. 229th Coy. R.E.
        11. S.O. for T.Ms.   23. Left Group Artillery.
        12. Commandant LOOS

Operation Orders by Lt. Col. B.J. Jones D.S.O
Commdg. 19th Batt. R.W.F.   22.

1. The 19th R.W.F. will be relieved by the 17th Welsh on the 1st Sept.
   19th R.W.F. will move into support in LOOS.
2. Companies will be relieved by the corresponding Coys. of the 17th Welsh in the following order.

R.W.F.	Welsh
A Coy.	B Coy.
B Coy.	A Coy.
C Coy.	C Coy.
D Coy.	D Coy.

3. C.S.M's of 17th Welsh will take over stores at 1pm. Care will be taken that petrol tins are carefully numbered.
4. A & C Coys. R.W.F. will move into the enclosure
   B Coy. will move into Duke St.
   D Coy. into Village line & LENS Redoubt.
5. A party of 1 officer 1 Sergt. 4 NCOs & 20 men from B Coy. will be at Batt. H.Q. at 3 pm. They will relieve the platoon of 17th Welsh in the WELLINGTON KEEP.
6. Bombers & Snipers will be relieved by 10 a.m.

P.E. Williams. Capt.
Adjt. 19th R.W.F.

31/8/16.

OPERATION ORDERS by Lt Col B. J. Jones D.S.O
Commdg. 19th R.W.F.

23

1. The Batt. will relieve the 17th Welsh in the Right sub-section LOOS tomorrow the 5th inst. Crescent area will be taken over by the 12 S.W.B.

2. Positions of the Coys will be as follows –
   Right Coy B. Coy.   Centre Coy A Coy
   Left "   D "   Support Coy. C Coy

3. A & C Coys will make their own arrangements for taking over stores &c from 17th Welsh.
   B & D Coys will take over stores at 3 (three) o'clock.
   1 N.C.O. from H.Q. will take over stores at the same time.

4. 1 N.C.O. from A Coy. will be at the East end of WREXHAM TUNNEL at 9 a.m. to conduct C.S. M4 (12 S.W.B) to A & C Coys 19th R.W.F. to take over stores.
   1 N.C.O. from B & D Coys (19th R.W.F.) will report at H.Q. 12th S.W.B. as guides to S.W.B. NCO's taking over.

5. One guide per Coys A & C will be at East end WREXHAM TUNNEL at a time to be notified later. One guide from each of B & D Coys and Hdqrs will be at Headquarters 12th S.W.B. at a time to be notified later.
   1 Guide for keep at MAZINGARBE will be at H.Q. 12th S.W.B. at 12 noon

P. E. Williams. Capt+ Adjt. 19th R.W.F.

S E C R E T.   COPY NO. ....

119th BRIGADE ORDER NO. 21.

1. The following internal relief will take place in the LOOS Section on Wednesday, September 6th.

    (a) 19th Bn R.W.Fusiliers will relieve 17th Bn Welsh Regt. in the right subsection.
    (b) 18th Bn Welsh Regt will relieve 12th Bn S.W.Borderers in the left subsection.
    (c) 12th Bn S.W.Borderers will move into support, taking over the various trenches, redoubts, keeps and billets vacated by the 19th Bn R.W.Fusiliers.
    (d) 17th Bn Welsh Regt will move into Brigade Reserve in N. Maroc.

2. (a) Route for 17th and 18th Bns Welsh Regt will be NORTH STREET.
    (b) Main body of 18th Bn Welsh Regt (going East) will be clear of the junction of NORTH STREET and PICCADILLY at G.34.d.55.95. by 3 p.m. before which hour the main body of 17th Bn Welsh Regt (going West) will not commence to pass that point.
    (c) Bombing and Snipers' Posts and Lewis Guns will be relieved by 10 a.m. Other reliefs will be complete by 10 p.m.
    (d) All other arrangements will be made between Os. C. Units direct.

3. Completion of relief will be wired to these Headquarters by the usual code.

                                                    Captain.
                                                    Brigade Major.
5th September 1916.   119th Brigade.

Copy No 1. O.C. 19th R.W.F.   Copy No. 13. Bde Transport Officer
       2. O.C. 12th S.W.B.   14. "   Intelligence Officer
       3. O.C. 17th Welsh.   15. "   Signals.
       4. O.C. 18th Welsh.   16. "   Bomb Officer
       5. Q.M. 19th R.W.F.   17. O/C 229th Coy. R.E.
       6. Q.M. 12th S.W.B.   18. 121st Brigade.
       7. Q.M. 17th Welsh.   19. 112th Brigade
       8. Q.M. 18th Welsh.   20. War Diary.
       9. 119th M.G.C.   21. Brigade Major.
      10. 119th T.M.B.   22. Staff Captain.
      11. S.O. for T.Ms.   23. Left Group Artillery.
      12. Commandant LOOS

S E C R E T.   COPY NO. 1.

119TH BRIGADE ORDER NO 22.

1. The 119th Brigade will be relieved by the 121st Brigade in the LOOS Section on the 10th and 11th instant, in accordance with the table overleaf, and will move into Divisional reserve in LES BREBIS and PETIT SAINS.

2. Brigade S.A.A. and Bomb Stores will be taken over under arrangements to be made by Staff Captains direct.

3. Brigade Snipers and Observers will be relieved under arrangements to be made by Brigade Intelligence Officers direct.

4. Carrying parties for 173rd and 258th Tunnelling Coys, R.E. will be found by 119th Brigade as follows:-

   No 1. Party. To 12 noon, when it will be relieved by party of 121st Brigade.
   " 2.   "   To night of 10th/11th September inclusive.
   " 3.   "   "   "   "
   " 4.   "   "   "   "
   " 5 & 6"   To 6 a.m. relief on 11th inclusive.

5. (a) The 100 men (25 per Battalion) attached to 229th Field Co. R.E. for dug-out construction will be relieved by 121st Brigade at 3 p.m. on the 11th instant, when they will rejoin their respective Units.

   (b) The 3 N.C.Os and 36 men, 17th Bn Welsh Regiment, similarly attached for work on Trench Mortar Emplacements, will be relieved at 4 p.m. by a corresponding party from the 13th Bn Yorkshire Regiment.
   Guides to meet these two parties will be found by the 229th Field Co. R.E., and will be at HATCHETTS at 2.45 p.m. and 3.45 p.m. respectively.

6. Working parties found by the Brigade in Reserve will be found by the 17th Bn Welsh Regiment in accordance with instructions issued separately to the O.C. that Unit.

7. Billetting parties of Battalions of 119th Brigade will report to the Town Major, LES BREBIS, at 12 noon on the 11th instant.

8. All movement will be by platoons or detachments, at 200 yards distance.

S E C R E T.

9. On completion of relief, Units of 119th Brigade will be billetted as under :-

18th Bn Welsh Regiment	Area A, LES BREBIS	A Bn
17th Bn Welsh Regiment	Area B, LES BREBIS	B Bn
12th Bn S.W. Borderers	Area D, LES BREBIS	C Bn
19th Bn R.W. Fusiliers	PETIT SAINS	D Bn

10. Completion of reliefs will be wired to these Headquarters by the usual code.

    G.O.C. 119th Brigade will hand over command of the LOOS Section to G.O.C. 121st Brigade on completion of the Brigade relief.

11. Acknowledge.

                                            Captain.
                                            Brigade Major.
                                            119th Brigade.

9th September 1916.

```
Copy No. 1. O.C. 19th R.W.F.          Copy No. 14. Bde Signals.
         2. O.C. 12th S.W.B.                   15. 40th Division. "G"
         3. O.C. 17th Welsh.                   16. 40th Division  "Q"
         4. O.C. 18th Welsh.                   17. 76th Brigade
         5. Q.M. 19th R.W.F.                   18. 120th Brigade
         6. Q.M. 12th S.W.B.                   19. 121st Brigade
         7. Q.M. 17th Welsh.                   20. War Diary
         8. Q.M. 18th Welsh.                   21. Brigade Major.
         9. 119th M.G.Coy.                     22. Staff Captain.
        10. 119th T.M.B.                       23. Commandant, LOOS.
        11. Bde Transport Officer              24. Town Major. LES BREBIS.
        12.  "  Intelligence Officer.          25. O.C. Left Group Artillery.
        13.  "  Bomb Officer                   26. 229th Company R.E.
```

Table to accompany. 119TH BRIGADE ORDER NO 22

Date	Unit 119th Brigade	Unit 121st Brigade	Guides from Units, 119th Bde. Time	Guides from Units, 119th Bde. Place	Number.	Outgoing Route 119th Brigade	Remarks.
Sept.10	M.G. Coy.	M.G. Coy.	5 p.m.	HATCHETTS	1 per gun	PICCADILLY, GRENAY (by permission of 120th Infantry Brigade)	Detailed arrangements between Os.C.concerned
do	Lewis Guns 19th R.W.F. 18th Welsh 12th S.W.B.	Lewis Guns. 21st Middlesex 12th Suffolks 20th Middlesex	4 p.m.	do	do	do	
do	T.M.Battery	T.M.Battery	6 p.m.	do	1 per mortar	do	Detailed arrangements between Os.C.concerned
Sept.11	12th S.W.B. 1 Company Bn. H.Q.	20th Middlesex 1 Company Bn. H.Q.	2 p.m.	Cross roads at G.13.d.1.4 PHILOSOPHE	1 per platoon 1 from Bn H.Q.	NORTHERN UP and PHILOSOPHE (by permission of 76th Infy. Brigade)	For LENS ROAD REDOUBT
do	12th S.W.B. 2 Companies	20th Middlesex 2 Companies	2 p.m.	HATCHETTS	1 per platoon	PICCADILLY & GRENAY (by permission of 120th I.Bde	For ENCLOSURE
do	12th S.W.B. 1 Company	20th Middlesex 1 Company	2.45p.m.	Junction of NORTH ST. and DUKE ST. G.35.b.0.7.	do	do	For DUKE STREET
do	18th Welsh	12th Suffolks	4 p.m.	do	1 per platoon 1 per Bn. H.Q.	do	Left Subsection.
do	19th R.W.F.	21st Middlesex	5 p.m.	HATCHETTS	do	do	Right Subsection.
do	17th Welsh	13th Yorks.	4 p.m.	GRENAY CHURCH	do	—	Bde Reserve.MAROC.

Control Posts to regulate traffic will be posted on the 11th by 19th Bn R.W.F. at the following points from 1.30 p.m. onwards :— (i) Junction of NORTH ST and DUKE ST. (ii) Junction of PICCADILLY and DUKE ST. (iii) HATCHETTS.

"A" Form.

MESSAGES AND SIGNALS.

Army Form C. 2121.

No. of Message _____

Prefix .... Code .... m.	Words	Charge	This message is on a/c of .... Service.	Recd. at .... m.
Office of Origin and Service Instructions.	Sent At .... m. To .... By		.... (Signature of "Franking Officer.")	Date .... From .... By

TO {

Sender's Number.	Day of Month	In reply to Number	A A A
*			

	From			
	Place			
	Time			

The above may be forwarded as now corrected.   **(Z)**

.... Censor.   Signature of Addressor or person authorised to telegraph in his name.

* This line should be erased if not required.

(688-9) —McC. & Co. Ltd., London.— W 14142/641. 225,000 4/15. Forms C 2121/10.

S E C R E T.   COPY NO....1.....

119TH BRIGADE ORDER NO. 23

1. The 119th Brigade will relieve the 120th Brigade in the MAROC Section on the 18th and 19th instant, in accordance with the table overleaf.

2. Guides will be provided by Units of the 120th Brigade.

3. (a) <u>Trench Stores</u>. 1 Officer per Battalion and 1 N.C.O. per Company will take over Trench Stores under arrangements to be made by O.C.Units direct.

   (b) <u>Brigade S.A.A. and Bomb Stores</u> will be taken over under arrangements to be made by Staff Captains direct.

4. Brigade Snipers and Observers will be relieved under arrangements to be made by Brigade Intelligence Officers direct.

5. All movement will be by platoons or detachments at 200 yards interval.

6. Carrying parties for 173rd Tunnelling Coy. R.E. will be found by the 18th Bn Welsh Regiment in accordance with instructions issued to the O.C. that Unit direct.

7. Completion of reliefs will be wired to these Headquarters by the usual code.

   The G.O.C. 119th Brigade will assume command of MAROC Section on the completion of the Brigade relief.

Acknowledge.

                                Hugh Reed   Captain.
                                              for Brigade Major.
17th Sept 1916.   119th Infantry Brigade.

Copy No. 1.O.C. 19th R.W.F.   Copy No. 14.Bde Signals.
         2.O.C. 12th S.W.B.   15.Bde Bomb Officer
         3.O.C. 17th Welsh   16."G" 40th Division
         4.O.C. 18th Welsh.   17."Q" 40th Division
         5.Q.M. 19th R.W.F.   18.120th Brigade
         6.Q.M. 12th S.W.B.   19.121st Brigade
         7.Q.M. 17th Welsh   20.111th Brigade
         8.Q.M. 18th Welsh.   21.War Diary
         9.119th M.G.Coy.   22.Brigade Major
        10.119th T.M.B.   23.Staff Captain.
        11.Bde Transport Officer   24.173rd Tunnelling Co.
        12.Bde Intelligence Officer.   25.Right Group Artillery.
        13.Bde Supply Officer.   26.Town Major.LES BREBIS

Date.	Unit of 119th Brigade relieving.	Unit of 120th Brigade to be relieved	Destination of Unit of 119th Brigade.	Guides to be found by 120th Bde			Remarks
				Time	Place	Number	
Sept 18.	119th M.G.Coy	120th M.G.Coy	—	8 p.m.	HOLE-IN-THE-WALL	1 per gun	
do	Lewis Guns 17th Bn Welsh 12th Bn S.W.B.	Lewis Guns 13th E.Surreys 11th K.O.R.Lancs	—	4 p.m.	do	do	
do	119th T.M.B.	120th T.M.B.	—	5 p.m.	do	1 per mortar	
Sept 19.	17th Bn Welsh	13th E Surreys	Right Subsection	4 p.m.	do	1 per platoon 1 per Bn H.Q.	
do	12th Bn S.W.B.	11th K.O.R.Lancs	Left Subsection	5 p.m.	do	do	
do	Bombers 12th Bn S.W.B.	Bombers 11th K.O.R.Lancs	DOUBLE CRASSIER	3-45p.m.	do	2	2 Officers, 6 N.C.Os and 60 men.
do	18th Bn Welsh	14th A & S Highrs	Support MAROC	5 p.m.	do	1 per platoon 1 per Bn H.Q.	
do	19th Bn R.W.F	14th H.L.I.	Reserve MAROC	6 p.m.	do	do	

19TH BATTALION.

Operation Orders by Lt. Col. B.J. Jones. D.S.O. Commdg.
19th Batt. R.W.F.

1. The 19th R.W.F. will relieve the 14th H.L.I. in Reserve at MAROC on the 19th inst.

2. Companies will move in the following order A, B, Headquarters, C & D. No.1 Platoon will pass Batt. Orderly Room at 4 p.m. Guides will be met at the ~~Hole in the Wall~~ IRON GATES. All movement will be by Platoons at not less than 200 yds. interval.

3. One officer & C.S.M. of each Coy. + 1 Officer + 1 N.C.O. of Headquarters will be at the ~~Hole in the Wall~~ IRON GATES at 3 p.m.

4. Lewis Gunners will move off at 1 p.m.

5. Snipers will move in accordance with arrangements made by Brigade Intelligence Officer.

6. Each Coy. will detail a party of 1 N.C.O. + 3 men to report billets clean to Billeting Officer at 5 p.m.

18.9.16

P.E. Williams. Capt.
Adjt. 19th R.W.F.

S E C R E T.   COPY NO. ....

119th BRIGADE ORDER No. 24.

1. The following internal relief will take place in the MAROC Section on Saturday 23rd September.

    (a) 19th Bn R.W.Fusiliers will move into support, taking over ST. JAMES'S & TRAVERS keeps and billets vacated by the 18th Bn The Welsh Regt.

    (b) 18th Bn; The Welsh Regt, will move into Brigade Reserve, taking over the billets vacated by 19th Bn R.W.F.

2. All details will be arranged by C.O's concerned.

3. Relief to be complete by 10 p.m.

4. Carrying parties for 173rd Tunnelling Company will be found by both Battalions in accordance with instructions issued to C.O's direct.

5. Completion of relief will be wired to these Headquarters in the usual code.

6. Acknowledge.

                                                    Captain,
                                                For Brigade Major,
22-9-16.   119th Infantry Brigade.

Copy No. 1. O.C. 19th R.W.F.   Copy No. 10. Bde Transport Officer
         2. O.C. 12th S.W.B.   11. " Intelligence Officer
         3. O.C. 17th Welsh.   12. " Signals.
         4. O.C. 18th Welsh.   13. O.C. 224th Field Co. R.E.
         5. Q.M. 19th R.W.F.   14. "G" 40th Division
         6. Q.M. 18th Welsh.   15. War Diary
         7. 119th M.G.Coy,   16. Brigade Major.
         8. 119th T.M.B.   17. Staff Captain.
         9. S.O. for T.Ms.   18. Town Major. MAROC.

Operation Orders by Lt.Col. B.J. Jones D.S.O.
Commanding 19th Batt. R.W.F.

26

1. The 19th Batt. R.W.F. will move into Support in [Mametz] on the 23rd inst. 19th Batt. Welsh Regt. will move into Reserve.

2. Companies will take over from the 19th in the following manner:
   R.W.F.   A   B   C   D
   Welsh Regt. A   B   C   D

3. Two parties each of 1 [N.C.O.] + 30 O.R. from B Coy. will take over the two [keeps] held by D Coy. 19th [Welsh Regt.] They will be met at the HOLE-in the-WALL at 3 p.m.

4. The guard of 2 N.C.O's + 12 men (B Coy.) will be relieved at 3 p.m. [parties] from B Coy. will meet this guard at the HOLE-in-the-WALL at 3 p.m.

5. First platoon of A Coy. will be at the HOLE-in-the-WALL at 3 p.m. Movement will be by platoons at 30 yards interval.

6. C.S.M's + [other] Headquarters will take over about 3.0 p.m.

7. Lewis Gun Section will be at HOLE-in the WALL at 3 p.m., they will provide a guide at [that hour].

8. 1 N.C.O. + 1 Signaller [from each Coy.] will be at the 19th Bn. Welsh Headquarters at 1.30 p.m.

9. 1 Guide per Coy. will be at the HOLE-in-the-[wall] at 3 p.m.

J. Williams Capt.
Adj. 19th R.W.F.

SECRET   Hule   WAR Diary   COPY NO...1....

119TH BRIGADE ORDER NO 25

1. The following internal relief will take place in the MAROC Section on Wednesday, September 27th.

    (a) 19th Bn R.W.Fusiliers will relieve 17th Bn The Welsh Regiment in the right subsection.
    (b) 18th Bn The Welsh Regiment will relieve 12th Bn S.W. Borderers in the left subsection.
    (c) 12th Bn S.W.Borderers will move into support, taking over the billets and keeps vacated by the 19th Bn. R.W.Fusiliers.
    (d) 17th Bn The Welsh Regiment will move into reserve, taking over the billets vacated by 18th Bn. The Welsh Regiment.

2. (a) Route for 19th Bn. R.W.Fusiliers will be TREIZE ALLEY and NEUF ALLEY, the main body being clear of junction of TREIZE ALLEY and PICCADILLY by 4 p.m.
    (b) Route for 18th Bn. The Welsh Regiment will be PICCADILLY and SOUTH STREET the head of the main body not reaching junction of TREIZE ALLEY and PICCADILLY before 4 p.m.
    (c) Route for 12th Bn. S.W.Borderers will be MIDDLE ALLEY.
    (d) Route for 17th Bn. The Welsh Regiment will be EDGWARE ROAD.

3. (a) The 12th Bn.S.W.Borderers bombers on the DOUBLE CRASSIER will be relieved by the bombers of the 18th Bn. The Welsh Regiment by 11 a.m.
    (b) Lewis Guns will be relieved by 10 a.m. Other reliefs will be complete by 10 p.m.
    (c) All other arrangements will be made between C.O's direct.

4. Carrying parties for Tunnelling Companies will be found in accordance with instructions issued to C.O's direct.
   O.C. 224th Field Coy. R.E. will make his own arrangements with Battalions in the line for working parties.

5. O's C. Support and Reserve Battalions will allot Lewis Guns to the "B" series M.G. emplacements as they are allotted at present.

6. Completion of relief will be wired to these Headquarters by the usual code.

7. Acknowledge.

                                                     Heshe Reed Captain.
                                                            for Brigade Major.
25th September 1916.   119th Infantry Brigade.

Copy No. 1. O.C. 19th R.W.F.	Copy No. 13. Bde Transport Officer
2. O.C. 12th S.W.B.	14. " Intelligence Officer
3. O.C. 17th Welsh.	15. " Signals.
4. O.C. 18th Welsh.	16. " Bomb Officer
5. Q.M. 19th R.W.F.	17. O.C. 224th Coy. R.E.
6. Q.M. 12th S.W.B.	18. 121st Brigade.
7. Q.M. 17th Welsh.	19. 111th Brigade.
8. Q.M. 18th Welsh.	20. War Diary.
9. 119th M.G.Coy.	21. Brigade Major.
10. 119th T.M.B.	22. Staff Captain.
11. S.O. for T.Ms.	23. Right Group Artillery.
12. Town Major, MAROC.	

27

Observation Report   Sept 7th 1916

TYPE	Our Troops	Enemy Troops
Artillery	6-8 pm Our artillery fired a no. of rounds of shrapnel 15 yds in rear of HARRISON'S CRATER into enemy's front line	5-6 pm about 12 whizz-bangs fired just behind its support line. 7.5 pm A few shells fired into WOS village & the village line
T.M's	5-6 pm About 8 medium T.M's fired into Enemy trench in front of Bogan 34. Stoke's gun also active. 9 have Stoke's near Bogan 37 in REGENT ST put out of action	7-8 pm No of medium fell in neighbourhood of Bogan 32. REGENT ST. prinly searching for No 2 Stoke's. HEAVY T.M. (SAUSAGE) 6 pushed fell near B074 in B074 in Bogan 36. No 6 am - 8.30 am Three Heavy T.M.'s fell near Bogan 36. No damage done
GRENADES	12-1 pm No of Rifle Grenades fired from near Bogan 32 on to Sap head at M.S.d 9.6.	6pm - 7pm Rifle Grenades very active — 10 fell in REGENT ST. 11.30 pm A few aerial torpedoes fell near Bogan 36.
Machine Guns	12-2 am No of rounds fired at Working Party at M.S.d 6.7	On the whole quiet. Gun active from Crellery Building at M.11 b.20.45.
Sniping & Rifle Fire	On the whole quiet. About 30 rds fired at Enemy Patrol at M.6.c 4.7	Practically non existent
Patrols	MANNING'S MOUND patrolled by Sec Lt J Dunny 2 am. Enemy patrol in NO Mans seen approaching during night. Approaches to a ground Flest Church — in neighbourhood of M.6.c at 7. M.G. rifle Thrown up in direction of enemy's line. No patrols fire opened on them. Patrol retired one working further into salient.	

7/9/16

P.E. Williams. Capt
Adjt. 19th R.I.F.

Report   (c) Nil   two
(b). for week 6/9/16 6 — 7/9/16

Operations:— (a) nil
(b) 5.15 pm. Enemy bombarded
our front line and supports
with T.M. & rifle grenades.
Our Artillery retaliation with
good effect.
5.20. Enemy tried to get down
one of our aeroplanes. It
seemed to have fire to a
...
6.30 pm Enemy dropped a
few heavy shells in vicinity
of point G.35 D4.36.
11.30 pm ...

2. Intelligence (a). 1 pm ...
         ... 176 C 8.6
         ...
         ...
         ...
         ...

a. [illegible] pit [illegible] M.6. D 5 9½.

b. nil

c. I. [illegible]

II. nil

III. [illegible]

IV. at M.6 D 4¾. 9½. [illegible]

[illegible]

[illegible] of [illegible] plate in

[illegible]. [illegible] a [illegible] hole in

centre of [illegible].

[illegible] was very thick at this

point.

@ 30 [illegible] (7/9/16) [illegible] appeared to

be a [illegible] [illegible] at M6.C77.

d. [illegible]

e. (i) nil

(ii). A [illegible] board was [illegible]

at M 6 D 1½. 9½. [illegible]

[illegible]. [illegible]

[illegible] investigated.

Sept 7th 1916

[illegible] 2nd Lt.

i/c. [illegible]

[illegible]

Operations Report. Sept. 8th 1916

TYPE	OWN TROOPS	ENEMY TROOPS
Artillery.	During the day our 18 Pdrs and Heavy + Cannon a good deal of damage to enemy's trenches.	4 pm. M.G. fire. A few rounds heavy exploded in neighbourhood of MANNING'S MOUND kiosk.
T.M's	7.15–7.30 pm Heavy artillery replied to enemy's T.M's. The result was effective + the T.M's were silenced. 5–7 pm. 2 Stokes + 4 Medium were sent you off fire on Enemy's trenches.	6–7 pm. Activity of Heavy T.M's from direction of "NAGS" Loop. Considerable damage caused to support line at M 6 a + 1 near Bryan 34. Effectively silenced by our Heavy Artillery.
Grenades.	During the day a no. of Rifle Grenades (25) were fired at enemy Sap at M 5.d.95.60. Caught 1 Rifle Grenade from near the CHALK PIT	6 pm. No. of enemy rifle-grenades fired in vicinity of Bryan 34 + Support line.
Machine Guns.	1 a.m. 2 a.m. M.G. fires on enemy working party near HARRISON'S CRATER. Working party immediately disperses. 11.30 pm. 3 magazines fired at working party near M 6 b 35/25.	Occasionally harassed our front line on M.G. on the CRASSIER. M.G. + M.S.C. fires on the Coy front near LOOS CRASSIER + Cause some annoyance.
Rifle fire Sniping.	No Whistle fired during the night by snipers from the parapet.	Very quiet, some little reply to our rifle fire.
Patrols.	MANNING'S MOUND Patrolled during the night under 2nd Lt. T. Drumm. Nothing to report see rough front. Capt T. Hitchburn, 2nd Lt Putwell fired here between Centre Sap + HARRIS CRATER + examines new front to the west, on an issue of a net in sight from our parapet in any time.	No comments.

8.9.16
P. Ewellyn. Capt
Capt 19 th Batt.

found a magazine, this silenced it.
(c) 4 S. Platz @ M 6 C 4½ 5½.
Riomic(was seen throwd anca
At about 2 yards interval. There
are two iron plates.
(d) Nil
(e)(a) Enemy observation balloon
was observed ascending, a direction
of Celt St Edouard time 3.30.
descending - 15.30.
(B) Gap in enemy y wire M 6 @ 8½ 6½
about 6 yards long

A.C.Morris 2o Lt.
y/o Scouts re
Warrior

8/9/16

Placed on Sheet 1 Trenches from
Noon 7/9/16 to noon 8/9/16.
(Conf. held at B.Hq.)

1. Operations. (a) At 9.15 a.m. machine
gunners spotted enemy
working party in no man's land
at 176 B 2 2. Rapid fire
heavily dispersed. Enemy no. of
casualties.

(b) Enemy trench mortar bombs
fell close to from M6A06.
& M6B 3 5½ causing considerable
damage. Our guns to retaliate
with good effect. (7pm – 8pm)

(c) 11.30 pm (7/9/16) enemy
bombarded our support line
with bombs not causing much
damage. An artillery [illegible]
result to record. [illegible]

2. Intelligence. (a) Periscope at 176 B 4. 5/9/3 cm.
(b) Nil
(c) 1. M.G. at M 5 d 9.5½ firing
all night. Saw four L.G.

Operations Report — Sept 9th 1916

TYPE	OWN TROOPS	ENEMY TROOPS
Artillery	4-6 pm A few 18 pdrs fired into enemy's trenches in neighbourhood of HARRISON'S crater.	Very quiet
T.M's.	4-6 pm Stokes very active traversing enemy front. Good damage done. 2am - 4 am Repetition of above	4-5 pm Few light T.M's fired in the vicinity of Bogun 3.2. Presently searching for Stokes Gun
Grenades.	12-2 am A number of rifle grenades fired into HARRISON'S CRATER. Proved very effective. A few more also fires at a working party at M.6.d.35.25 + also fires to party	9-10 pm About 10 Aerial Darts fires near M.5.c.15.5.65 between front + support lines. 1 am Two rifle grenades fell immediately behind MANNING'S mound in our front line - no damage
M.Gs.	8-8.30 pm M.guns fired at working party near HARRISON'S crater. The party quickly dispersed. 12.30 am M.guns fires from HARRISON'S crater (?) enemy's working party hastily dispersed 12.30 am 3 m.guns into fires at enemy working party near M.6.b.35.25. M.Gfire seemed effective as casualties were seen being taken over the parapet	9-10pm Indirect fire on LENS-BETHUNE rd on approach from transport during the rest of the night very quiet
Rifle fire.	About 1 pm no fires at working party near M.6.c.90.55. A hit is doubtful	very quiet
PATROL	MANNING'S MOUND was patrolled during night by a party under Lt. L Keddie very [gud?]	Nil —

9.9.16

P. Williams Capt
Adjt 19th R.W.F.

Books badly damaged.
Otherwise the whole of the ci— is one
mass of thick ——

Sept 9th 1916

A Williams Mr Lieut
o/c "Supvs"
"Warrior"

(b) Nil
(c) 14. At M 6 D 8. 9½ a bypass plate but no movement could be seen behind same. Enemy wire very thick at this point. 3 loophole plates or what appeared to be same, with no movement behind at T 7.5 D 9½. 5
(d) iii. At T 7.6 C 3.5. a small box arrangement was observed. It was carefully watched for a time & the enemy commenced a bombing a shaft of light appeared. We suspect it to be an OP for TM'S.
(e) (i). Enemy appears but sparingly on front line in his own all along our front. A numerous party was seen (too late to report at time) in broad day light in front of our left company. Hun sentries slain [?] tips.

At M 03 9½ a gap it to be seen in enemy wire at this part it

Report on enemy trenches noon 8/9/16 to
noon 9/9/16. Loos (Pt Bath) Sector

Operations (a). During the whole of last night
our M.G's were active dispersing many
German working (chiefly wiring) parties
& patrols causing many casualties.
Very quiet 24 hours.

(b) Enemy bombarded for about 10 mins
causing no damage. Our artillery
retaliated outnumbered the enemy.
It has been reported a time that
for the past 24 hours the "Saucy Minnie"
has been sent over from this Hun
line. A somewhat unusual occurrence
in this sector.

2. Intelligence (a) Man looking over parapet
M6D1¼9½ out of range for our
snipers firing (6.30pm) A periscope
is also in use at this point.
M5D9½ 5½ men looking over
parapet (9.30am 9/9/16) also 2
periscopes.

Army Form C. 2118

Operation Report

WAR DIARY
or
INTELLIGENCE SUMMARY
(Erase heading not required.)

Instructions regarding War Diaries and Intelligence Summaries are contained in F.S. Regs., Part II. and the Staff Manual respectively. Title Pages will be prepared in manuscript.

Place	Date	Hour	Summary of Events and Information	Remarks and references to Appendices
Lys			Our Loop (A few Trench Mortar shells in area of Harrisons Crater about M.C.5.4.	Enemy Trench Mortars slightly active today. 17 TM's fired. (A.4.) 11.15 to 12pm no. of shrapnel + TM's Ger burst M.C.5.4
		9.5am	About 12 Mauser fires in retaliation after having a round	
T.M's		10.45pm	Cancelled	8.30-9.30pm TM's fire on Regd SF from Bogan 35
		9.5am	About 8 shrapnel fell in rear of HARRISON's crater	
		3.30pm	On stokes active fire from near HAYMARKET	3.30 Heavy TM's active near SP on regd SP off Bogan 32. TM's activity near M.5.d.75.25
		6pm	Good shooting with Stokes from Regd SP. Enemy's line well straddled.	4pm 7.30pm TM Loos active in Support line near Bogan 34. Apparently more active than usual.
				10.15 2 light trench mortars (TM) fired burst of fire near HART'S crater etc.
Grenade			Started at M.5.d.95.62 fired in as interlocking They dumb fires into enemy's trench in rear of HARRISON's crater	6-7.30pm Lively Stock Mg active on front line near Bogan 34.35. 11.45am Several activity of enemy TM's Apparently in crater Cy near Bogan 34 Q Jew's crossed the canal at 4.5am
		6.30pm	M.G.d.40.2.5. (considerably harassing the enemy's gun).	MG fires on a considerably active in near HART's crater towards the River occasionally during the night
M.G's		11.30pm		
Rifle Grenade			About 2 also a couple showing above the ear it (WELKINS) was fired at (SUCKLING)	Sniping fairly active during the night

PATROLS ATTACHED

Observations.

1. About 10.15 p.m. a small CAMOUFLET was blown near HART'S CRATER. The Germans immediately sent up a large no. of Very Lights rockets indicating that they were taken by surprise. They also put up a barrage of T.M's & shrapnel for about 4 min. when they instantly ceased before our retaliation was brought to bear on them. Part of the gallery of the mine under HART'S CRATER was destroyed & some miners overcome by fumes. There is no change in either of the craters (HARTS & HARRISONS). Things were quite normal by 11 p.m.

Information.

B. A roll of papers was dropped in "No Man's" land about 3 p.m. on the 9th inst. from a BOSCHE Plane (evidence not quite definite whether British or Bosche). Copies were forwarded to Brigade Headquarters.

10.9.16.

F.C. Williams Capt.
Adjt. 19th R.W.F.

"A" Form.　　　　　　　　　　　　　　　　　　Army Form C. 2121.

MESSAGES AND SIGNALS.

No. of Message _____

Prefix _____ Code _____ m.	Words	Charge	*This message is on a/c of*	Recd. at _____ m.
Office of Origin and Service Instructions. _____ _____ _____	Sent At _____ m. To _____ By _____		_____ Service. (Signature of "Franking Officer.")	Date _____ From _____ By _____

TO { _____

Sender's Number.	Day of Month	In reply to Number	A A A
*			

[message body — blank ruled lines]

From			
Place			
Time			

The above may be forwarded as now corrected.　　(Z)

_____
　　　　　　　　　　　　Censor.　|　Signature of Addressor or person authorised to telegraph in his name.

* This line should be erased if not required.

(688-9) —McC. & Co. Ltd., London.— W 14142/641. 225,000 4/15. Forms C 2121/10.

Report on enemy trench in from 7/9/16 to noon 10/9/16. Loos Sector, 1st Bn.

1. **Operations** (a) 4.30pm our stokes guns fired on enemy line to cut gap in enemy wire at M6D1.9£. At 7.5pm our Artillery & T.M's bombarded Hulluch line. Effect could not be determined but enemy retaliated at intervals with Howitzers.

(b) 12 noon enemy bombarded our support line for about 15 minutes. 4pm He also bombarded both our front line & supports with T.M's & rifle grenades. Our artillery retaliation but results could not be seen.

9.30am enemy bombarded our supports and at intervals to noon. Our artillery retaliated.

At 9.30pm – 10pm enemy threw a few rifle bombs blowing in the side of one of our

enemy galleries in the vicinity
of Hawk Crater. The enemy, for
a period of 3 mins put up a
barrage of shrapnel over their
own shaft entrances. One
or two were gassed otherwise no
damage was done.

Intelligence (a) 1.30 pm periscope at entrances
at M6 O 3½. 9½.

(b) M6 C 4¾ 5½ 3 snipers plates
were seen also a large Box periscope
M6 C 2 5. another snipers plate
is apparently seen behind same.
A periscope is also seen here.

(c) M6 B 4¾. ½ smoke seen
behind enemy other TM fired
on our lines. suspected emplacement

(d) What appears to be a
wireless apparatus is attached
to spire of St Laurent church.
During last night enemy have
put up new wire M6 C 2½ 5.

Sept 10th 1916   A.C. Morris Lieut
                              Offr Scouts
                              Loomis

Operations Report — Sept 11th 1916

TYPE	OWN TROOPS	ENEMY TROOPS
Artillery	5.15–5.30pm Retaliation with shrapnel on TM howitzers new chalk pit Round as good TMs retaliation considerable fire	4pm 2 rnds of HE shrapnel & TM's in reply fired from HARTS CRATER & Boyau 39 mainly on Saphut Trenches
T M'S	5.15pm A few Medium TMs fired on HARRISON'S CRATER.	3.45pm 8 heavy TM's fell in recent chalk pit. Lines retaliation by heavies TM's heavy been very quiet. TMs fell M16 @ 10.50. 4.30–5pm Few
Rifle Grenades &c	2.0pm–2.45pm 30 effect new enemy's gun at HART'S CRATER	2.3pm 30 rifle grenades fired near CHALK PIT.
Machine Guns	11 pm no of rounds fired at enemy working party at M 5 d 50.50. 11 pm 20 working party view HARTS CRATER fired on superiors. They did not re-appear	Intermittent he was on several occasions during the night. 12.2am Irradiance actioned fire direction of MANNING'S MOUND also fire left of HARRISONS CRATER. Machine gun developed from M6 eq.91
Rifle Fire Sniping	1.0am 6 working party left of 1 Sap L and in 24 no occasion 9 enemy party made movement	Normal and Sniping especially at dawn & dusk 17 left and right lines
Patrols	HANCACKS mound fired on by rather rural the LI & G Patrols in Day of rifles Fisher	Some missionaries.

P. Williams Cap?
Capt 19th ???
11.9.16

Report on Snipers from noon 10/9/16
to noon 11/9/16. Woodstock Avre.

1) Operations (a) ...
   ...
   ...
   ...
   an appeared line row artillery
   platoon observing the guns.

2) Intelligence (a) Snipers seen at M6c2.5
   at same time shot was fired
   from loophole M6c 2.5 sniper
   was removed.
   (c) 4. At M6a 3½ 9½, observed
   a hole in the parapet which
   appears to be an O.P. now
   aspect probably a loophole
   was seen there.
   (d) 2. At 1.30pm smoke again
   issued from behind wiring
   at M6 B14½ 4½, at same time
   which water was dripping

on our lines.
(2) Our M.G's again dispersed
several enemy wiring parties in
the vicinity of saints Bator

Sept 11th /916

Acumoms grad.
O/C "Scouts
Borneo"

Report on Enemy Trenches. noon
19/9/16 to noon 20/9/16. "Marve"

1. Operations.
(a). Our artillery shelled enemy
front line between M 10 A 6.4½.
and M 10 A 6½. 9. at 10.20 am
20/9/16. Enemy retaliated causing
us damage.
(b) Our artillery fired several rounds
of shrapnel at Double crassier
M 4 D 1.4½. at 12.50 (noon) 19/9/16

2. Intelligence (a) Three men were seen apparently
observing at 1710 C 2.6¾ at 12 noon
19/9/16. One had his head well
above the parapet & looked around
for a considerable period.
At 4 p.m. two men were seen at 17 d 9.4
(b) nil
(c) nil
(d) nil
(e)(a) nil
(b) Smoke was seen rising from
between two houses at 17 10 D 9 6¾
at 3.15 p.m. 19/9/16.
(c) M 10 C 3.7. A fire was seen burning
at this point for at least 2 hours
& giving thick clouds of smoke.

20/9/16.   A. Moore. 2nd Lt.
                                        3D. "Warrior"

Report on enemy trenches noon 20/9/16
noon 21/9/16.   MAROC.

1. <u>Operations</u>:- (a) M.10.c.3.9. at 10am (20/9/16).
our T.M. bombarded enemy wire
causing a gap. Trench mortars bombarded
M.10.c.1½.5½. and ~~Trench mortars bombarded~~
enemy's ~~gun~~ T.M. at this point
silencing it for a time, but
it was heard to fire again from 9-10 p.m.
(b) Enemy dropped heavier but over lines.
Results could not be determined.

2. <u>Intelligence</u> (a) nil
(B) nil
(c) i. At 7 p.m. we observed an M.G.E.
at M.10.A.6½.3, a faint smoke
was also seen when the gun was
fired.
at M.10.a.6.6. M.G.E. but not
seen firing.
ii. nil
iii. Enemy O.P. built in sand bags
suspected. Careful watch is
being kept on the spot. M.10.A.9.7.
iv. at M.10.A.9½.6½. S.P. seen also
a large white cat on parapet
at this point.
v. At 4 p.m. at M.10.C.1½.5½. a T.M. was

seen before from this point.
Shell appeared to be very large &
caused a big explosion.

a. nil
2.(a) nil
(b) Smoke seen coming from enemy
trench at M.5.c.3½.0. at 10.3 a.m.
9/9/16.

A. Cooper D/Lieut
O/C Leuchars Trenchmortars
"WARRIOR"

Sept
9/9/16

Report on Enemy trenches from 21/7/16
Anson 22/7/16.   MAROC.

1. Operations. (a) Our artillery bombarded M11A 6.9½
   front-line trench at 2 pm (21/7/16)
   Also between M4C 9.7, M4D 2.3½.
   Very high explosive at 2.35 pm.
   (b) Trench mortars bombarded our
   lines at M7B 6.4 at 10.15 this
   morning & in reply but little damage.

2. Intelligence a. nil
                b. nil
                c. (i) nil
                   (ii) nil
                   iii. An O.P. at M10C 4.7½
                        Watched by a tel. scope were
                        seen here.
                   iv. S.P. seen at M10A 9½.6
                       A periscope observed in
                       use here.
                d. nil
                e. nil. Gaps before reported
                   are still to be seen.

Work. O.P's.
No.7. Select O.P. has had some
slight improvements made & the murder
has been newly fixed.   A.Morris 2/Lt
                            "WARRIOR."

War Diary

Report on enemy trenches Noon 22/9/16
to noon 23/9/16.   'Maroc'.

1. Operations: (a) At 3.30 p.m. our T.M. bombarded
enemy front line at M.10.C.2.7.
causing considerable
damage, also at M.10.C.1.5.
here causing a fire which
was likely to be a dugout.
Our artillery shelled M.4.D.8.6.
very heavily at about 5 p.m.
(b) nil

2. Intelligence. (a) At M.4.C.8.5½ a small
red flag appears on parapet
at dawn. Also a periscope
was in use here. There appears
to be some fresh [brown] earth
thrown up here.
A man was seen looking over
the parapet at M.10.C.4.6½
wearing a grey uniform but no
hat at about 4.30 p.m.
At M.16.A.6.5. a horse & cart
was seen going along road,
two men in uniform were with
cart and another in rear.
(b) nil
(c) i nil
    ii nil

iii at M6D 6¾.1 something was seen glittering in Forge 12 are LENS! Possibly a telescope.
iv nil
v nil

(1) nil

(2) (a) nil
(b) Gap in wire fence at M.10.c.2.7¼
Large Gap also at M.10.C ¾. 5.
"   "   "   " M 9 D 9½ 3¼.
(this is evidently under repair as fresh wire is (b) seen there)
Wire Badly damaged between M.10.C.2.7.
+ M.10 C.14.
Wire very thin at M.10 A. 6½, 6½.
Enemy transport seen on road at N.8.A.16
At M.10 C 5.6½, a fire was seen burning lasting about 15–20 minutes at about 7pm 22/9/16.

General. Owing to a heavy mist observation this morning was rendered practically impossible.
WORK &c. Minor Repairs & improvements O.O.P's & Billets.

Sept 23rd 1916

A.C.Morris 2nd Lieut
O/C Scouts Snipers WARRIOR

Report on enemy trenches noon 23/9/16
to noon 24th/9/16.   "Maroc."

1. Operations: (a) Our artillery shelled
enemy's front line with
shrapnel at 3.30pm on
point M.10.A.6.4.
Also shelled the double Crassin
at 4pm point M.4.D.2.5.
At 4pm 16 Fosse de Lens was
shelled by heavies causing
serious damage. M.10.C.8.5½.
(b) nil

2. Intelligence (a) Two men seen walking past
point M.16.C.8¾.4¾. at
2.30 pm, over open ground
wearing grey uniforms & round
hats.
At 5.30pm parties of Germans
were seen walking past M.16.A.6.1.
also wearing grey uniforms
& round hats. Also a large
party of 25-30 men who
appeared to be civilians clad
in dark blue clothes one or two
wearing straw hats. Appeared
to be very young.

at M10 A6.½. Periscope seen
also at M10 B 6¼. 1 and being put
up & down at intervals

(b) nil
(c) i. MG E at M10 A 5.4 with box
care suspected to be used by snipers
in day time. Movement seen behind
it.
ii. nil
iii. nil
iv. nil
v. nil
(d) 1. Suspected M.G.E. with steel or iron
case fixed with sliding door at
nose end. M10 B.37
Also a suspected M.G.E at M9 8.4
ii iii iv v. nil.

(e) (a) nil
(b) At M4 C 9.4 wire very thick
also a slit through the wire at this
point. Probably infront of M.G.E.
Smoke was seen coming from 2 houses
at M 16 C 8.6. time 2 pm.
Also from house M 29 A 7.8. time 3pm.
M.10 A. 6¾. 1 Bocke wire very thick
M 10 A 6. 8.   "   "   " thin
M 10 A 6. 2.   "   "   " thin.

General Work :- Continuation of repairs & improvements
b OP No 8 (Railway). Observation bad owing
to mist this morning.   A.C.Morris 2nd/Lt.
Sept 24/1916   S/O "WARRIOR"

Report on Enemy trenches noon 24/9/16 to noon 25/9/16.   MAROC.

1. Operations. (a) M.4.C.8.6. at 12.30 noon our artillery dropped a few bombs on this spot.
At M.10.C.1¼.4¾ our T.M. badly damaged enemy trenches
M.10.C.7½.8½ at 11 am (25/9/16) our artillery fired one round at this point.
(b) nil.

2. Intelligence (a). Periscope in use at point M.4.C.8.4.
Box periscope also in use at M.10.A.6½.3½
At M.10.C.8½.4¼ periscope on stick observed.
(b) Fresh soil has been thrown up at M.10.A.9.1. making parapet very high.
(c)(i) M.10.A.5.4 movement was seen behind M.G.E at this point.
(ii) nil
(iii) nil
(iv) nil
(v) nil.

(a) (i) nil
(ii)(iii) nil
(iv) Suspected snipers plate at this point.
(v) nil

(2) (a) nil
(b) Enemy wire badly damaged at M.10.c.3.5. & M.10.c.0.4. by our T.M.B.

M.16.A.6.4. Road in use. The road is constantly in use. Traffic at all times of day & presumably night is to be seen making use of it. Both military transport & what appear to be civilian vehicles (similar to Bread vans) are often seen. Women (two) were seen yesterday at 5.30 pm wearing white blouses & black skirts. This road has been mentioned before in my reports.

WORK re Improvements to O.P's still carried on (Imp alley). Rifle Batteries in use nightly, one is being set on Road above mentioned.

25.9.16.

a. Morris 2nd Lieut
O/C Scouts Snipers
WARRIOR

1

Report on Enemy Trenches noon 25/9/16.
Noon 26/9/16. "Maroc"

1. <u>Operations</u> (a) Our T.M. bombarded Enemy
   trenches with good effect
   M.10.c.7.6. time 2.35pm.
   Our Artillery fired a few rounds
   at M15.B.8½.4. At 2.30pm
   Our T.M. shelled this point
   causing considerable damage
   M16A.6.5. at 5pm.
   At 5.45 our T.M's bombarded
   trenches M9.D.9.3. at 5.45pm
   (b). N.1.A.5.9. at 2.10pm what
   was thought to be a mine
   was sprung at this point causing
   a large cloud of white smoke.
   A man appeared immediately
   after on trench near by, & quickly
   disappeared. T.G's were heard
   firing in the focs visually &
   our artillery bombarded the
   whole of the Boche front line
   from M6.c.25. & N1.A.5.9.
   continuing till 3 pm.

2. <u>Intelligence</u> (a). Smoke was seen
   issuing from enemy's trench
   at 2pm. M10C.2½.2½.

Y

* M16A3½.9½. Three of the Enemy were seen riding past this point on cycles. also a covered own presumably Officers Mess cart (twice. 3 p.m.)
* (A Fixed rifle battery is being set on this point).

A man was seen looking over parapet at M4C7½.6.

(b) nil
(c) i. nil
ii. nil
iii. nil
iv. Snipers plate at M4C6½.).
v. nil
(d) i. nil
ii. nil
iii. Suspected O.P. M4D3.4½ aimed about 40° to the left of this a yellow flag was seen ⌐

iv. Suspected S.P. at M10A6½.5
v. nil

(e). N25D.27. A Red X was seen. Evidently a new dressing station.
At 5.10 p.m. Observation Balloon seen to rise over this point M17A9.
It descended in about 1 hour. Over St Pierre.

3

It appeared to be a brand new
balloon, never been up
at this point before.

General being mist + fog observation
of any importance was rendered
impossible this morning.

Sept. 26th 1916

AEllicott 2nd Lieut
O/c Scouts & Snipers
WARRIOR

Report on Enemy trenches noon 26/9/16
to noon 27/9/16   "MAROC"

1. Operations (a) Our artillery bombarded
enemy's line at M4.C. at
3 p.m.
            (b) Our TM's bombarded
            [illegible] vicinity of Post 16
            at 11.15 this morning.
(b) nil.

2. Intelligence (a) Looking party was observed
at M4.C.8.5. They were seen
using a periscope. Fresh brown
soil is also seen thrown up
at this point.
Man was looking through windows
at M11.D.4.
Our observed one of M's [illegible]
placing sand bags on parapet
at M10.A.6½.3½.
Small working party at M10.C.0.4.
Movement seen at this point
appears to be ripening trench here.
Periscope seen at M10.A.9½.7.
Enemy is very new continually
exposed M16 A. 9. 9½. Between 4
& 6 p.m. at least 30 Boche were seen.

Two Germans were seen looking
over parapet at M10.c.1.5. wearing
grey uniforms & round dark hats.
(b) nil
(c) D. MGE seen to fire at point
M10 A.6½.3½. early at also seen
ii. nil
iii. nil
iv. S.P fired at point M10 A.6.6
  Flak broken observed whilst
v. nil
(d) nil
(e) (a) nil
  (b) Enemy were seen flares at point
  M10 A.6.3.6.6.
  M10 A.6.6 both saw lay out to
  be seen at this point.
  M16 C.7.5½. flares seen at this
  point, in addition at intervals of track.
  hrs.
  M10 A.6.3½ Gap in parapet
  also a hole green, been lain.

Sept 27/16
A. Moore, Lieut.
O/c Scout & Snipers
WARRIOR

Operations Report — 25th September 1916

TYPE	OWN TROOPS	ENEMY TROOPS
Artillery	From 11.15 am 6 Rounds of Shrapnel were fired at enemy's support line; appeared to drop right in support trenches	M. gun about 6 whizz bangs fired at support trenches but no damage was done
T.M's	1 am Gun Stokes fired on Enemy's lines east of Cenacle during 16 heavy mist	— Nil —
	11.5 am Heavy T.M fired at Enemy lines in front of Pad 16. Three splendid hits received	
Grenades	No. of Newton Pippins & Rifle Grenades fired at Enemy's trench during the night from Right Coy (Edgeware Rd – BONAVIO)	— Nil —
M. Guns	M.G's fired concentrated at gaps in enemy's wire throughout the night. Burst of fire opened on enemy about M.4.C.7.6.	6.30 pm – 6.30 pm Enemy M.G's active traversing from line about Bayonet 15 +16. Very quiet otherwise
Rifle Fire	No. 17 rounds per man fired throughout the night	Few fired at Sub heard throughout the night
Patrols	Patrol under Lce Sgt G.E. Roberts went out at 9 pm in broad patrols manoeuvre; strong working party on enemy's road line at 11.20 p.m M.10 a.5.6. Firing returned at (R–R) Pictures	Own patrol (cont) wire & returned at Bank Sap. Enemy's fork out appeared at 50 yds in front of second situation. concertina pattern & fairly thick.
	Patrol under Lce C. Hutchinson (R–R) Pictures from head of Sap G along enemy's	

P. Russellaine Capt
OC 1st/19th R. (left?)
25/9/16

Report on enemy from noon
27/9/16 to noon 28/9/16. "17ARDC"

1. Operations
   2.(a) → (i) One sniper observed in enemy
                front line at M10.C.1½.6½ advancing
                in parapet. Two shots were fired
                at moving object inside. No
                further movement was seen. (5.30pm)
             (ii) Our T.M's & L.T.M's during afternoon
                bombarded enemy's front & support
                lines this morning from 11am - 12 noon
                causing considerable damage to
                line in M10A. & M10.C.
        (b) nil.

2. Intelligence (a) M10 A 6½, 7½. Two men
                looking over parapet at 12 noon
                27/9/16. One appeared to be an
                officer wearing a peaked cap with
                coloured band around.
                Three horses & a wagon seen at
                M24 A 7.2. also a Mechanical
                Transport wagon going along
                this road. Three also returned.
                from 2.30 pm.
                At 5 pm two of the enemy were
                seen looking over parapet at
                M.Q. D9.3. wearing grey uniforms.
                & round hats.

at M16 A 3½. 9¾. About 24 of
the enemy were seen at 5.36pm.
Also observed wagon drawn by
two horses.

(b). Recent alterations have been
made at this point. There appears
to be a S.P. here. M10A6¾ 4¾.
~~S.P. here.~~ M10 A 6¼ 2¾. Sandbags
have been piled up here with
a emergency loophole plate at bottom
of them.

(c) nil
(d) nil
(e) nil
(f) S.P. with a curtain behind plate
at M10A 6¼ .6.
(Another see above in NEW WORK)
(g) At 2.35 pm a white box was seen
at M10A 9½ 5½. Wire coming thick
here & partly covers the box.
At 4.10pm. the shock of a mine
exploding was felt, but our
observers were unable to state where
it was.
Also about 9 pm another mine
exploded & it is found to be on
this side of the double crater
(M4 c.77) forming a small

crater.
Owing to very heavy mist observation
was rendered impossible up till
10.30 a.m. this morning.

A. Albright Lt.
O/C Scouts & Snipers
WARRIOR.

Sept 28th 1916

Operations Report   Sept 29th 1916

TYPE		OWN TROOPS		ENEMY TROOPS
Artillery	3 to 4.0 pm & 10.20 pm	A fair number of heavy & shells of light calibre were fired at enemy's support line - all appeared to fall in our trenches	7.50 pm	2 HE & Shrap. (approx) at our front line (mostly right Coy) both fell behind front line & no damage was done
T.M's	3.10 pm to 4.30 pm	Stokes at intervals of 10 mins in front of Thiepval on enemy trench at M4.C.75.15. At same time some enemy occu. new line of intervals own enemy B700 new support line. B700 new Stokes fired at enemy new front & 115 support line	3.20 pm to 4.50 pm	A few T.M's retaliated from direction of M4 D 4 3 on our support line near junction SEVENTH AVENUE & LIVERPOOL STREET
M.G's		Covering fire by M.G's on enemy worked. Also frequent bursts at the two gun emplacements. Rifle Grenade right of Thiep. & there was a working party near front & a working party near front.	9.0 pm to 11.0 pm	6 M.G. bursts were opened at the heads of our saps & sample often traversed
Grenades:		30 Meaden Pyrenia & Rifle Grenades were fired during night by own Right Coy. Edgware Rd — Boyeau to [?] at enemy trench. Number of rifle grenades fired at enemy trench by left Coy. Rifle reported ineffective to replies.	8.30 pm	1 Rifle Grenade fired & fell between front & support line
Rifle Fire		Average of 4 rounds per man fired at suspected groups on enemy front line.		Occasional shots from direction of CRASSIER & M.M. C.65.20
Patrols		Party of 2 Officers & N.C.O.s, Roberts, W. & Rev. men (wiring) 3 N.C.O's & 20 men went out of Sap C at 11 pm to reconnoitre [?] ??? movement. Stay to M.7. a 1.5 - M.10 A.0 where they ??? ??? in enemy wire. Party got into enemy front & ??? ???. Sniper Party (1 Officer 2 N.C.O's & 7 men) failed to reach. No movement & ??? party was of ???? anything of the enemy. Party returned 1.15 am		A working party (enemy) was seen just to right of ??? to connecting sap near northerly with front & stood in the front of the two shell houses

P. Williamson   Capt. M.I.

29.9.16

Report on enemy trenches noon 28/9/16
Noon 29/9/16.   "Marse".

1. Operations:- (a) A 112 (squadron) (28/9/16) M10 C 3½.5.
   our T.M's bombarded enemy's trenches
   causing much damage.
   Also M. Battery M10 C 4.6. ran
   but [shoots] with apparently no
   effect.
   M10 A 9.0) our artillery fired a few
   M10 A 9.1.) rounds about these points
   M10 C 4.7) causing but little damage.
   [struck out] —— enemy's trenches at 2pm
   At 4.30pm one of our shells burst
   at M4 D 2¾. 14. causing serious
   damage to enemy trench.
   From War Bulletin (29/9/16)
   (b) Enemy dropped some leaves
   at intervals a/c our trenches, but
   owing to mist results could not
   be determined. Our guns
   retaliated. Effect not seen.

2. Intelligence (a) At 1pm. shot in Royat (?) 6
   an officer looking over the
   parapet M4 D. 5¾ 2¼. He was
   wearing a round peaked hat.
   at 1.30 One of the enemy was

at M10A 6½.5. waving a round hat.
He seemed to be peering over parapet.

At 3.5 a party of the enemy were seen at M12 A7.5. They appeared to be in a garden of some description.

At 5.45 pm. A man appeared above parapet at at M10 C. 9.3. wearing a grey uniform. what looked like a white peaked hat. He was about 6' in height.

(b) M10B.1.1. Ten cart is to be seen thrown on parapet at this point.
M11.A 2.1. Landscrapers displaced at this point yesterday. Today they have been replaced. A trip of wire suspected.

(c) nil
(d) nil.
(e) nil.
(f) nil.
(g) M10B. 22.8. Small gap in enemy wire.
    M 10 C 2.7.   "   "   under repair.
    M 10 C 2. 6) Large gaps, enemy wire
    M 10 C 2. 5) Badly damaged
    M 10 C 2. 5) Gaps. Also no wire here.
    M 9 D 9 & 3)
    M 10 A 6 & 6)

A box affair was seen at 1710. C.4.2.
also movement was seen here.

[sketch of box]

During this morning movement
was rendered impossible owing
to heavy mist & rain.

29:9:16

A.C.Moore Lieut
O/c Scouts & Snipers
"WARRIOR."

Operations Report   S/W 30/9/16

TYPE	OWN TROOPS	ENEMY TROOPS
Artillery	5.15 pm Our Artillery opened fire on the trenches in neighbourhood of Guns 18 Sch. Much damage was done. Also fire in neighbourhood of Double Craters.	3-6 pm Whizz bangs fired in dropped line in retaliation for Heavy T.M. activity in our front.
Trench Mortars	9.30 am. Few Stokes fired at enemy line near M.4.c.75.30. 5-6 pm Bombardment of enemy trenches at M.1.c.c. Considerable damage was done to enemy's front support trenches.	5-6 pm Enemy retaliated with 4 Rumjars near Liverpool Street Little Ridge.
Machine Guns	Machine guns active on gaps in enemy's wire active throughout the night. Pouched also traversed.	Enemy M.G's not very active. Bursts fired apparently from Pearl 16.
Rifle Grenades	No. 1 Rifle grenades fired at enemy trenches near M.4.c.73 to also fired through the day at trenches to the right of Pearl 16.	Entire absence of enemy activity.
Rifle Fire	No Rifle fire during the night at snipers. Snipers active at noon M.4.c.70	Snipers active firing at our trench at M.3.d.90.15. Shots very low.
General Information	A red light seen showing from 9 pm to 9.40 pm. Slightly to left of Pearl 16. Apparently our aiming candle flame. Nothing seen of it after 9.40 pm.	

30/9/16

D.F. Williams. Capt
Adjt 19th Reft

1) Snipers.
At 5 pm our snipers hit a man
looking over parapet at
M.10.A.6½.3½.
Also two prisoners M.10.A.6.9.1.

Sept 30th/916

A. Elliott Lt.
O.i/c Scouts.
"WARRIOR"

Report on Enemy trenches opposite
29/7/16 to 30/7/16. "Mark"

1. Operations. (a) From 3-6 pm our T.M's bombarded
   M10c ? from C.6. and
   support. (?) ? ? did
   considerable damage.
   ? ? ? and
   bags could be seen flying through
   the air. M4C
                M4D.
   Enemy retaliated with few
   T.M's & rifle grenades.
   We also bombarded I.11.C.C. doing
   ? damage.
   At 11 am our artillery fired a
   ? ? ? considerable
   damage at the enemy's line
   M10.c.1½.6.? where there was
   fresh soil on the parapet.
   (b) ?

2. Intelligence. @ M10A Barrage ? 6½.6.
              at 2.50 pm
              at 7.15 am. M10 B7 3. a party
              of about 13 men were seen
              ? ? ? ?

(a) M10 A 6.1. Rocks looking out
perhaps an O.P. pl. un easy, a
jumper boat.
Two men seen at point M9D 84.22.
at 10.30 a.m. Appeared to be
preparing parapet.

(b) Loophole M10 C 12.5.
     "   17 C C 7.4.
     "   M10 C 3.2. Sandbags
placed here.

(c) M.G.E. M4.C9.3½ almost concealed
by wire.
M.G.E. M4C7½.6. Suspected here.
M.G.E. M10A6½.3½. forward
spots still in use.

(d) M4 C 9.3½ Res. T.M. emplacement
loaded from old ammunition
dump & used, post 11.10 this morning.
Artillery can't find it.

(e) Nil.
(f) Nil
(g) Gap in enemy wire M10A 52.6½.
Enemy wire very badly damaged
at M4 C 7½.3½
Smoke seen rising from front
line trench at M10 C 39. also
M10 A 6.3.

On His Majesty's Service.

SECRET

19 RWF
Vol 5
Oct 16

5-H.
96 sheets

SECRET

SECRET

COPY NO......

119TH BRIGADE ORDER NO 26.

1.   The following internal relief will take place in the MAROC Section on Sunday, October 1st :-

(a) 17th Bn, Welsh Regiment will move into Support, taking over ST JAMES'S and TRAVERS KEEPS, and billets vacated by the 12th Bn South Wales Borderers.

(b) 12th Bn South Wales Borderers will move into Reserve taking over the billets vacated by the
    17th Bn Welsh Regiment.

2.   All details will be arranged by Os. C. concerned.

3.   The reliefs will be complete by 10 p.m.

4.   Carrying parties for 173rd Tunnelling Company, R.E. will be found in accordance with instructions issued to Os. C. direct.

5.   Completion of relief will be wired to these Headquarters in the usual code.

6.   Acknowledge.

[signature]
Captain.
Brigade Major,
119th Brigade.

29th Sept 1916.

Copy No. 1. O.C. 19th R.W.F.
2. O.C. 12th S.W.B.
3. O.C. 17th Welsh.
4. O.C. 18th Welsh.
5. Q.M. 19th R.W.F.
6. Q.M. 12th S.W.B.
7. Q.M. 17th Welsh.
8. Q.M. 18th Welsh.
9. 119th M.G.Coy.
10. 119th T.M.B.
11. S. O. for T.Ms.
12. Bde. Transport Officer

Copy. No. 13. Bde Intelligence Officer
14. Bde Signals.
15. O.C. 224th Coy. R.E.
16. "Q" 40th Division.
17. "G" 40th Division.
18. 173th Tunnelling Coy. R.E.
19. Brigade Major.
20. Staff Captain
21. War Diary.
22. Town Major. MAROC.

SECRET   119th Bde. No.6/71/G.L.

    O.C. 18th Welsh.   O.C. 224th Coy. R.E.
    O.C. Right Group Artillery   Brigade Bomb Officer
    " " 40th Division.   do   O.C. 119th M.G.Coy.
    "G" 40th Division.   O.C. 119th T.M.B.
    H.Q. 121st Brigade.   S.O. for T.Ms.
    O.C. 19th R.W.F.   Office.

                - - - - - - - - - - - - -

1.   A minor enterprise will be carried out by troops of the 18th Bn, Welsh Regiment, in square M.5.d. on the night of the 30th Sept/1st Octr, for the purpose of

    (1) procuring identifications,
    (2) causing casualties to the enemy,
    (3) causing damage to hostile trenches.

2.   3 parties will be employed :-

    1st party, 2 Officers & 18. O.R.
    2nd party, 1 Officer & 20. O.R.

    These two parties will be divided into bombers, bayonet men, carriers, rifle men, and men to procure identification.

    3rd party, 1 Officer & 10. O.R.

    Total employed :- 4 Officers and 48. O.R.

3.   The 1st party will enter the German trenches at M.5.d.15.40 and will work outwards in 2 detachments.

    The 2nd party will reinforce the 1st party as soon as the latter have entered the German trenches, and will also deal with dug-outs.

    The 3rd party will extend in NO MAN'S LAND with the object of,

    (1) protecting flanks;
    (2) collecting stragglers and wounded;
    (3) collecting prisoners;
    (4) covering withdrawal.

4.   These parties will be in positions allotted to them by zero minus 30.

5.   At zero minus 2, the Artillery will bombard the hostile front line.

    At zero, the Artillery will lift to a barrage, and the first party will enter the German trenches. The barrage will be maintained until the raiding parties are clear of hostile trenches.

    The points of bombardment and barrage have been fixed by O.C. 18th Bn Welsh Regiment in consultation with O.C. Right Group.

6. Supply of mobile charges, mats, ladders, phosphorus bombs, ammunition supply and evacuation of wounded have been arranged for.

7. Code words will be as follows :-

Raid	SALMON
Operation will take place.	TROUT
Operation postponed until.......	WHALE ....
Operation cancelled	GRAYLING
Barrage to slacken	PIKE
Barrage to cease	GRILSE
Zero time	KELT.......
Resume normal conditions	SARDINE

Captain.

Brigade Major.

29th September 1916. 119th Infantry Brigade.

SECRET   COPY NO. 1

War Diary

119TH BRIGADE ORDER NO. 27.

1. The following internal reliefs will take place in the MAROC Section on Thursday, October 5th.

    (a) 17th Bn Welsh Rgt. will relieve 19th Bn R.W.F. in the right Subsection.
    (b) 12th Bn S.W.B. will relieve 18th Bn Welsh Rgt in the left Subsection.
    (c) 18th Bn Welsh Regt will move into support.
    (d) 19th Bn R.W.F. will move into reserve.

2. (a) The bombers of the 18th Bn Welsh Regt on the DOUBLE CRASSIER will be relieved by the bombers of the 12th Bn S.W.B. by 11 a.m.
    (b) Lewis Guns will be relieved by 10 a.m.
    (c) Reliefs will be complete by 10 p.m.

3. O's C. Support and Reserve Battalions will allot Lewis Guns to "B" Series M.G. Emplacements as at present allotted.

4. All other arrangements will be made between O's C direct.

5. Completion of relief will be wired to these Headquarters by the usual code.

6. Acknowledge.

                                                       Captain.
                                                       Brigade Major.
3rd October 1916   119th Brigade.

Copy No. 1. O.C. 19th R.W.F.   Copy No. 13. Bde Transport Officer
        2. O.C. 12th S.W.B.   14. Bde Intelligence Officer
        3. O.C. 17th Welsh.   15. Bde Signal Officer.
        4. O.C. 18th Welsh.   16. O.C. Right Group Artillery
        5. Q.M. 19th R.W.F.   17. O.C. 224th Company R.E.
        6. Q.M. 12th S.W.B.   18. O.C. 173rd Tunnelling Coy. R.E.
        7. Q.M. 17th Welsh.   19. War Diary.
        8. Q.M. 18th Welsh.   20. Brigade Major.
        9. 119th M.G.Coy.   21. Staff Captain.
       10. 119th T.M.B.   22. 111th Brigade.
       11. S.O. for T.Ms.   23. 121st Brigade.
       12. Town Major, MAROC.

ack'd

S E C R E T.   COPY NO... 1 .....

119TH BRIGADE ORDER NO. 28.

1.   The right subsection, MAROC Section, will be handed over to the 111th Infantry Brigade on the 9th instant.

2.   The 17th Bn Welsh Regiment will be relieved by the 13th Bn Rifle Brigade on that date, and will move into temporary billets in LES BREBIS, Area D.

3.   Guides at the rate of 1 for Battalion Headquarters, 1 per platoon, and 1 per Lewis Gun (8 guns) from the 17th Bn Welsh Regiment will be at the IRON GATES, MAROC, at 9 a.m. on that date, at which hour the 13th Bn Rifle Brigade will commence to arrive.

4.   1 Officer per Battalion and 1 N.C.O. per Company of the 17th Bn Welsh Regiment will meet a corresponding party of the 13th Bn Rifle Brigade, to whom all trench stores will be handed over, at the IRON GATES, MAROC at 7 a.m. on that date.

5.   All other arrangements will be made between O's C direct.

6.   The Brigade S.A.A. and Bomb Stores in MAROC will not be handed over.

7.   Relief of all Vickers Guns in MAROC right subsection will be arranged direct between O's C. 111th M.G.Coy and 119th M.G.Coy. to be complete by 4 p.m.

        Series B Emplacements in the subsection will also be handed over.

8.   Relief of Stokes Guns in the same subsection will similarly be arranged direct between O's C. 111th and 119th T.M.Batteries, to be complete by 4 p.m.

9.   Brigade Scouts and Snipers in the same subsection will be relieved under arrangements to be made between Brigade Intelligence Officers direct.

10.   The 19th Bn Royal Welsh Fusiliers, at present in Brigade Reserve, will move into billets in LES BREBIS, Area A tomorrow.

        This move will not commence till 12 noon, and will be complete by 4 p.m.

11.   Billetting parties of the 17th Bn Welsh Regiment and 19th Bn Royal Welsh Fusiliers will report to the Town Major, LES BREBIS, at 9 a.m. and 12 noon respectively.

12.   All movement on the MAROC - GRENAY - LES BREBIS Road will be by platoons or detachments at 200 yards interval.

13.   Completion of reliefs will be wired to these Headquarters by the usual code.

14.   On completion of the relief, G.O.C. 119th Brigade will hand over the command of the right subsection, MAROC, to G.O.C. 111th Brigade.

The boundary between Brigades will then be

BANK SAP inclusive to 111th Brigade.
M.4.c.50.75.
SEVENTH AVENUE inclusive to 119th Brigade.
M.3.a.45.30.
M.1.b.9.5.

                                              Captain.
                                              Brigade Major.
8th October 1916.   119th Infantry Brigade.

Copy No. 1. O.C. 19th R.W.F.
2. O.C. 12th S.W.B.
3. O.C. 17th Welsh
4. O.C. 18th Welsh.
5. Q.M. 19th R.W.F.
6. Q.M. 12th S.W.B.
7. Q.M. 17th Welsh.
8. Q.M. 18th Welsh.
9. O.C. 119th M.G.Coy.
10. O.C. 119th T.M.B
11. S.O. for T.Ms.
12. Bde Transport Officer
13. Bde Intelligence Officer
14. Bde Signal Officer.

Copy No. 15. War Diary
16. Brigade Major.
17. Staff Captain
18. "G" 40th Division.
19. "Q" 40th Division.
20. O.C. Right Group Artillery.
21. 37th Division.
22. 111th Brigade.
23. 121st Brigade.
24. 173rd Tunnelling Coy. R.E.
25. 224th Field Coy. R.E.
26. Town Major. LES BREBIS.
27. Town Major. MAROC.

SECRET.   COPY NO. 1.

119th Brigade Order No 29.

1. The 119th Brigade will take over the new LOOS Section from BANK SAP at M.4.c.5.6. to BOYAU 40 at M.6.b.4.6. both exclusive on the 11th and 12th October, in accordance with the table overleaf.

2. The boundaries of the new Section will be as follows :-

   On the South: As in 119th Brigade Order No 28 of 8/10/16, para. 14.

   On the North: BOYAU 40 - NORTH STREET - LONDON ROAD all exclusive.

3. The new 14 BIS Section (North of NORTH STREET inclusive) will be held by the 121st Brigade.

4. The new LOOS Section will be divided into two subsections, designated right and left subsections, at the trench junction M.5.5. - M.5.6.

   The boundary between the two subsections will be HAYMARKET and PICCADILLY, inclusive to the left subsection.

5. Each subsection will be held by one Battalion. In addition, one Battalion will be in support and one Battalion in reserve.

6. Dispositions will be as follows :-

   Right subsection.   A Battalion, with Headquarters at M.3.b.3.5.
                       2 Companies in front line
                       1 Company in support in DUG-OUT ROW.
                       1 Company in support in PALL MALL and in SOUTH STREET between TRAVERS KEEP and HAYMARKET.
                       Bombing parties on NORTH and SOUTH CRASSIERS.

   Left subsection.   B Battalion, with Headquarters at HATCHETTS (G.35.d.5.5.)
                       2 Companies in front line.
                       2 Companies in support in ENCLOSURE.

   Brigade Support.   C Battalion, with Headquarters at M.3.a.9.4.
                       1 Company in DUKE STREET.
                       1 Company in O.G.1, North of PICCADILLY.
                       2 Companies in SOUTH STREET, West of TRAVERS KEEP, finding garrisons for ST JAMES'S and TRAVERS KEEPS.

   Brigade Reserve.   D Battalion, in billets in N. MAROC with Headquarters at M.2.b.6.9.

7. Brigade Headquarters, permanent billets of 119th M.G.Coy and 119th T.M.B., Quartermasters' Stores, and Transport will remain as at present.

8. PICCADILLY will be used for traffic towards LOOS only between the hours of A and B.

9. Completion of reliefs will be wired to these Headquarters in the usual code.

On completion of relief numbers 1, 2, 3, 4, 5, and 8, G.O.C. 119th Brigade will assume command of the new LOOS Section.

Captain.
Brigade Major.
119th Brigade.

9th October 1916.

Copy. No. 1. O.C. 19th R.W.F.
2. O.C. 12th S.W.B.
3. O.C. 17th Welsh.
4. O.C. 18th Welsh.
5. Q.M. 19th R.W.F.
6. Q.M. 12th S.W.B.
7. Q.M. 17th Welsh.
8. Q.M. 18th Welsh.
9. O.C. 119th M.G.Coy.
10. O.C. 119th T.M.B.
11. S.C. for T.Ms.
12. Bde Transport Officer
13. Bde Intelligence Officer
14. Bde Signal Officer.

Copy No. 15. War Diary
16. Brigade Major.
17. Staff Captain.
18. "G" 40th Division.
19. "Q" 40th Division.
20. 111th Brigade.
21. 121st Brigade.
22. O.C. Right Group Artillery.
23. 173rd Tunneling Coy. R.E.
24. 224th Field Coy. R.E.
25. Commandant, LOOS.
26. Town Major, MAROC.
27. Town Major, LES BREBIS.

Date	Unit 119th Brigade	Unit to be relieved	Taking over	Guides 121st Bde Time	Guides 121st Bde Place	Relief to be complete
1. 11th	119th T.M.B.	121st T.M.B.	—	—	—	Details to be arranged between O's C. concerned by 12 midnight, 11th/12th October.
2. "	119th M.G.Coy.	121st M.G.Coy.	—	—	—	do do do
3. 12th	19th R.W.F. B.Bn	13th Yorks Rgt Left Subsection C	HATCHETTS	—	—	Route via PICCADILLY. Note:— Duke St. Coy, SWB
4. "	12th S.W.B. C.Bn 1 Coy.	21st Middlesex 1 Coy.	DUKE STREET	D	Junction of DUKE ST. & PICCADILLY.	do do to follow 19th R.W.F.
5. "	do	12th Suffolks 1 Coy.	O.G.1.	E	Junction of O.G.1 and PICCADILLY.	do do to follow DUKE ST Coy. 19 R.W.F.
6. "	12th S.W.B. 2 Coys.	18th Welsh.	SOUTH STREET ST JAMES'S & TRAVERS KEEPS	—	—	Details to be arranged between O's C concerned The front line, Right Subsection, ST JAMES'S and TRAVERS KEEPS will not be left without a full garrison. Relief to be complete by 6 p.m.
7. "	18th Welsh	A Bn 12th S.W.B.	Right Subsection	—	—	do do do
8. "	17th Welsh	D.Bn 12th Suffolks less 1 Coy.	N. MAROC	—	—	Billetting parties to report to Town Major, MAROC. Relief to be complete by 2 p.m.
9. "	Bde Snipers	Bde Snipers 121st Brigade	—	—	—	Details to be arranged between O's C.concerned

NOTES.

1. In the case of reliefs Nos. 3, 4, and 5, the usual parties for taking over Trench Stores will be at the rendezvous shown in Column 8 one hour before the time shown in Column 7.

2. The hours A, B, C, D, and E will be notified later.

SECRET.   COPY NO......

Supplement to 119th Brigade Order No 29.
- - - - - - - - - - - - - - - - - - - -

1. Reference para. 6. Brigade Support. 2 Companies in SOUTH STREET. Personnel of these 2 Companies for whom there is not sufficient accommodation in SOUTH STREET, ST JAMES'S and TRAVERS KEEPS will be billetted in N.E. MAROC pending the provision of such accommodation.

   Platoons will not be broken up for this purpose.

2. Reference para.8.   A - 4-30 a.m.
                          B - 9 a.m. 12th October.

3. Reference Table of Reliefs.   C - 7 a.m.
                                 D - 6 a.m.
                                 E - 9 a.m.

   Relief 1. Last Column. For "12 midnight 11th/12th October" read "6 p.m."

      do   3.   do   After "PICCADILLY" insert "to follow DUKE ST Coy. 12th S.W.B."

      do   4.   do   Delete words "to follow 19th R.W.F".

      do   5.   do   For "DUKE ST Coy" substitute "19th R.W.F"

      do   6.   do   For "a full" substitute "the normal".

                                            [signature]
                                            Captain.
                                            Brigade Major.
                                            119th Brigade.

10th October 1916.

Copy No. 1. O.C. 19th R.W.F.   Copy No. 8. War Diary
         2. O.C. 12th S.W.B.   9. Brigade Major.
         3. O.C. 17th Welsh.   10. Staff Captain.
         4. O.C. 18th Welsh.   11. 40th Division. "G"
         5. O.C. 119th M.G.Coy.   12. 121st Brigade.
         6. O.C. 119th T.M.B.   13. Town Major, MAROC.
         7. O.C. 119th Signals.

SECRET   COPY NO...1.....

War Diary

119TH BRIGADE ORDER NO 30
- - - - - - - - - - - - -

1. The following internal reliefs will take place in the LOOS
   Section on Monday, October 16th.

   (a) The 17th Bn Welsh Regiment will move into Support.

   (b) The 12th Bn South Wales Borderers will move into
       Reserve in N. MAROC.

2. All arrangements will be made between O's. C. direct.

3. Completion of the relief will be wired to these Headquarters
   in the usual code.

                                            [signature] Captain.

                                                 Brigade Major.
14th October 1916.   119th Infantry Brigade.

Copy No. 1. O.C. 19th R.W.F.   Copy No. 11. O.C. No.2. Coy, A.S.C.
         2. O.C. 12th S.W.B.   12. Bde Transport Officer
         3. O.C. 17th Welsh.   13. Bde Intelligence Officer
         4. O.C. 18th Welsh.   14. Bde Signal Officer.
         5. Q.M. 12th S.W.B.   15. O.C. 224th Field Coy. R.E.
         6. Q.M. 17th Welsh.   16. O.C. 173rd Tunnelling Coy.
         7. O.C. 119th M.G.Coy.   17. War Diary.
         8. O.C. 119th T.M.B.   18. Brigade Major.
         9. S.O. for T.M's.   19. Staff Captain
        10. Town Major, MAROC.   20. 111th Brigade.

SECRET.   COPY NO......

119TH BRIGADE ORDER NO.31.

1.   The following internal relief will take place in the LOOS Section on Friday, the 20th instant.

    (a) 17th Bn Welsh Regiment will relieve the 18th Bn Welsh Regiment in the right subsection.
    (b) 12th Bn South Wales Borderers will relieve the 19th Bn Royal Welsh Fusiliers in the left subsection.
    (c) 18th Bn Welsh Regiment will move into Support.
    (d) 19th Bn Royal Welsh Fusiliers will move into Reserve.

2.   Lewis Guns, Snipers and bombers will be relieved by 12 noon. All other reliefs will be complete by 10 p.m.

3.   From 2 p.m. onwards SOUTH ST (for traffic towards MAROC) and PICCADILLY (for traffic towards LOOS) are allotted to the 19th Bn Royal Welsh Fusiliers and 12th Bn South Wales Borderers. These trenches will not be used for traffic in the opposite direction to that shown above, from that hour until completion of relief in the left subsection.

4.   All other arrangements will be made between O's C. Units direct.

5.   Completion of relief will be wired to these Headquarters by the usual code.

                                                           Captain.
                                                           Brigade Major.
18th October 1916.   119th Brigade.

Copy No. 1. O.C. 19th R.W.F.   Copy No. 13. 121st Brigade.
        2. O.C. 12th S.W.B.   14. 4th Canadian Brigade.
        3. O.C. 17th Welsh.   15. Brigade Major.
        4. O.C. 18th Welsh.   16. Staff Captain.
        5. Q.M. 19th R.W.F.   17. War Diary
        6. Q.M. 12th S.W.B.   18. Bde Transport Officer
        7. Q.M. 17th Welsh.   19. Bde Intelligence Officer
        8. Q.M. 18th Welsh.   20. Bde Signal Officer.
        9. O.C. 119th M.G.Coy.   21. O.C. No.2 Coy. A.S.C.
      10. O.C. 119th T.M.B.   22. Commandant, LOOS
      11. S.O. for T.M's.   23. Town Major, MAROC.
      12. O.C. Right Group Artillery.

SECRET.   COPY NO...1....

119TH BRIGADE ORDER NO.34.
----

1. The following internal reliefs will take place in the LOOS
   Section on Wednesday, October 25th.

   (a) The 19th Bn Royal Welsh Fusiliers will move into
       Support.
   (b) The 18th Bn Welsh Regiment will move into Reserve
       in N. MAROC.

2. All arrangements will be made between O's C. Units direct.

3. Completion of the relief will be wired to these Headquarters
   in the usual code

4. O.Ps will not be changed.

ackld.

                                                    Captain.

                                              Brigade Major.

22nd October 1916.   119th Infantry Brigade.

Copy No. 1. O.C. 19th R.W.F.   Copy No. 11. O.C. No. 2 Coy. A.S.C.
         2. O.C. 12th S.W.B.   12. Bde Transport Officer.
         3. O.C. 17th Welsh.   13. Bde Intelligence Officer
         4. O.C. 18th Welsh.   14. Bde Signal Officer.
         5. Q.M. 19th R.W.F.   15. O.C. 224th Field Coy. R.E.
         6. Q.M. 18th Welsh.   16. O.C. 173rd Tunnelling Coy.
         7. O.C. 119th M.G.Coy.   17. War Diary.
         8. O.C. 119th T.M.B.   18. Brigade Major.
         9. S.O. for T.M's.   19. Staff Captain.
        10. Town Major, MAROC.   20. 111th Brigade.

SECRET.   COPY NO. 1

                    119TH BRIGADE ORDER NO 35.
                    ----

1. The 40th Division will be relieved in the line by the 24th
    Division during the period October 25th - 29th, and will
    move into G.H.Q. Reserve.

2. The 119th Brigade will be relieved in the LOOS Section by the
    73rd Infantry Brigade on the 29th October, in accordance with
    the table overleaf, and will move into billets in LES BREBIS
    and PETIT SAINS until the 31st October.

3. (i)   All trench stores and equipment in O.P's, Emplacements,
           etc., will be handed over on relief.
    (ii)   All air photographs, log books, trench maps, defence
           schemes etc., will be handed over on relief. Complete
           lists of such articles handed over, with receipt
           attached, will be forwarded to these Headquarters by
           10 a.m. on the 30th.
    (iii) Brigade S.A.A. and Bomb Stores will be handed over by
           arrangements between Staff Captains direct.

4. All other arrangements will be made between O's C. Units
    direct.

5. Billetting parties from each Battalion will report to the
    Town Major, LES BREBIS, at 9 a.m. on the 29th.

6. (i)   Carrying parties will be found by 119th Brigade up to,
           and including, the following (Reference Defence Scheme,
           Appendix L) :-

                Support Battalion. Party No. 13. 9 a.m. 29-10-16
                Reserve Battalion. Party No. 1. 10 a.m. 29-10-16

           The parties after these will be supplied by the 73rd
           Brigade.
    (ii)   Party No. 6. (permanent) ~~and cable burying party~~ will be
           relieved by the 73rd Brigade at 12 noon, by arrangement
           between Units direct. O.C. Reserve Battalion will
           report arrangements made to this Office.
    (iii) O's C. Support and Reserve Battalions will arrange to
           leave sufficient guides with relieving Battalions to
           guide parties for 173rd Tunnelling Coy. R.E. to their
           rendezvous. Arrangements will be made between
           O's C. Units direct. These guides will lead one party
           to each rendezvous, and then rejoin their units.

7. Completion of relief will be wired to these Headquarters in
    the usual code.

8. On completion of relief, the G.O.C. will hand over command of the LOOS Section to the G.O.C. 73rd Infantry Brigade.

[signature]
Captain.

Brigade Major.

24th October 1916.   119th Infantry Brigade.

Copy. No. 1. O.C. 19th R.W.F.
       2. O.C. 12th S.W.B.
       3. O.C. 17th Welsh.
       4. O.C. 18th Welsh.
       5. Q.M. 19th R.W.F.
       6. Q.M. 12th S.W.B.
       7. Q.M. 17th Welsh.
       8. Q.M. 18th Welsh.
       9. O.C. 119th M.G.Coy.
     10. O.C. 119th T.M.B.
     11. S.O. for T.M's.
     12. Bde Transport Officer.
     13. Bde Intelligence Officer.
     14. Bde Signal Officer.
     15. 40th Division. "G"

Copy No. 16. 40th Division. "Q"
       17. 24th Division "G"
       18. 24th Division "Q"
       19. 73rd Brigade.
       20. 17th Brigade.
       21. 4th Canadian Inf. Bde.
       22. O.C. No. 2. Coy. A.S.C.
       23. Town Major. MAROC.
       24. Town Major. LES BREBIS.
       25. Commandant, LOOS.
       26. O.C. Right Group Artillery.
       27. War Diary.
       28. Brigade Major.
       29. Staff Captain.
       30. O.C. 173rd Tunnelling Coy. R.E.

No.	Unit 119th Inf.Bde.	Disposition	Unit 73rd Inf.Bde.	Guides 73rd Bde Time	Guides 73rd Bde Place	Route 73rd Inf.Bde.	Route 119th Inf.Bde.	Billetting Area. 119th Bde.	Remarks
1	12th Bn S.W.B. (Less Lewis Guns)	Left Subsection	9th R.Sussex Rgt. (Less Lewis Guns)	11 a.m.	Cross Roads PHILOSOPHE G.13.d.05.35	NORTHERN UP. RAILWAY ALLEY.	NORTH ST. LONDON RD.	LES BREBIS AREA D.	DUKE ST will not be used by either of these Battns
2	17th Bn Welsh Rgt (Less Lewis Guns)	Right Subsection	7th Northants Rgt (Less Lewis Guns)	11 a.m.	GRENAY CHURCH M.1.b.25.00	PICCADILLY to SOUTH ST or MIDDLE ALLEY.	PICCADILLY	LES BREBIS AREA B.	
3	19th Bn R.W.F. 1 Coy.	Support DUKE ST.	2nd Leinster Rgt. 1 Coy.	12 noon	do	PICCADILLY	NORTH STREET. LONDON RD.	PETIT SAINS	
4	do	Support O.G. 1.	do	do	do	do	do	do	
5	19th Bn R.W.F. 1 platoon.	TRAVERS KEEP.	2nd Leinster Rgt 1 platoon.	12-30 p.m.	do	do SOUTH ST.	do	do	
6	do	ST JAMES'S KEEP	do	do	do	do	NORTH ST. LONDON RD.	do	
7	Remainder 19th Bn R.W.F.	Support	Remainder 2nd Leinster Rgt	do	do	PICCADILLY	PICCADILLY	do	
8	18th Bn Welsh Rgt	Reserve	13th Middlesex.	2 p.m.	do	-	-	LES BREBIS AREA A	
9	Lewis Guns 12th Bn S.W.B.	Left Subsection	Lewis Guns 9th R.Sussex Rgt	9-30 a.m.	As in 1.	As in 1.	As in 1.	As in 1.	
10	Lewis Guns 17th Bn Welsh.	Right Subsection	Lewis Guns 7th Northants Rgt	9-30 a.m.	As in 2.	As in 2.	As in 2.	As in 2.	
11	119th M.G.Coy.	-	73rd M.G.Coy.	-	-	As required	As required	Permanent Billets	Details to be arranged between O.C. Coys direct. Routes shown in 1,2,3, are available before 9-15a.m.

No.	Unit 119th Inf.Bde	Disposition	Unit 73rd Inf Bde.	Guides 119th Bde		Route 73rd Inf.Bde	Route 119th Inf.Bde	Billeting Area 119th Bde.	Remarks.
				Time	Place				
12	119th T.M.B.	-	73rd T.M.B.	-	-	As Required	As required	Permanent Billets	Details to be arranged between O.C. Batteries direct. Routes shewn in 1 and 2 are available between 10 a.m. and 10-45 a.m.
13	Bde Snipers & Observers	-	Bde Snipers & Observers	-	-	-	-	-	Details to be arranged between Brigade Intelligence Officers direct.

NOTES.

1. Parties of 73rd Brigade to take over trench stores, in the case of reliefs Nos 1 and 2, will be at the rendezvous shown in Column 6, 1 hour before the hour shown in Column 5, where they will be met by representatives of Units of 119th Brigade.

2. All movement will be by platoons or detachments, at 100 yards interval.

3. Guides will be found by Units of 119th Brigade at the rate of 1 per Bn H.Q. platoon, gun and mortar.

March Table to accompany 119th Brigade Order No. 56

No. 1. Route. Cross roads L.22.d.8.6. - NOEUX LES MINES - Cross Roads K.15.c. - railway bridge J.18.b. - Cross Roads J.10.d
- Cross Roads J.16.a.6.7.

Unit.	Present billets.	Instructions.
136th Field Ambulance (less 3 ambulance wagons)	BRAQUEMONT	To be South of Road J.15.b.5.4. - J.16.a.6.7. - J.16.d.8.4. by 11 a.m.
No.2. Coy.40th Div.Train. (less baggage wagons of Units)	do	To be in billets and clear of roads in BRUAY by 11 a.m.
119th M.G.Company.	LES BREBIS.	To be clear of square L.35. by 8 a.m.
224th Field Coy. R.E.	GRENAY	Not to pass LES BREBIS Church till 9-10 a.m. To be clear of square L.35. by 9-45 a.m.

No. 2. Route. PETIT-SAINS - HERSIN - BARLIN - Cross Roads K.19.b - RUITZ - level crossing J.16.d. - cross roads J.16.a.6.7.

Unit.	Present billets.	Pass Starting Points			
		A	B		
Brigade Headquarters	LES BREBIS	8-0 a.m.	8-40 a.m.	Starting Point A.	Road Junction L.35.a.5.2.
Signal Section.	do	8-2 a.m.	8-42 a.m.		
19th Royal Welsh Fusiliers	PETIT SAINS		8-45 a.m.		
17th Welsh Regiment	LES BREBIS Area B	8-34 a.m.	9-24 a.m.		
12th South Wales Borderers	do Area D	9-13 a.m.	10-3 a.m.		
119th Trench Mortar Battery	do	9-42 a.m.	10-32 a.m.	dc B.	Cross Roads PETIT SAINS. R.2.b.5.8.
18th Welsh Regiment.	do Area A	10-3. a.m.	10-43 a.m.		

Copy No. 1. O.C. 19th R.W.F.	Copy No. 12. War Diary
2. O.C. 12th S.W.B.	13. Brigade Major.
3. O.C. 17th Welsh.	14. Staff Captain.
4. O.C. 18th Welsh.	15. Camp Commandant.
5. O.C. 119th T.M.B.	16. Signals.
6. O.C. 119th M.G.Coy.	17. Town Major. BRUAY.
7. O.C. 224th Field Coy. R.E.	18. Town Major. LES BREBIS.
8. O.C. 136th Field Ambulance.	19. A.P.M. 40th Division.
9. O.C. No. 2 Coy. Divisional Train.	20. C.R.E. do
10. 40th Division. "G"	21. A.D.M.S. do
11. 73rd Infantry Brigade.	

SECRET.   COPY NO...1...

119TH BRIGADE ORDER NO. 36

Reference Map Sheet 36.B. 1/40,000

1. The 119th Brigade Group will march from its present billets on Tuesday, the 31st instant, to temporary billets in BRUAY, in accordance with the march table attached.

   1st Line Transport and baggage wagons will accompany Units.

2. All movement East of the Railway Line L.20.a. - Q.6.d. will be, in the case of Infantry, by platoons or detachments at 100 yards interval; in the case of R.E., M.G.Company and T.M.Battery, by sections or detachments at 100 yards interval.

3. On clearing the above Railway Line, each Unit will close up to a normal march formation, and will proceed without waiting for the Unit following.

4. O.C. 131th Field Ambulance will detail 3 horse Ambulance Wagons, to be North-West of the Cross Roads at PETIT SAINS R.2.b.5.3. at 9-30 a.m., facing South-East. These wagons will join the rear of the 17th Bn Welsh Regiment, 12th Bn South Wales Borderers and 18th Bn Welsh Regiment respectively under the orders of the M.O. attached to those Units.

5. Billeting Officers of Units (except A.S.C. and R.A.M.C., who will make their own arrangements) will report to the Staff Captain at the Cross Roads in BRUAY, J.16.a.6.7. at 11 a.m., where they will meet their respective Units and lead them without halting or checking to their billeting areas.

6. Units of the 119th Brigade will render a marching-out state showing actual ration strength in Officers and O.R. (including attached) to these Headquarters by 8 a.m. on the 31st. 119th T.M.Battery will be shown separately from 12th Bn South Wales Borderers.

7. Attention is drawn to Brigade Standing Orders for War, para 4 (a) and (b).

   The Brigade Headquarters guard will be found by 18th Bn Welsh Regiment on arrival at BRUAY.

8. Brigade Headquarters will close in LES BREBIS at 8 a.m., and open in BRUAY J.9.d.8.9. at 10 a.m.

9. Units will observe the usual halts - i.e. at 10 minutes before every clock hour, resuming the march at the clock hour.

28th October 1916.

Captain.
Brigade Major.
119th Infantry Brigade.

```
Copy No. 1. O.C. 19th R.W.F.        Copy No. 12. War Diary
        2. O.C. 12th S.W.B.                 13. Brigade Major.
        3. O.C. 17th Welsh.                 14. Staff Captain.
        4. O.C. 18th Welsh.                 15. Camp Commandant.
        5. O.C. 119th T.M.B.                16. Signals.
        6. O.C. 119th M.G.Coy.              17. Town Major. BRUAY.
        7. O.C. 224th Field Coy. R.E.       18. Town Major. LES BREBIS.
        8. O.C. 136th Field Ambulance.      19. A.P.M. 40th Division.
        9. O.C. No. 2 Coy. Divisional Train. 20. C.R.E.    do
       10. 40th Division. "G"               21. A.D.M.S.  do
       11. 73rd Infantry Brigade.
```

Operation Orders by Capt. J.H.R. Downes-Powell
Commanding 19th Batt. R.W.Fus.

1. The 19th Batt R.W.F. will be relieved by the 17th Welsh Bn. in the Right Sub-section MAROC on the 5th inst. The Batt. will move into Reserve & occupy billets as vacated by 12th S.W.B.

2.
19th Batt.	17th Welsh	Guides	Time	Place	C.S.M.
A	C	1 per platoon	2.30 pm	Maroc	
B	A	Nil	—	J. Irving	
C	B	1 per platoon	2.30 pm	Albert &	
D	D	Nil	—	Piccadilly	

3. Coys will occupy same billets in Reserve as during previous tour in that area.
1 N.C.O. from each Coy & 1 N.C.O from Headquarters will take over Stores from 12th S.W.B. at 11 a.m.

4. 1 Officer 2 NCO's and 30 men (A Coy) will report at 12th S.W.B. Headquarters at 12 noon and take over CABLE LAYING fatigue.

5. 1 Sergt, 1 Cpl & 12 men (C Coy) will report at Headquarters at 1.30 pm & take over guards & traffic control.
1 Cpl & 3 men (C. Coy) will report at OREN BRIDGE at 1.30 pm. & take over the standing guard the Bridge.

6. Lewis Gun Sections & Snipers will make their own arrangements for relief.

7. Completion of Relief will be notified by runner.

H. Williams Capt.
A/Adjt 19th R.W.F.

4.10.16

Movement Orders by Capt P.E. Williams Adjt.

1. The 19th Batt R.W.F. will move into billets at LES BREBIS tomorrow the 9th inst.
2. Battalion will move as follows:—
   Leaving MAROC.
   D Coy.   12.30 pm
   B "   12.50 "
   C "   1.15 "
   Headquarters   1.45 "
   A Coy.   2.0 pm.
   L. Gunners.   2.30 "

   All movements will be by Platoons.
3. Billeting Officer & N.C.O's will report at Batt Headquarters at 10.30 am on the 9th inst.
4. Officers Valises will be stacked near the Regimental Aid Post by 3 p.m.
5. Lists of French Stores will be handed in by 12 noon. Billets will be left in a clean & sanitary condition.
6. Completion of move will be notified to Bde Hqrs by 3.30

Baths — Tomorrow the 9th inst.

A Coy.   Leave MAROC.   10.15 a.m.
Stretcher bearers, Pioneers,
Bombers, Scouts & Snipers }   —   11.15 a.m.
Lewis Gunners   —   11.45 a.m.
Runners, Signallers,
Police, Sanitary }   —   1 p.m.
D. Coy. After   in trenches   2 p.m. at the Bath
B. Coy.   —   3 p.m.
C. Coy.   —   4 p.m.

P.E. Williams Capt
Adjt 19th Bn R.W.F.

8-10-16

Operation Orders by Lt. Col. B.E. Jones. D.S.O.
Commanding 19th Batt. R.W.F.   No. 30.

1. The 19th Batt. R.W.F. will relieve the 13th Yorks in the LOOS Sector to-morrow, 12th inst.

2. Dispositions of Coys. will be as follows:

R.W.F.		13th Yorks.
A Coy.	Right Coy.	D Coy.
C Coy.	Left Coy.	C Coy.
B Coy.	Right Support	B Coy.
D Coy.	Left Support.	A Coy.

3. Breakfast will be at 4.30 a.m.; the Battalion will move off in the following order. Route: MAROC, PICCADILLY.

  A Coy. 5.15 a.m.   C Coy. 5.30 a.m.
  B Coy. 5.45 a.m.   D Coy. 6.0 a.m.
  Headquarters 6.15 a.m.

Coy. Signallers will accompany first platoon of each Coy.

4. A party of 1 N.C.O. & 3 men from each Coy. & 1 rep. from each Detail will report to the billetting officer at the Z.M. St. at 6.30 a.m. that all billets have been left in a clean & sanitary condition.

5. A meal will be served at 8.30 a.m. at LOOS. Coy. Cooks are situated at the ENCLOSURE.

6. Lists of Trench Stores will be handed in to Batt. Headqrs. by 10. a.m.

7. Scouts & Snipers will be relieved according to Brigade arrangements already issued.

8. Completion of relief will be notified by runner.

P.E. Williams. Capt.
Adj. 19th R.W.F.

11.10.16.

O.C. A Coy   Copy   31

1. Our Internal Relief will take place tomorrow – 16th Oct. 1916.

2. B. Coy will relieve A Coy in the Right Coy Sub section.
   D Coy will relieve C Coy in the Left Coy Sub-section.

3. Trench Stores will be handed over by 9.30 am.
   Os. C. Coys will make their own arrangements between themselves.

4. Relief will be complete by noon

5. Completion of relief will be advised to Bn HQ by runner.

O Lloyd Roberts Lieut.
Actg Adjt.
19th R.W.F.

15. 10. 16.

Operation Orders by Lt. Col. R. J. Jones. D.S.O.
Commanding 19th Battn. Royal Welsh Fusiliers.

1. The 19th Bn R.W.F. will be relieved by the 12th Bn S.W.B.s in the Left Sub-section. LOOS. on the 20th inst.
   The 19th R.W.F. will move into Reserve & occupy billets te in N. MAROC, vacated by the 12th Bn S.W.B.s.
   The Route will be via SOUTH STREET.

2.

R.W.F	S.W.B	Guides	Time	Place	O.S. Mo 12th S.W.B
A	C	—	—	HATCHETTS.	2 pm.
B	A	1 Per Platoon	2.45 pm.		
C	D	—	—		
D	B	1 Per Platoon	2.30 pm.		

3. 1 N.C.O from each Coy & 1 N.C.O from H.Q. will report at Hdqrs. 12th S.W.B. at noon to take over Stores.

4. 1 Officer, 2 NCOs & 48 men (A. Coy) will report at Bn Hdqrs (HATCHETTS) at 8.30 am to take over Cable laying Fatigue.
   1 NCO & 14 men (C. Coy) will report at Hdqps. 173rd Tunnelling Coy. SUNKEN ROAD and relieve a similar party of the 12th S.W.B.

5. 1 Sergt, 1 Corpl, & L/Cpl + 15 men (C Coy) will report at the HOLE IN THE WALL at 12.30 pm. to take over guards & traffic control.

6. Lewis Gun Section & Snipers will make their own arrangements for relief.

7. Completion of relief will be notified by Runner.

19.10.16.

Lloyd Roberts Lieut.
A/Adjt.
19th R.W.F.

Operation Order by Capt John Gamon Platt
Commdg 19th Bn RWF

1. The 19th Battn Rt will move into billets at LES BREBIS tomorrow the 9th inst.

2. Battalion will move as follows
   Leave MAROC.
   D Coy   12.30 pm
   B   12.50 "
   C   1.15 "
   Headquarters 1.45 "
   A Coy   2.0 pm
   L. Gunners   2.30 "

   All movements will be by Platoons.

3. Billetting Officer & NCO's will report at Bn Headquarters at 10.30 am on the 9th inst.

4. Mens valises will be stacked near the Regimental Aid Post by 3 p.m.

5. Lists of Trench Stores will be handed in by 12 noon.
   Billets will be left in a clean & sanitary condition.

6. Completion of move will be notified to Bn Hqrs by 4.3

Baths   tomorrow the 9th inst.

A Coy.   Leave MAROC   10.15 a.m.
Stretcherbearers, Pioneers,
Runners, Scouts & Snipers   11.0 a.m.
Lewis Gunners   11.45 a.m.
HQ Staff, Signallers,
Police, Sanitary   1 pm.
D Coy. after arrival in billets   2 p.m. at the Baths
B. Coy.   3 p.m.
C. Coy.   4 p.m.

                              P.E. Williams Capt
                              Adjt 19th Bn RWF
8-10-16

War Diary

33

Battalion Orders by Lt Col. S. Jones DSO.
Tuesday 24th Oct 1916

1. The following internal Relief will take place tomorrow 25th Oct. 1916.
2. The 19th R.W.F. will relieve the 8th Welsh Regt. in Support.
   8th Welsh Regt.   9th R.W.F. - Reserve
            Routes as South Gd. Rd. - PICCADILLY

3.   R.W.F.   Welsh.
      A   D   1 Officer 1 Sergt 1 Cpl & 28 men of A Coy will
      B   A   take over Trenches &c.
      C   B   1 Officer 1 Sergt 1 Cpl & 28 men of C Coy will
      D   C   take over St Luis &c.

   Guides for A Coy (R.W.F.) will be at Support Bn Hdqrs at
   9.30 a.m. to be in turn taking over the troops in each sector for
   the remainder, who will be in billets.

   Guides for B Coy (R.W.F.) will be at the junction of S.G.1.
   and PICCADILLY at 10.30 a.m.

   Guides for D Coy (R.W.F.) will be at the junction of DUKE STREET
   and PICCADILLY at 10.30 a.m.

   NCOs per Coy and NCOs from Hdqrs will report at Support
   Battn Hdqrs at 9.30 a.m. to take over stores.

   Signallers will go with the first platoon of each Coy.

   Relief will be complete by noon.

   Completion of Relief will be notified to Bn. Hdqrs by
   runner.

24-10-16.

                                Lloyd Roberts Lieut
                                Actg Adjt 19th R.W.Fus

OPERATION ORDERS
by Lt Colonel A.J. Jones D.S.O. Commanding
19th Bn Royal Welsh Fusiliers

Oct 27 1916.

1. The 19th Bn. R.W.F. will be relieved by the 2nd Leinster Regiment on the 29th inst.
   The 19th Bn R.W.F. will move into billets at PETIT SAINS

2. Guides 1 pr platoon and 1 from each keep will be at Batt Orderly Room at 10.30 a.m.
   Route for 2nd Leinsters PICCADILLY.
   PICCADILLY and SOUTH STREET for the two keeps
   Route for 19th R.W.F.

   DUKE ST Coy
   O.G.1 Coy   } NORTH ST
   TRAVERS KEEP   } & LONDON RD.
   St JAMES'S KEEP

   REMAINDER OF BATTALION — PICCADILLY

3. Billeting Officer and 1 NCO from each Coy and Headquarters will report at Batt Orderly Room at 8 a.m

4. French stove lists will be handed in by 10 a.m.

5. Completion of relief will be notified to Batt H.Qrs by runner

(sgd) P.E. Williams Captain
Adjutant 19th Bn Royal Welsh Fus.

SECRET

On His Majesty's Service.

A.G's. Office
BASE

19 R.W.F
Vol 6
Nov 16

Operations Report. Oct 1st 1916

TYPE	Own Troops	Enemy Troops
Artillery.	9.30 p.m. An intense bombardment fired on enemy trenches - 18 pounders shown 2 broken about 1 hour. 11.0 a.m. Intermittent bombardment of enemy trenches. Few shells of light calibre went over Puits.	7 a.m. Few shells fell into Mazur Veedage.
T.Mos.	1 hr to 5 pm. Fired 30 rounds for bombardment with medium from B87/AV 16. at enemy sap 4.30 p.m. at M.4.C.80.50. 3 pm to 10 pm. Medium activity at same spot - 30 rounds. 10.30 pm. 8 stokes - 66 rounds. 3 pm to 6 pm. 179 rounds Stokes, 3 rounds Medium t 4 rounds Heavy at enemy front line t support opposite right Coy front. 2 Heavies fell in enemy wire 1 in our own wire t 1 a few yards in front of our support.	3 hr to 5 hr. Retaliation with g.m. minenwerfer at front line at M.4.B.55.63. No material damage.
Grenades.	Simultaneous with T.M. bombardment our batteries fired 15 rounds at enemy wire and trenches at M.4.C.80.60.	— NIL —
M.G.s.	During the night our M.G. fired 3700 rounds at saps in enemy's wire.	Enemy's guns traversed our trenches at intervals during night - especially during major Ts. bombards intent of this trenches returned up to 11 p.m.
Rifle.	Sentries fired occasional shots at suspected sniper at M.4.D.44.20	Enemy's snipers much on the alert. Snipers pits range on SAP H. These come from SP 5617 in FOSSE 16. machine gun located here.
Patrols.	A patrol of 1 Officer t 1 N.C.O. reconnoitres ground in front of BANY sap. Another party went out at 1 am. (1 Sergt t 2 men) to ascertain if there was a gap in enemy's wire at M.10.A.6.8. Returned at 3 o'clock t reported no gap. They lay upto about 20 yds each side of their trench with same result.	No enemy patrols or working parties or encounters or seen.

O.P. Williams
Capt. + Adj. 19 R.W.F.

19th R.W.F.

Army Form C. 2118

WAR DIARY
or
INTELLIGENCE SUMMARY

(Erase heading not required.)

October 1916

Place	Date	Hour	Summary of Events and Information	Remarks and references to Appendices
MAROC	1-4		In right subsection. A very quiet tour. Enemy's artillery and trench mortars were generally quiet & inactive. A small raid against the enemy's trenches near PUITS 16 was attempted on the night of the 3rd/4th with object of obtaining identifications. It was unsuccessful owing to want of experience of those taking part. Total casualties during tour — 3 killed, 4 wounded.	J.O. 26. (3rd Oct)
"	5th		MAROC LES BRÉBIS. The Battalion went into reserve in LES BRÉBIS on relief by the 17th WELSH Regt.	27. 28
"	13th		The Battalion relieved the 13th YORKSHIRE Regt. in the MAROC left subsection. The enemy's snipers and trench mortars were extremely active during this tour. From 7am till noon on the 17th he bombarded our front and support lines with trench mortars, field guns, and aerial darts. Most of the shells burst about REGENT STREET and HARRISON CRATER and the trenches between, and at times they were falling at rate of 50 per half hour. The trenches were much	29. 30
"	17th			

Army Form C. 2118

WAR DIARY
or
INTELLIGENCE SUMMARY

(Erase heading not required.)

October 1916

Place	Date	Hour	Summary of Events and Information	Remarks and references to Appendices
MAROC	17th		damaged, but the casualties were few in number.	
	19th		On the evening of the 19th a small raid was carried out against the enemy's trenches just north of HART'S CRATER. The enemy had much on the alert and the garrison over which the party had to advance was swept by his machine guns. Nevertheless 2nd. Lt. P.G. DANIELS though wounded succeeded in entering the German trench with some of his men. Three Germans were accounted for and searched for identifications. A helmet and some papers were brought back. There were twelve casualties - mostly slight. Total casualties during tour - 9 killed, 50 wounded.	31. 32. 33.
"	20th		The Battalion moved into reserve. One casualty (wounded)	34.
"	23rd		The Battalion moved in support. Two men wounded	34.
"	29th		The Battalion was relieved by the 2nd Welsh tonight and marched to billets in PETIT SAINS	35.

Report on Enemy Trenches. noon
30/9/16 - noon 1/10/16. Maia.

1. Operation. (a) Our artillery badly damaged
   enemy M.G. at M.4.O.½.1½.
   At 5.5 pm. Enemy T.M. at about
   M.7.C.D.3.4, was seen firing again.
   Our T.M's replied causing much
   damage.
   Our T.M's bombarded enemy Bay's
   at M.10.A.5.½.9½, at 6 pm. also
   damaged some of the enemy wire.
   At 6.30 pm our artillery shelled
   M.4.D.9.2, & D.3 & 8½ with shrapnel
   and other causing some damage.
   Our T.M Shells were seen to fall
   short at M.7.C.D.? M.7.9.D.7.9½
   M.10.A.5.1½. at 3.30 pm.
   (b) Nil.

2. Stillness. (a) A man was seen walking
   along railway at M.7.C.5.7.7.
   time 2 pm.
   A man was seen throwing
   soil on parapet M.7.C.3.½.½.
   at 3.30 pm.
   2 men were seen at M.10.C.2½.4.8.
   at 8.30pm carrying Ivy rod shield

(b) Enemy lookout post noted
at M.10.a.6.2½ on parapet.
Fresh sandbags have been placed
on parapet also fresh soil has
been thrown up at M.9.D.7½.1½ at
Dawn.

(c) Suspected M.G. at M.10.B.9½.7.

(d) nil

(e) nil

(f) Snipers post at M.4.D.1.5.

(g) A van was seen at M.6.A.6.4.
at 3.45 pm. Being loaded up with
furniture by civilians. Later men
returning. They were working very
hurriedly.
Green flag at M.6.D.6½.½. [sketch].
Enemy observation balloon rose
in direction of Lens 12 kilos
at 6 pm.

(h) Our snipers claim a hit at
a man who appeared well over
the parapet, at M.9.D.8½.3.
A man was seen on near side of
double craters going up the oggs
at 6 m.sh. Our snipers fired but
owing to double parallel could
not be seen. No further movement
was seen however.

1st Oct 1916

Allcott Lt
O/C Scouts Warwick

Operation Report   Oct 2nd 1916

TYPE		
Artillery	Own troops heavy shelling (Road)	4-10 pm Gun fire of 8/Essex/Scots n/z of Hoop Bend near Bogan 12-16 near Bogan 3.
	6am-9am two of 18pdrs fired near Pnt 16	9-9:30 pm 15-20 Rds fired in retaliation general bombardment in vicinity of Bogar 2 & Pt and Bogar 3.
T.M.'s	Loops in wire kept open during the day	
M.G.'s		Active only during the main operations. Our front line was not touched.
Grenades.		Slight retaliation between 9-10 pm
Rifle fire- Sniping		Fair amount of Rifle fire between 9-10 pm

Report on enemy trenches noon 1/10/16
to noon 2nd/10/16.   M a r e l

1. Observations (a) Our TMB Bombarded
   enemy line at M10A 6 2 4 2
   at 12.30 pm enemy seen
   running.
   At 3.0 our artillery shelled
   at Double Crassier. Effect
   cannot [be] judged M9SC 4 2.
   2.6 p.m. party seen carrying out
   at 8.55 pm our post
   M10C.   M7.10.A M14C. Double
   Report of snipers fire Hill 70.
   M10 C.6.1 has been badly damaged
   during the Bombardment and also
   Point 16. M710C75
   Also trolley line broken at
   M10C 75
   (B) Enemy retaliation to our Bombardment
   was very little slight. A few minenwerfers
   were used and three were
   seen to fire from near refinery
   crassier about M14.07 2
   No other from about M9CC 94.

Intelligence (a) At 12.45 pm an airman
   was seen on parapet waving a flag
   or piece of cloth at M12 B 3 2

Ten minutes late he again
appeared but would not stay.

At 10ʰ 6ᵐ 23ˢ Movement was
seen to have its culmination
at 3 2 ——

At 9 30 as one of the comparison
was suffering for its star
a gap the right of 10ʰ 68 64.
It was worrying about one.

② 57ᵐ 13 24/14. Just out on
parapet

⑦ 10ʰ 76, 56. Just out on
parapet then point to clock
a face the I would have been
put up.

③ all
③ ...
④ ...
⑤ ... appears to this one
⑥ At noon (12ʰ 45ᵐ) a term
shown ... one ... one ... when
... was seen from the
building. M6ᴺ 76 16
M10 C 12 but no body no good
at a faint
M10 C 12 D. Bags papa
M 7 B 7 = 32. Aurora.

M/C B4 5¾. Shell shot observed was a direct hit on parapet of P. Gun, observation below gun at 3 pm over Fuse 12 or Lens

A tree is you on skyline north west behind S.P. M.L. 71 B. Shell was fired on Fuse 12 seconds in sea time base.

Oct 8th 1906

A. Adams Lt.
O/c S. gun Island
Nepean

1. Report on enemy trenches noon 2/10/16 noon 3/10/16.   Havre.

   (a) Operations (i) 2nd T.T.: Bombarded enemy trenches at M.10.c.3.9. causing no damage. (11am)
                  (ii) nil
                  (iii)

2. Intelligence (a) A man seen carrying something up the parapet at M.10.b.2¼.7.

   [illegible] an observatory [illegible] tested at M.10.c.3½.4 at 11 (am) appears to be [illegible] and battered down 2pm. M.10.A.6½.2½. 2 men seen apparently busy with machine gun in side the emplacement at this point. 5.30 pm. A party of men observed walking past this man [illegible] dusk. M.10.A.6½.2½.

   (b) No work seen to be thrown up at this point. Our artillery dropped a few rounds here also after dark. No man was seen. M.10.B.2½.9.
   Men were to be seen at M.10.B.¾.7½

(a) So picked up ? E at M6C)1½
(b) nil
(c) nil
(d) Suspected S.P. at M4D3. 2¾.
    "   "   " M4D1½. 5.
    [illegible] unable to head
    up.
(e) [illegible] too much
    [illegible] at M10A 9½ 9
    being taken [illegible] formation
    [illegible] impossible this
    [illegible].
(f) [illegible] M10A 6.9 ½
    [illegible] 3.50 pm.

Oct 3rd /916

A.C. [illegible] Lt.
WARRIOR

Operation Report   Oct 3rd 1916.

TYPE	OWN TROOPS	ENEMY TROOPS
Artillery		10 am 4 Lozenge bays in new support line near Bryant 43.
T.M.s	12 (heavy) Stokes fired 150 rounds at enemy trenches 15 9 am 11 mm 25 " " M10C.3.9	— NIL —
Grenades.		— NIL —
M Gs	Fired intermittently at Saps in enemy wire throughout the night No 4 Gun 158 rounds, No5. 47 rounds, No6. 423 rounds.	Traversed parts of our front during night
Rifle & Sniping	Occasional shots during the night.	Occasional shots.
Information.		Enemy sent up 3 green lights at M.10 A & C at 7pm. MG located at PUIS 16 Trench. Left lg. at intervals during the night.
Patrols.	1 NCO & 3 men went out at 10 pm to examine Sap in enemy wire from Bryant 12 15 SAPS. no enemy were moving parts seen. 1 NCO & 3 men went out at 9.30 pm to examine our mmg pm Bryant 12 to SAP 6 to report where enemy sentry being done later.	

J.E. Williams Capt
Adj 19th R.W.F.

Operation Report. Oct 4th 1916.

TYPE	OWN TROOPS	ENEMY TROOPS
Artillery	2 bursts our artillery fired 30 heavy shells + 17-18pdrs 4 pm on enemy trench opposite left Company front. Fire to heavy shells 6-18 pdrs on left of Coy front.	— NIL —
T.Ms.	2 bursts Bombard went off enemy trenches front 4.15 pm line + vicinity of Pairs 16. — Stokes fires 152 rounds.	2 bursts 12 enemy T.Ms (2 duds) between E.O.C. & map at 4 pm. ROAD + BOYAU C₉ (front line) 5 Rifle Grenades from opposite BOYAU 9. Fell between Enemy front & right of front trench of own unit.
Grenades	6 pm 10 grenade fires on enemy front line round Pair 16	
MGs	Traverse bursts as above several times throughout the night. Private pairs at intervals during night at Site in enemy line. No. 4 Gun. 304 rounds, No.5. 376 rounds No.6. 376 rounds.	Traversed our www several times during the right. Coss fire from left of Right Coy front, direction of DOUBLE CROSS, B2
Rifle + Sniping	Intermittent fire during the night	Sniping www active than usual
PATROLS	2 Officers, 3 NCOs + 2 men went out from M9.0.6.5.9.2 + move by M10.A.4.5.10 where they lay in ammo and curformation. Entering Aflank. Enemy working very hard in vicinity of Plac 16. A heavy Cwt (which is assumed by these www heavy) to be going backwards + forwards in vicinity with flats returns to Sank point. Much droping with flats returns to Sank point. Much droping + snipping of wistal about this point.	Another return of rifle grenades were fired at the front — none hit — 30 yet away they worps round to their left + come in at SAPC (M9.C.L.a.78)

P. E. Williams Capt

19th R. W. F.

Oct 19th R. W. F.

Report on enemy trenches from 3/10/16 to
4/10/16.   "Maroc".

1. Operations (a) Our artillery shelled a round
                    this point M.c 9½.¼ & caused
                    what was thought to be an
                    explosion of ammunition or bombs.
                    Our T.M's & others badly
                    damaged enemy trenches at
                    the following points. M.10c ½.5½
                                          M.10c 2.6¾
                    and at 3.0 p.m.
                    M.4.7.4½, a shell dropped
                    on O.P. at this point causing
                    little damage.
                    at M.10c.2.4 and M.8.6.3
                    the ground is very bad, cut
                    up by our shell fire.
              (b) Nil

2. Intelligence (a) Observed enemy working behind
                    hill as reported on 2.30 p.m.
                    at M.10h.6.4.6.
                    Enemy were apparently relieving
                    at point M.9½.1½. at 3.15 p.m.
                    Men seen were carrying
                    some a rifle and fully equipped.
                    Our artillery & M.G's opened
                    a heavy fire on them.

M.16 A.3½.9h. a armoured car was seen at this point.
M.22.B.7½.9½. Five Mechanised transport vehicles were seen going along the road at 6pm.
M.24.A.7.2. five horse transport vehicles seen at this point. Enemy were observed standing by at these.

Ⓑ. M.10 A.7½.6½. Much soil has been thrown up at this point. Also at M.10.B.1½.1. Our artillery shelled this point at 2.10pm. Enemy seen damaged.

M.10 C.4.6½. Enemy suspected to be sappy at this point having gassed with heavier wire at 5 am. Horsemen have been placed round here, or what appeared to be a map or an advancing front line tunnel. Periscope was in use but M/G etc.

M.10 C.3.7. No enemy wire.
M.10 C.7.3. " " "
M.10 A.4½.3½. wire badly damaged

Ⓒ. M.10 A.5½.8½. The enemy's bit M.G.'s here are supposed to be firing one & the other unnaturally to front.

(1) nil
(2) M.10.B.4.3 at evening look out post observed.
(3) 3 enemy patrols seen under cover of [?] and thought to be at S.P. M.4.9.9.4.5.
(4) M.4.B.7.b. a flash was seen at this point but to suspect it to be a gun fired at 3.45 pm M.11.a.9.6. Suspected heavy guns put out of [?] line of [?]
(5) nil

A.E. Morris Lieut
o/c Scouts
1st K.R.R.

Oct 4th 1916

Operations Report   Aug 5th 1916

TYPE		Own troops		Enemy troops
Artillery	2-3 pm	19 Howitzers burnings/parts bns mm shafts S. of D CRASSIER	11 am	4 shrapnel at our front line & support trench 180°Av 17. 6 high shells on support line between 180°Av 5v3.
T.Ms	3-5 pm	Stokes fired 10 rounds & shaking up enemy front line N. of D CRASSIER. Stokes fired 10 rounds on retaliation on enemy front line N of D CRASSIER.	10 am	12 Rum fire between front line & B.O.C.in Ap. 5. 2 B.O.C. in Ap. 5.
	3.45pm & 5pm	4 rounds from stokes on enemy work front line in support opposite Sigis tag point. Machine guns 12 rounds on enemy front line 180°Av3. Stokes -- 172 -- do -- ct -- 180°Av 3.	6 pm	2 Rum guns at support line near 180°Av 5v3.
Grenades	12 am 4 pm 8 am & 11 am	3 Hales at enemy front line opposite 180°Av 16 -- do -- 7 pm front line -- do -- -- do -- 20 Rifle Grenades -- do --	5.45 pm	3 rifle Grenades into RANK SAP from direction of CRASSIER.
M.Gs.	7pm to 7 am	Vel Gun Hems 9.10am fired at half his intervals except flares towards enemy front line & Saps in west near CRASSIE & tures field 56.5 -- do -- do -- fired 470 rounds -- do -- do -- 370 Rapid fires at intervals at enemys Saps & puts 16.	7pm to 5 am	Hostile MG fire. It. traversing our front line 3 short sharp bursts from near M10A to 40.
Rifle & Sniping.		100 rounds fired by sentries at M40.10 to & puts 16 where sniping hostile supports were shown.	9 pm 9.15 pm 10 pm	Short fires from near M4C, 10.6 & puts 16.

5.10.16.   P.E. Williams Capt
                            6 RWF
                            Aug 19th RWF

Report on enemy trenches noon
4/10/16 - noon 5/10/16.   Maroc.

1. ~~Intelligence~~
   Operations (a) Our artillery shelled
   this point M4 D 9.2½. at
   3.20pm. The third shot
   seemed to cause an explosion.
   Our T.M's shelled enemy
   lines at M15 B 9.9½. causing
   some damage.
   M10 C 3.1½. & M9 D 8. 2½. our
   T.M's shelled enemy lines at
   these points causing considerable
   damage.
   At 11.30 a.m. our T.M. was firing
   in enemy lines at this line.
   (b) nil.

2. Intelligence (a). At 6.10pm. men were seen
   passing to & fro at this point
   M15 A 6 4.
   M13 A. 3 1. Steam was seen
   as of coming from an engine
   shunting.
   M 24 A 7 2. Motor lorries / transport
   were seen being disposed, at
   6.30am.

At 8 am a party of about 25 men
were seen passing Kite point
M.16.A.5½.8½. wearing grey caps.
At 9.5 a.m. Man looking over parapet
at M.71DA.6½.1. he appeared to be wearing
a dark round hat.
At 10 am. Transport drawn by two
horses was seen proceeding in the
direction of LIEVIN at M.2hA.7.2.
also a man on horseback going
in same direction.
At 10.30 am. Two men were seen
on horseback as if returning from
the direction of LIEVIN at the
gallop on the same road.

(b). M.16.C.8½.9½. Fresh work in
sandbags at this point.

(c). ~~nil~~ ~~~~

(d). Glass again seen shining in
FOSSE 12. DE LENS probably an
O.P.

(e). M.9 at M.71DA.6½.2½. still in use.
M.8.E. suspected at M.10.C.7½.7.

(f). nil

(g). M.11.A.5½.1½. S.P.
M.10.A.6½.6½. S.P. firing South.

(g). M.11.A.9½.5½. a door in trench
is now here large enough for
a man to get through.

3

Smoke seen issuing from a dugout
at M10c.9.2½.
Thick clouds of smoke at M4c.7½.2½.
Trench board at M10A.9½.5½.
apparently used as a lookout.
M9D.8½.4. Smoke seen issuing
from trench at this point.

(6) Two of the enemy looking over
parapet at M4c.8½.3½. wearing
peaked caps similar to officers
caps worn. Two snipers fired
one found & one wounded, disappeared,
the other disappeared before a
second shot could be fired.
Periscope lit at M10c.2.7

A. Morris Lieut
O/C Scouts & Snipers
WARWICK

Oct 5" 1916

1. Report on enemy trenches noon 5/10/16
to noon 6/10/16.   "Maroc."

① Operations (a). 170c.0.2½. at 12 noon
5/10/16. our T.M's. caused a fire
to break out at above point, which
lasted one hour.
Our T.M. damaged enemy O.P.
at 170.C.3½.6. time 2.30 pm.
at 11.30 A.m. our T.M's bombarded
enemy trenches in front of Pait 16.
(b) nil.

2 Intelligence (a). 12.30 (noon) man wearing
peaked cap looking over parapet
at 174 D.8.2 using field glasses.
Two men seen at 175 C 3¾.5.
wearing white round hats & white
tunics similar to chefs.
Corn drawn at 17 24 + 1/2.
drawn by two horses. time
4.30 pm.
(b). Green sandbags placed at
this point 174 C.8.5½.
Fresh lumps of chalk have
been thrown up at 170 B 36⅞.).
Fresh earth at 170 A. 9½.5.
(c) Suspected M.G. E at 170 C.5½.4½.

(1) M.G.E. suspected at 174.D.5½.4½
(2) 174.D.15½ suspected T.M. emplacement as smoke was seen to rise in spurts when enemy mortar was firing.
(3) nil.
(4) Snipers plate at 17.10.A.6½.5¾. also man seen looking over parapet at this point. Time 2.30 pm.
(5) Small red & white flag at 174.C.7½.5¾.
   [sketch of flag: WHITE / RED / WHITE / RED]
   a snipers plate was also seen 1 yd left of same.

17.5.C.3¾.2¼. Red & yellow flag in enemy trench.
Movement seen behind loophole plate at 17.10.A.6½.3¾.
Enemy wire very thick at 17.10.A.6½.3¾ & also 17.10.C.8½.9½.
Periscope in use at 17.10.C.2.7½. at 5.45 am. also at 17.10.C.1.5.

(6) nil.

A.C. Morris Lieut
o/c South
"Warrior"

Oct 6th 1916

Report on Enemy trenches noon 6/10/16.
to noon 7/10/16.   "Maroc".

1. **Operations**. ⓐ Our TM's bombarded enemy trenches at M10.C.3½.8 causing serious damage. Trench boards & articles of every description were seen flying through the air.
Also the Berthier M10.C.7.6. received on shell of TM's causing but little damage.
Our TM's bombarded enemy communication & front line trenches at M10.C.1½.6. M10.C.24.7. M10.C.4.3 causing much damage. M10.C.0.1. our TM's shelled enemy's second line with good effect.
ⓑ also at M.10.A.6.1. and at M14.C.7.2.
ⓒ Enemy TM fired two or more from M14.D.9½.1. into the Double Crassier, at 5pm.

2. **Intelligence** ⓐ. M14.C.7.7. Two men were seen at 8 noon 5/10/16 one using a shovel & the other appeared to be on the look out.
Mechanised Transport going along

2

road at M24A.7.2. was seen. also transport drawn by horses.
M10A6½.2¾. at 5.4am. several men were seen "standing to." at this point one wearing steel helmet. A man was also seen at this time standing near the M.G.E at M10A6½.2¾. A man was seen block over parapet at 7.15am, point M10A9½.3½ wearing a round cap with light blue band.
M9D8¾.3. Two men seen apparently on the look out.

ⓑ. M10A6¼.6¾. More fresh work is being carried out at this point.
M4C.7.½. Fresh soil has been thrown up at this point.
M10A6½.6¾. Fresh chalk thrown up here.

ⓒ. nil.

ⓓ. M4.D.2½.3½. Enemy T.M. seen to fire from here. Our T.M.'s retaliated 2 shells bursting very close to the emplacement.
M4.D.9½.1. T.M.E. mentioned in I.B.

ⓔ nil

ⓕ What appears to be a S.P. was seen at M4 C 9½.1.

ⓖ. M10A9½.4¾. Movement seen behind loophole here.

3

6.30pm. Observer noticed that the
fingers on clock of LENS CATHEDRAL
had been set back 5 minutes.
This clock has long since stopped going.
N20 C.6.4. what appeared to be the
smoke of an engine was seen.
Large clouds of smoke seen to
rise from large chimneys in
LENS.
M10 A6½.4½. Movement seen behind
loopholes at this point.
A Red & yellow screen seen at
this point M4 C.7 & 6.

```
| RED    |
| YELLOW |
```

Report on Wire (Enemy)
M10 C 3½ 9½.   Thick wire.
M9 D 1. 8.   Any "Do"
M9 D 0.4.   "Do"
M10 A 6½.4.   Good wire partly hidden by grass
M10 A 6½ 4.   Do
M10 A 6½ 5.   Do
M10 C 1.5.   New wire
M9 D 9.3.   Do
M9 D 8½.2½.   Do

Also an officer was seen wearing
a round peaked cap with a light
blue band and a red and white
button as a badge, at the same
point.

M10 A 6½ 5 a man wearing a round
cap with white button on top
looked over a short plank at this
point.

M9 D 9½ 3½ Man seen looking
over parapet wearing grey round
hat.

M10 C 9 5 at 5pm. a man was
seen with full pack equipt.
probably relieving.

At 6 pm. M9 D 8½ 2½. a man
was seen over parapet apparently
watching our Aeroplane.

At 6.30 a.m. two men were seen
passing point M10 C 3½ 6. The
french trench appears to be very
much broken down.

3.

(b). Fresh earth has been thrown up at M10B 7 7.
M10 B 6½ 7. also him.

(c). M10 B 8½ 2½. M.G.E. has fired both.
M10 A 6.4. This appears to be a M.G.E.

(d). nil

(e). nil

(f). M10 C 1½ 6. Snipers loophole plate here.

(g). M4 C 8 5½. The Germ. sandbags here previously reported have been covered with white stones. It is evident that work of some description is being carried on here.

CE Morris / Lieut.
O/C Scouts.
WARRIOR

Oct 8/16

Report on enemy bombing, noon
7/10/16 to noon 8/10/16. "Mairè"

1. Operations (a) Our T.M's bombarded
enemy lines at M.10.C &
M.11.A but results could
not be seen. time 11.45 a.m.

(b) A few 77m.m. were dropped
in our lines causing no
damage, at 4.30 p.m.
At 5.15. the enemy shelled
with very light stuff our
lines at M.9.a. causing
no damage.

M.9.B.89 } enemy shelled
M.9.B.6.0 } our lines between
these points causing but
little damage.

2. Intelligence (a) Two men seen at
M.10.A.62.4. One wearing
a steel helmet, & the other
a round ~~~~~~~ cap.

4

M10 C 2.7.   large gap
M10 C 1.6.   d⁰ gap
M10 C 3.9.   small gap.
M9 B 8½.2½.   small gap.

A.C.Morris Lieut
o i/c Scouts & Snipers
WARRIOR.

Oct. 7th 1916.

Report on enemy trenches noon
8/10/16 to noon 9/10/16 "Maroc"

1. **Operations** ⓐ Our T.M's bombarded enemy lines in front of Pnet-16 D.T. & N.9. 12 noon. Our Artillery shelled the Double Crassier at 10.50 am.

2. **Intelligence** ⓐ M10A 62.68. Working party seen at Noon throwing up brown earth. Our Artillery fired 2 H.E. on spot. Work ceased (See form attached)
M10 A 6½.6½. Six men seen at this point all wearing round black caps. Also an officer wearing peaked cap with light blue band.

21

2.

At 5.30pm. A man wearing dark brown hat was seen to look over parapet at M9D8½.2¼.

Two men seen to walk down trench at M10A.95.45 & 1955 a looking party seen M10B ~~~~ 5¼.8¼.

Man looking over parapet wearing dark round hat with a button or badge on at M10A1.5½

(b). Alteration in trench at M4C.76½. New wire previously reported has been broken or blasted a large gap is at M9B.9.3. M4C.8.5½. Fresh sandbags built up here.

(c). Machine Gun was heard firing from Point 6 D. S. Lens at 16.30 wow.

(d) nil
(e) nil.

8. nil
9. Small puff of smoke was
seen to emerge from centre
of the Beehive appearing as
bow one was smoky haze
M10 C 12.4. Wire very thick & dam
post & second line.
M10 C 18.7. ⎫ Wire badly damaged
M10 C 17.6. ⎬ Enterr. trops
M10 C 12.5. ⎭ bombs.
M10 C 3.9. Wire badly damaged
here.
M11 A 11. at 6.15 am a fire
was seen at this point.

R.E. [signature]   A. Mont, Lieut.
                         o/c Scouts
Oct 9th 1916   WARRIOR

27

Report from Trenches taken
2/10/16 Aviation 13/10/16 1.00 S.

1 Operations @ [crossed out] Our guns
& TM's bombarded enemy
lines at 2.30 pm.
B.M. saw open trench chopped
of artillery shells in
the Cyril Redoubt
sector. in & retaliated
1.16 & 58. Enemy bombard-
our trench & TM's RE
at 2.30 pm.
1.16 (2) 42. at 4.15 pm
Enemy dropped some
heavy TM's Res. Our
artillery & TM's replied with
full force effect.
1.16 (2) 92. at 3.15 pm
heavy TM's were dropped
at this point doing very
little damage.
At 10.30 his morning enemy

T.M. shells dropped in our lines of intrench doing little damage.

① nil
② nil
③ nil
④ nil
⑤ M6c9.5. Tape in rear of own
   M6c2.4. Trench did very little
                        trek hor.

M6D1.9
M6B4.   Wire (enemy)
M7B20.   along trench line
M6D 12.9½
M6D 1.9
M6c9.8
M6c9.7½   D°
M6c62 SE
M7c3 SE

Fired en enemy post. Enemy trailed in thin cloud at M6D4.9 at 4 pm.
Semaphore Key seen M6B4.2. probably one of our own.

WORK
C.P. under construction at
M 35 D 9, 6². Preparations to take
work carried out last night.
S.P. on transverse tube commenced
last night.

A. Morris Lieut.
O/c Scouts & Snipers
Oct 13ᵗʰ 1916   WARRIOR

Oct 13th 1916.

Operations Report.   13-10-16

Type	Own Troops.		Enemy Troops.
Artillery.	10 AM. Fired 25 to 30 rounds 18 pdr shell into enemy trenches in front of GORDON MOUND about 18 pdrs into enemy position, enemy	10.20 AM.	Gfew rounds 77mm into our gun positions. Little damage
T.M.s.	12 noon 12 noon Fired 26 rounds into enemy front line. Also 16mm into enemy front line opposite HAM & CRATER. Crater on fire	1.30 pm	Enemy heavy burst of fire into CRATER, then on H.T.&W.T. S.P. & T. No enemy seen. No damage.
	12.30pm 6 meeting of 8 S.P.M. on enemy front line opposite POTS 31	2.30pm	7.T. Three rounds of no damage fire between trenches, no damage
	3.15. 14 medium m on enemy front, support line	4pm	7.T. rounds on mornings mound CRATER & mornings mound
	3.45pm	5.30pm	7. N.T. rounds also in same between lips of POTS 31
	12 bought 12 Stokes on enemy support	12pm	1 HT rounds on POTS 31 between lips of POTS 31 at RAIN gun on POTS 31
	12.15pm 6 "		
Grenades.	6am. 14 Newton Pippins & 8 Mills fired at enemy front line.		Enemy fired rifle grenades intermittently between HAY GARDENS CRATER, mornings mound all on our part line CRATER support line
	between trenches 12 noon 30 Grenades fired on enemy front line between CRATER & GREEN MOUND	5.30 & 7.30am	Enemy fired a few lines from POTS 31 & 6 POTS 43 a little Sacred fire a No damage. Weapons used. Fell short.
		8.00am	Enemy 11 ridges C.T. rounds fired Sacred & 6 on also between trenches Between left of GT Bombing Post, grenades CRATER. No damage done
M.Gs.	Throughout run bursts fired 290 rounds at taps in enemy wrist of hidden corners of mound trenches	throughout night	Enemy m.g. bursts on our line at intervals night to left of GREEN MOUND, front of our line in long, SHEP'S S.A.P., they seemed to have no trouble
Rifle.	"do" bus anothers & centuries fired occasional shots at enemy working parties.	-do-	enemy anothers & centuries very busy.

J. Williams Cap.
11th Royal Scots

Report from [illegible] 13/10/16
[illegible] 14/10/16 LOOS

1. Operations (a) TMC S7 [illegible] TMs:
[illegible]
enemy lines at the front.
[illegible]
[illegible]

(b) Enemy [illegible] at [illegible]
our lines [illegible] TMs [illegible] at
~~[illegible]~~ 1pm
2-4pm [illegible]
[illegible] support line at
intervals [illegible] left of
Harrison's Crater.
Also at [illegible] today
a few [illegible]
[illegible]
of [illegible]
damage. Our guns
retaliated effectively [illegible]
[illegible]

2. Intelligence (a) ~~[illegible]~~ MG seen [illegible]

2

... from the direction
of 176B 5½. Careful
watch to any kept on this
spot.

ⓓ nil

ⓔ Our [?] suspect enemy
OP [crossed out] at 176C)½6½
[?] ... that [?]
has [?] was seen ....

ⓕ nil

ⓖ [?] ... in [?] parapet
at 176C 8)½ ... [?]
... any ....
171B 3¼ 2½   } [?]
17 6C 5½ 3   } any thick
17(C 4¾ 5½ 17(C9) at [?]
176C 5½ [?] ....
17(C 3)) ... ...

ⓗ Main ... 176B 7.4.4 ... on
... will ... parapet.

ERRATA 2. ⓐ Men seen at 176D½ 9½ may

② 6 Coy.   3

WORK.   Construction of C.T. + S.P. carried
on with best of light.

                        A.J. Morris Lieut
                          o/c Sentry party
Oct 14th 1916   19th Bttn R. W[els]

1. Operations (a) 176 (B.L.Bn) TMs bombarded enemy positions keeping enemy under cover at time of op at 1715 also bombarded the left my bn Bound with good effect.

But M.G fire in enemy lines continued harassing Effects could not be determined.

(b) nil

2. Intelligence (a) African officer wearing round peaked cap with light blue band looked over parapet at 176C 3.6.
(b) Enemy seen standing to at 5.45pm along their front line at intervals.
(c) nil
(d) Suspected M.G at M 6C 4.6

		OUR TROOPS		ENEMY TROOPS
H.E. Hy.	12 m/n	Fired 5 rounds of Lyddite & then enemy gun fired several shots. B.97a03 31	8.45 am to 9.15 am	Fired 12 rounds Shrapnel & HE searching the Sulphur Kingdom & Kilsels
	1 am	"		
	1 pm	Fired to relieve an enemy front line & line HARTS CRATER.		
	2.55 pm	Fired several silence enemy TMs by vicinity of Stockham.		
	9 am	Fired 6 rounds HE into enemy trenches to B.H. of CRASSIER.		
T.Ms.	1.3 pm	12 medium rounds	1.3 pm	6 rounds on B.97a4 31.
	3.55 pm	4 "	3.55 pm	7 " on B.97a03 31A. (drainage ? case the 9 Sulphur)
	1.55 pm	46 Light	7.45 pm	4 " B.97a3 31
	8.1-12 am	18 medium		3 " m. support line - between Humphrey's CRATER & Humphrey's Rd
	enemy day		8.5-10 am	4 " supports line (B.9.c.)
		Mortar fired 15 rds at Safa in enemy line & enemy trenches beyond Roumana's Sunken Twp	10.8-12 am	14 " the front & front line on Hillsby Road
			2.10-4 pm	Enemy heavy T.Ms. continues S. on trenches near QUESTED & Bayonet no damage.
			10.10 am	5 rounds slow on B.97a03 31 A - B.97a03 31.
Grenades.	10-11 am	Fired 20 Grenades on enemy trench w opposite HARTS CRATER	1 to 3 pm	5 " " "
			3 to 5 pm	7 "
			7.6 pm	Enemy threw grenades at our crew camp
	Thought	Fired rifle . 16 1st enemy front trench	9.5-11 pm	3 Riffle Grenades on front line between B.97a03 31A.3A.
	day.	M. 169.no 16 "		
		M.269.no 30	5.45 am	6 " (feed slap)
			Intermittently at enemy hy. area 24 yds.	12 yds. fired 4 round of T.Rifles o.p.4 T.P.B. - bearing no our trench
M.Gp.		shoot . Fires report to at Safa on enemy - were Snipers & dispersing enemy working parts	throughout night.	Fairly quiet.
Rifle.	do	Occasional shots - to mortar shots in enemy front line & 150 rds at Safa in enemy line	" "	Very quiet - Sniping occasionally during daylight.

Information: Enemy had several more shoots reported moving parts on out a different parts of this line most of last night. Clear has fairly anything in his front line hands opposite BHP MANS SAP.

E.Laghdank Capt.
a/adjt. 19th RWF.

2

loophole appears to be covered with
light shrubs.
ⓑ 176 DN 12. A faint blue smoke
was seen to rise at this spot.
We suspect a T.O.? and careful observation actually being kept on this
spot in order to verify it.

ⓒ nil
ⓓ 176 C st. 5½. Snypers L.P.
ⓔ 176 C 3.5½. Movement seen
thru loophole at this point.
176 C ¾ ½. A Snyper's Post
was seen. he behind [coil?] of
wire. Movement was seen
thereon.
ⓕ On a ripper from Moore and
Cable observed one of the enemy
looking well over the parapet
at 176 C 2. 6½ at 2.30 p.m.
We saw one person from the same
spot at 3.25 pm. observed another
of the enemy at 175 DN 3½. Look-

3

got over the fence & obtained Blank
from the face trench. Also enemy
observed an enemy sniper behind
spot hole having the enemy sniper
fixed on our map. No one
was really fired & taken to H.Q.
Point M 6.13.6½. 4. Drive 1 pm
Snow recure spot our sniper fired
at a man who looked over parapet
at M6 B 5½.3½. He came a bit
short afterwards he said he was
come with own spot & from where
he could see (one) of (?) (?his had?)
lifting something. He fired again
but could not see any result.

WORK   Mill day workers in
         S.P. & O.P.

oct 13 ?9?   AMorris Lieut
                          He points Supt
                          WARRICK

OPERATION REPORT — October 18 - 19/10.

TYPE	OWN TROOPS.		ENEMY TROOPS.	
Artillery.	12 noon to 1 pm.	5 shells of light calibre on enemy front line opposite BOYAU 31.	6.15 am.	4 shots (bursts) between front line & B.H.Q. Bjw.g of BOYAU 32.
	11.45 am.	15 rds - 18 pdrs into enemy front line in front of GIBSON MOUND	11.50 am.	Enemy retaliates with a few 77 mm (abt into B.O.S. VILLAGE from direction of GLITZ 31 & 32
T.Mo.	2 to 4 pm.	Our med.trench mortars retaliated on enemy front & supports near N.A.O.Ts CRATER & 16 rounds fired.	2.30 to 4.	Retaliation with 2 Weapons - 1. T.mo. abt. 8" to right from direction of CRESSY M. & A.D. emplacement behind CRESSIER (Russian Pn Olive + Helga)
	5.30 pm.	6 rounds - do -		
	10 to 12 am.	2 rds medium on enemy front line opposite		
	During night.	Stokes fired 54 rounds on gaps in enemy's wire & trenches near CROSSIER 2		
			10 to 2 am. 3 minutes fire in front of mine near BOYAU 2. Stokes with showers falling behind Stokes emplacement.
Grenades.		34 halls. Set enemy front subs opposite, with mustn't 30 rifle grenades on enemy trench to left behind GRESSY MOUND		Enemy persistently fired 2 howitzers the left of mortar
			12 noon. 14 rifle grenades on our line - part of trench between BOYAU 3 & 31.
			2 am. 2 rifle do - do.
			4.15 am. 2 shells do - do. -
M.Gs.	During night.	Fired 2500 rds of enemy aircraft few Fw's & Scho Parties were observed.		Reconnaissance bursts in all directions to our line - Fires at our own wires very far
			7 to 7 pm. 8 to 10 pm.	Generally harassed.
Rifle.		Occasional firing		Fair, quiet + somewhat night.

Information: The enemy had made every (effort?) past. We were stood up quite at the knees. It was not occurring, but wish to be more careful than before or prevented by any combination sounds of digging. It was doubtful to one LG field - in too cover digging. It was doubtful to some cond was here is very little doubt that we inflicted casualties. Wire in our mine near BOYAU 33.

At 12 pm. two parties were observed on opposed side of HARRISON'S CRATER. A Lewis gun was turned on them.

At about 12.30 the morning the officer & J am Corporal were four along the whole line. The enemy seemed to have abandoned return so prisoners out of made down

O. Wyldbelton Lieut
V.C. Capt. 19 N. Batt

2nd [...] 15/7/16
[...] 10/7/16   LOOS

1. Operations (a) Gun [...] dropped near
   M.6.c.9.7. nearly [...]
   [...]
   [...]
   At 11.30 [...] enemy [...]
   TM's fired [...] on
   M.15.c.6.3. [...] causing some
   damage.

   (b) At 5 pm. No enemy [...]
   [...] our [...] of our T.M.
   [...]
   At 9 pm [...]
   [...] with [...]
   [...] of [...] trenches,
   doing some slight damage.

2. Intelligence (a) [...] women are
   seen [...] every night
   [...] M.16.c.15.

2

A 16:30 a man was seen at
173094 carrying a round helmet.
Also at 173042 3½ a man was
seen who appeared to be carrying
something.
At 17:45 at 1750 [crossed out] 2½ a German
was seen carrying black &
+ khaki from trap. They are
believed to be the parapet.

B. 176 B 2 70. No one was seen
at this point.

C. nil

D. nil

E. nil

F. 160 29½ Small dry
loophole arrangement seen
in parapet at this point
be suspect a S.P.

3.

(1) Small secure enemy from trench at the point S 30 d 5½ 3½ at 9.15 am. Sentries now at M 5 c 6½ 1½ M 5 c 9 2½ } Snipers giving trouble M 5 d 1 6 2 } at last point.

(2) Our snipers & Lewis guns claim a hit at M 6 K 5 3. Men were working & not enemy, were so few & no one was seen after firing 5, they took no notice of.

WORK. —

Being carried out at C.P. 6350716 H.S. to dawn under O my. A new profile parados ELLE work carried on last night.

A. C. Mansfield
O/c Lewis d-gun
R. F. Rev?n

Oct 16/1916.

OPERATION REPORT — Oct 16. 1916.

Type	Own Troops	Enemy Troops
Artillery	2.6 4 pm 5 light field Howitzers on enemy outpost opposite BRITISH SAP 4.16 am — do — — do — 4.30 pm 6 rds Shrum enemy trenches left sector of BRITISH MOUND	2.6 4 pm 10 rds H.E. Bomb on supports near ROYAL 31 3 pm 4 rds 77 mm on front line and support trenches left Bay front trenches S1 TR.ST 31 AUGUST.
T.M.	Our officer fired 24 shells at various times during night at co-operation with enemy new MINED + 2 rds on BRITISH HEAD of SAP 12 Medium east of Autumn.	2.6 4 pm Enemy snipped 4 P mm fires on CRATER R from direction of MUIRO (LOC + OLIVE) 10.15.2 am 8 " near from direction to CRATER L situated during day scattered shooting R (F.6 15 pm 11 9 mm on British R night N ROYAL 31 4.56 am 4 Medium Two vicinity ROYAL 31 6.5 pm 3 " 31 11 am 18 " " IMPRESSIONS CRATER 72.
Grenades	2/5 6 pm Fired 40 Rifle Grenades on enemy trenches from various fronts 35 mm line.	Enemy retaliated with Rifle Grenades on BRITISH 2/5 6 pm 6 Rifle Grenades on front line near ROYAL 32
M.Go.	Enemy fired 1320 rds at Saps on enemy wire + night Enemy working at SAPS 12 + 14 (right)	Enemy Enemy Traverses) Occasional + long S.A. fire fired at SAPS 12 + 14.
Rifle	Occasional shots at Saps + workings from Front	Enemy snipers busy over LONG SAP from the action of GREEN MOUND.

O.W.C. Roberts Lieut.
A/Adjt. 19th Rifles.

Rifle on enemy trenches near 16/7/1?
Trenches 7/10/16   L65

1 Operation Order   ... ...
                 enemy Line at P5c66
                 5Ms (2.9?) caught considerable
                 damage to our trenches ...
                 ... our losses slight, we
                 were opening around ...
                 P11c1152, with good effect.

@ 3-5pm Enemy bombardment
 line at T11 Harrisons Crater
 with T.M.s caused considerable
 ... craters.
 From 4am, this morning, enemy
 bombardment ... continually,
 both Front, Support, + lines
 of Communication with
 T.M.s, H.E. + Shrapnel. Also
 using some 77mm, ..., causing
 considerable damage.

2

Our stokes gun retaliated with
good effect. Artillery fired one
or two small shells (B.M.)

9. Intelligence (a) Man seen looking over
parapet at this point T15 D 6½.
3. at 1.30 pm.
Also at T15 D 5 3½. 2 men
were seen looking over parapet
at 3 pm.

(b) nil

(c) nil

(d) @ 11.39 & 9. A.M. enemy
T.M. was seen to fire from
here. It has been firing on several
occasions of late & now its
position has been confirmed.
a T.M. has also been seen

3

party from point 176 B 52.12
which appears to be set in the
Railway Embankment.

ⓐ nil

ⓑ nil

ⓒ 175 C 52 5½ at 12·30 pm.
Smoke was seen issuing from bush
at this point probably a dugout.
Also at point 175 O 4½ 3½
at 1·30 pm.

ⓓ Whilst testing telescopic sights
for moonlight firing a working
party of ~~enemy~~ two were spotted
with large telescope working
in front of enemy sap in
front of Warwick Craters.
Our snipers fired once &
observer noticed party fall over

4.

faces. In about 10 mins —
heads appeared &, of they
saw another showing fired.
On moving further down to left
to mins what appeared to be a
crowd of four were seen hurriedly
carrying something & they were
immediately rifle bombed. Before
before reasonable to get a rifle
turned off. Enemy retaliated
with one rifle grenade which
fell in no man's land.
One hit is certain. The other could
not be determined.

WORK:-

O.P. still going on.
S.P. on Parkinson's Crater is evidently
being watched. Our party, as soon as
goes up there than it is obliged
to come away because of rifle grenades

5

During the bombardment
this morning the lead wires of
6" at ?????? broken near ????
???? ???? ??????? ??? ???????
???? at 9.30am

Oct 17" 1916   A. Morris Lieut
                     19" R.L.

OPERATION REPORTS.

Type.	OWN TROOPS.	ENEMY TROOPS.
Artillery.	defensive shooting	5-8 pm. 10 shrapnel on left of line. 8-12 noon. Occasional shrapnel along whole front.
T.M.	About 160 rounds (Stokes utilisation)	5-6 pm. About 12 medium and heavy TM along REGENT Street. Occasional TM during night. From 7 to 12 noon – Bombardment on whole front, but especially on LOOS CRASSIER, REGENT STREET, HAY HILL and Bargues road front line from HARTS to HARRISONS. Estimated number of TM at 30-40 per hour. At times they were bursting at the rate of 7 or 8 every five minutes.
"		Fairly active during night 8 am to 12 noon
Grenades.	About 40 rounds	
M.G.	During night 47 magazines fired at working parties & patrols & gaps in enemy wire	7 to 11 pm. Fairly active – Traversing 6 to 11 am. About 3 magazines at one aeroplane
Rifle.	5.30 to 6 am. 60 rounds steady firing by sentries	Very quiet throughout night

Morris Lt Colonel
Comdg 1/5 R.W.F.

Report on Enemy tonight from 1/11/16
to 2 ? /11/16. Kev?

1. Operations @ nil

@ 8.15am at 17.6 D. Enemy
dropped a few shells in our
lines. Our dishes retaliated
with good effect.

2. Intelligence @ Sherman seen at 17.5 D
6½.3½ at 1.15 pm standing
near stakes. All in a
round hut. One was a
sniper.

@ 9.45 a.m. man stood
on parapet front trench smiling
with his hands in his
pocket 17.5 D.5½.12. wearing
dark chocolate round cap
& gum boots. He then walked
to the front line & got in.

3

Last night enemy was heard
bombing provisions at
point of right of Maurice Salm
Wood. Report that it has
examined him.

At 4.45 am a gun and shell were
sent up from town. Since in
vicinity of H.Q. M do suspect
fire and a bit ankten was
observed, on known that
the 77 m.m gun ceased sending
peppering our line well strapping
our Lewis gun and gave gas
on camps corn.

6 an C. Quo hite us learned from
Core Country, his men are out
looking in response of 17 6.3.32. 3.
The Qoo anyone found were ineanwalk
and men were seen to fall back into
trench.

2.

Two squadrons yeomanry are today
bivouacked here. I went forward
to you again Nos K, L & M.
One Squadron on the Boer Gracht
your front are [illegible].
I think this is doing [illegible] moral
effect. Helio went [illegible]
[illegible] [illegible]
[illegible]
Again our snipers fired at
[illegible] on a man [illegible]
[illegible] to any of his bodies
[illegible] to come [illegible]

Oct 18/1914

A Elliott, Lt.
O/C Scouts,
19th Regt.

7.30 am to 12.30 pm. — 8 rds. 18 pdrs on enemy's front line opposite HARTS CRATER.
— do — Lines 18 pdrs on CRASSIER.

2–5 pm — 24 rds. 18 pdrs on CRASSIER (many duds)

Occasional rounds with light field gun (about 12 pdr) during day on [illegible] in front of HARRISONS.

T.Ms. 8 am — 20 at Old [illegible] at Enemy's front (Stokes) opposite CRASSIER.

Very quiet.

Grenades. 6 to 9 am. — 30 [illegible] on enemy front opposite right Coy.
10 to 12. — 10 [illegible] [illegible] ditto.

5.30 to 6.30. — 10 Rifle Grenades vicinity of DEADMANS SAP & front line by BOYAU 32.
2 am to 5.30. — Numerous Grenades at intervals at DEADMANS SAP, front line by BOYAU 32.

M.Gs. 5.30 pm to 5.30 am. — 22 [illegible] in enemy wire & traversing front line.

4 am. M.G. fired at our aeroplane.
5.30 pm to 5.30 am. — traversed front over long, short Sap, Saps in CRASSIER.

Hs. during night. — 210 rounds fired by sentries.

[illegible] [illegible] fired.

18.10.16

[illegible] [illegible]
[illegible]
19th R.F.

Report on enemy trenches noon 16/10/16 to noon 17/10/16.   200³

1. Operations (a) Our guns were firing (heavies) intermittently on enemy trenches between the hours of 10 & 12 this morning.

(b) From 3-4 pm enemy dropped a few T.M.'s in our lines at intervals. Results could not be determined.

2. Intelligence (a) Man seen looking over parapet wearing a round grey cap, at M 6 D 27½ at 12.30 pm. Man was previously fired at by a Lt Fallon on mirror at block at M 5 D 4 4.6.

3.

(g) M11 Dg 32. Whd moved was at the point on top of crater with raised ledge on it. Movement could be seen behind it.

M11 C. 29. Thin blue smoke seen but probably a dug out.

(h) At 12 noon yesterday at M 76 B 3½ 4½ man seen, from of our anger SP, looking over parapet. wearing ribbard tipped cap with red band seems to be gold braid round peak. Sniper fired believed to have hit. After our snipers fired. Enemy sniper fired 5 rounds rapid at top head in rifle at our SP.

A hit is also claimed from same spot on man body over parapet from waist up at about M 76 B 6½ 3½.
at 8.30 a.m. this morning.

A

was told at about
4 & 10 a.m. which was looking over
Sandbags at M6 B33. 3. (from
Sans 66) wearing a black cap
& grey jacket. Sniper hit & claimed
at 11.15 a.m. Man was very short
blunt & grey coat with brass buttons
looking over a land bag sort of
M6B 6.3½. Our sniper fired
& again claim a hit.

A Wright
O/C Snipers

Oct 19th 1916

OPERATION REPORT

Time	OWN TROOPS	Time	ENEMY TROOPS
2 to 4 p.m.	18 rounds on enemy front line vanishpoint opposite HARTS CRATER	12 to 2 a.m.	8 H.E. shells on front line transport between HARTS CRATER & LOOS CRASSIER
4 to 6 p.m.	30 rounds into front transport trenches to night of MANNING'S MD NP	6 hr.	4 rifle grenades on front line near HARRISONS
10 to 12 mid.	3 rounds into enemy trenches right of HARTS CRATER B.		
10 a.m.	6 rounds at enemy's vanishpoint between HARRISON'S TRAP.T.		
9 to 10 p.m.	3 shots into enemy front line behind HARTS CRATER	2 to 6 a.m.	12 T.Ms. (Heavies) rear front of CRASSIER
12 to 2	15 shots at enemy " " to right 57 HARTS		10 Rum. Jam at rest trench near BOYAU 32N
2 to 4 p.m.	30 rifle grenades fired on enemy front land opposite HQ Ports	2 to 6 a.m. afternoon night	8 grenades (rifle) into CRASSIER front 20 rifle grenades CRASS into HARRISONS along HQ - CRASSIER Rly at line between BOYAU 31 - 32.
7 to 11 a.m.	6 rifle grenades } opposite BOYAU 31.		
11 to 12 p.m.			
5.20 to 6 } 5.30 a.m. }	11 magazines traversing enemy lines at gaps in enemy wires	2 to 4 p.m. 10 to 12 p.m.	Enemy fired at our aeroplane on M.G. vanishpoint line vanishpoint
do	10	2 to 4 p.m.	2 rum jars fired by M.G.
	No. 1 2 3rd Runs fired 23 rounds each into Gaps in enemy wires & at enemy parties. Very effective in stopping their working	4 to 6.50	
5.30 p.m. to 5.30 a.m.	150 rounds desultory firing by sentries.		Very quiet. matters

Alfred Roberts Lieut
Capt. 19 4 Ont.

Report on enemy trench mortar on
29/10/16 between 30/10/16 4.p.o.

1. Operations @ Preliminary cannonade
    be sent, of full report
    to be sent after trench mortar
    fires.

    @ 016.30 am. Enemy
    dropped a few bombs
    (3 L [illegible]) in our
    [illegible] no damage.
    Point 175 0.9.3.4.

2. Intelligence @ M5 D.3.4.5.2 Men looking
    over parapet.
    M75 C.4.2.6 men looking
    over parapet wearing
    an overcoat. So much
    of ground next to it being
    colour.
    M5 D 5½.4 Men looking

over page position enemy's pipe.

② M75 O63½ Observed aircraft
have been thrown up at this
point.

③ nil

④ nil

⑤ nil

⑥ nil

⑦ Smoke arising from bank
M11 B22.9
Also from M75 O93.4
+ from M6 B 3.0

⑧ M6 D3¾ 9½ at 4.10 pm was
hooked gun pos pick of landtrap
An snipers fired on camera(?) [illegible]

OPERATION ... REPORT

Type	Own Troops		Enemy Troops	
Artillery	3-4 pm	Shelled enemy in position behind HARRISON'S CRATER	1 to 2 pm	3 shells ineffective behind HARRISONS
	12-2 pm	4 shells fired into enemy's trenches near CRASSIER	8 pm to 10 pm	6 on our support-line right of [?]
	2-4 "	30-40 such — do —		6 CRASSIER
				Intermittent shelling throughout the night & fake wire-cutting barrage between HARRIS.COMM & HARRIS.
	8.30 to 10 pm	Barrage on enemy's trenches & front line & support near H.6.d. 20.90		
	16.5 am	6 WHIZZ BANGS on enemy support line opposite CRASSIER	8 to 9.30 pm	6 9 mm. Jam pots left of HARRIS.
			—do—	14 " " " near REGENT ST
T.M.	12-2 pm	8 rds. D/B fire into enemy's front appr. ls CRASSIER & HARR PTS		
	8.30 - 10 pm	65 Stokes on enemy front line at H.6.d.10.90		
Grenades	5 to 8 pm	10 Newton Pippin fired into enemy front	2 to 4 pm	10 Aerial dart kitchen bomb near CRASSIER B
	9 to 11 am	8 do	—do—	12 Rifle grenades & small percussion HARR & HARR
	11.30 am	2 Hales grenades " " "		4 Hang Hang also enemy CRATER PT
	7 pm	4 " " " "	8.30 to 9.30	5 Aerial darts & 9 rifle grenades behind HARR
	5 pm	10 " " " between HARR & Crass.		
M.G.	5.30 pm	16 Magazine at Sniper in enemy snipe opposite HARR Pts	11.45 am	Barrage on our front line to limits CRASSIER
	5.50 am	20 " on Sniper HARRIS.	6.30 am	30 rounds traversing front line near CRASSIER to HARR PTS
	—do—	No 12 M.G. fired into 10 supports & communicating enemy front line	11.15 pm	Very active traversing our front line
Rifle	—do—	130 rounds at loopholes & snipers		Snipers active

Fairly quiet night.
[signature] Lt
[signature] 19 K.R.R.
20.10.16

Report on enemy trenches. noon 20/10/16
to noon 23/10/16.   LOOS & MAROC
                    Mine Alley. O.P.

1 Operations @ M4 D 9.6. Our artillery
              dropped 6 or 7 heavies at this
              point causing much dirt &c
              to be thrown up.

              ⓑ. The enemy dropped a few
              shells on Harrison & Crater
              Results could not be seen.
              abt 2 pm yesterday.

2. Intelligence @ Man observed looking
              over parapet as aiming
              around hot M4 C 9.1½.
              M4 D 8½.5. Two men were
              seen looking over parapet
              here both wearing steel helmets

(b) nil

(c) nil

(d) nil

(e) Object was seen shining on Sorse 12 do lens possibly a telescope. Suspect an O.P.

(f) nil

(g) 75 C 1.8 ¾. Periscope seen here at this point being put up at intervals

Owing to heavy ground mist observation was rendered impossible this morning.

A.C.Morris Lieut
do
19th D.W.ths

Oct 23rd 1916

19th R.W.F. November 1916

Army Form C. 2118

WAR DIARY
INTELLIGENCE SUMMARY
(Erase heading not required.)

Instructions regarding War Diaries and Intelligence Summaries are contained in F.S. Regs., Part II. and the Staff Manual respectively. Title Pages will be prepared in manuscript.

Place	Date	Hour	Summary of Events and Information	Remarks and references to Appendices
PETIT SAINS	Oct. 31		Marched to billets in BRUAY	A, B
	Nov. 1st		" from BRUAY to OSTREVILLE	C, D
	2nd		" OSTREVILLE to BUNEVILLE	E, F
	4th		" BUNEVILLE " BUIRE-AU-BOIS	G, H
	5th		" BUIRE-AU-BOIS " HEUZECOURT.	I, J
	15th		" HEUZECOURT " BUIRE-AU-BOIS	K, L
	17th		" BUIRE-AU-BOIS to VILLERS L'HOPITAL	M,
	18th		" VILLERS L'HOPITAL to NEUVILLETTE.	O, P
	19th		" NEUVILLETTE to BOUQUEMAISON.	Q, R
	22nd		" BOUQUEMAISON to GEZAINCOURT.	S, T
	23rd		" GEZAINCOURT to SAINT OUEN.	U, V
	24th		" SAINT OUEN to BELLANCOURT.	W, X
	25th to 30th		In billets at BELLANCOURT.	

SECRET.   A   COPY NO. 1

119TH BRIGADE ORDER NO. 36

Reference Map Sheet 36.B. 1/40,000

1. The 119th Brigade Group will march from its present billets on Tuesday, the 31st instant, to temporary billets in BRUAY, in accordance with the march table attached.

   1st Line Transport and baggage wagons will accompany Units.

2. All movement East of the Railway Line L.20.a. - Q.6.d. will be, in the case of Infantry, by platoons or detachments at 100 yards interval; in the case of R.E., M.G.Company and T.M.Battery, by sections or detachments at 100 yards interval.

3. On clearing the above Railway Line, each Unit will close up to a normal march formation, and will proceed without waiting for the Unit following.

4. O.C. 130th Field Ambulance will detail 3 horse Ambulance Wagons, to be North-West of the Cross Roads at PETIT SAINS R.2.b.5.3. at 9-30 a.m., facing South-East. These wagons will join the rear of the 17th Bn Welsh Regiment, 12th Bn South Wales Borderers and 18th Bn Welsh Regiment respectively under the orders of the M.O. attached to those Units.

5. Billeting Officers of Units (except A.S.C. and R.A.M.C., who will make their own arrangements) will report to the Staff Captain at the Cross Roads in BRUAY, J.16.a.6.7. at 11 a.m., where they will meet their respective Units and lead them without halting or checking to their billeting areas.

6. Units of the 119th Brigade will render a marching-out state showing actual ration strength in Officers and O.R. (including attached) to these Headquarters by 8 a.m. on the 31st. 119th T.M.Battery will be shown separately from 12th Bn South Wales Borderers.

7. Attention is drawn to Brigade Standing Orders for War, para 4 (a) and (b).

   The Brigade Headquarters guard will be found by 18th Bn Welsh Regiment on arrival at BRUAY.

8. Brigade Headquarters will close in LES BREBIS at 8 a.m., and open in BRUAY J.9.d.8.0. at 10 a.m.

9. Units will observe the usual halts - i.e. at 10 minutes before every clock hour, resuming the march at the clock hour.

Captain.
Brigade Major.
119th Infantry Brigade.

28th October 1916.

```
Copy No. 1. O.C. 19th R.W.F.          Copy No. 12. War Diary
         2. O.C. 12th S.W.F.                   13. Brigade Major.
         3. O.C. 17th Welsh.                   14. Staff Captain.
         4. O.C. 18th Welsh.                   15. Camp Commandant.
         5. O.C. 119th T.M.B.                  16. Signals.
         6. O.C. 119th M.G.Coy.                17. Town Major. BRUAY.
         7. O.C. 224th Field Coy. R.E.         18. Town Major. LES BREBIS.
         8. O.C. 136th Field Ambulance.        19. A.P.M. 40th Division.
         9. O.C. No. 2 Coy. Divisional Train.  20. C.R.E.      do
        10. 40th Division. "G"                 21. A.D.M.S.    do
        11. 73rd Infantry Brigade.
```

March Table to accompany 119th Brigade Order No. 36

No. 1. Route. Cross roads L.22.d.8.6. - NOEUX LES MINES - Cross Roads K.15.c. - railway bridge J.18.b. - Cross Roads J.10.d - Cross Roads J.16.a.6.7.

Unit.	Present billets.	Instructions.
136th Field Ambulance (less 3 ambulance wagons)	BRAQUEMONT	To be South of Road J.15.b.5.4. - J.16.a.6.7. - J.16.d.8.4. by 11 a.m.
No.2. Coy.40th Div.Train. (less baggage wagons of Units)	do	To be in billets and clear of roads in BRUAY by 11 a.m.
119th M.G.Company.	LES BREBIS.	To be clear of square L.35. by 8 a.m.
224t Field Coy. R.E.	GRENAY	Not to pass LES BREBIS Church till 9-10 a.m. To be clear of square L.35. by 9-45 a.m.

No. 2. Route. PETIT SAINS - HERSIN - BARLIN - Cross Roads K.19.b - RUITZ - level crossing J.16.d. - cross roads J.16.a.6.7.

Unit.	Present billets.	Pass Starting Points	
		A	B
Brigade Headquarters	LES BREBIS	8-0 a.m.	8-40 a.m.
Signal Section.	do	8-2 a.m.	8-42 a.m.
19th Royal Welsh Fusiliers	PETIT SAINS	-	8-45 a.m.
17th Welsh Regiment	LES BREBIS Area B	8-34 a.m.	9-24 a.m.
12th South Wales Borderers	do Area D	9-13 a.m.	10-3 a.m.
119th Trench Mortar Battery	do	9-42 a.m.	10-32 a.m.
18th Welsh Regiment.	do Area A.	10-3 a.m.	10-43 a.m.

Starting Point A. Road Junction L.35.a.5.2.
B. Cross Roads PETIT SAINS.R.2.b.5.8.

SECRET.   COPY NO. 1

                      119TH BRIGADE ORDER NO. 37

Reference Map. Sheet 36.B. 1/40,000

1. The Brigade Group order of march as set forth below, will march
   to billets in Area "A" on Wednesday, November 1st.

   Starting point - Cross roads J.15.c.0.7.

   Route   - OURTON - DIEVAL - road junction N.23.b.3.0

2.

Units in order of march.	Pass Starting Point.	Route from N.23.b.3.0	Billet in	Distance in Miles
Brigade H.Q.	9. a.m.	-	LA THIEULOYE	7¾
18th Welsh.	9.3 a.m.	N.30.d.9.7., Q.26.	MAGNICOURT.	10⅛
19th R.W.F.	9.12 a.m.	BRYAS.	OSTREVILLE	10½
12th S.W.B.	9.21 a.m.	N.30.d.9.7.	MONCHY BRETON	8¾
119th M.G.C.	9.30 a.m.	N.30.a.7.5. N.29.b.9.0.	ORLENCOURT	9
119th T.M.B.	9.33 a.m.			
17th Welsh.	9.34 a.m.	-	LA THIEULOYE	8
136th Field Ambulance.	9.43 a.m.	BRYAS	OSTREVILLE	10

3. The 224th Field Company R.E. will march independently, via
   HOUDAIN and MAGNICOURT to billets in Area "B", where they will
   join the 121st Brigade Group.

   They will be clear of the railway crossing J.15.d.0.4. by 9 a.m.

4. No. 2. Coy. 40th Divl Train will march independently via HOUDAIN
   and LA COMTE to billets in HOUVELIN.

   They will not pass the cross roads J.15.b.5.4. before 9-45 a.m.,
   or until such time as the rear of the 136th Field Ambulance is
   clear of that point.

5. The main road through BRUAY from J.16.a.6.7. to the starting
   point will be used by troops moving to the starting point only.
   In moving to the starting point the order of march given in para.
   2 will be observed.

6. Baggage wagons will accompany Units.

7. Billeting Officers will meet Units on the outskirts of their respective billeting areas.

                                                                  Captain.

                                              Brigade Major.

31st October 1916.   119th Infantry Brigade.

Copy No. 1. O.C. 19th R.W.F.   Copy No. 8. O.C. 136th Field Ambulance.
        2. O.C. 12th S.W.B.   9. O.C. No. 2. Coy. Divl Train.
        3. O.C. 17th Welsh.   10. War Diary
        4. O.C. 18th Welsh.   11. Brigade Major.
        5. O.C. 119th M.G.Coy.   12. Staff Captain.
        6. O.C. 119th T.M.B.   13. Camp Commandant.
        7. O.C. 224th Coy. R.E.   14. 40th Division. (G)

War Diary.

D

OPERATION ORDERS BY
Colonel B.J. Jones D.S.O. Commanding
19th Bn Royal Welsh Fusiliers

Oct 31 1916.

1. The 19th Batts. R.W.F. will move out of billets in BRUAY on the 1st November and will proceed to OSTREVILLE.

2. Breakfast will be at 6.30 sharp and all dixies immediately returned to the Field Kitchens.

3. All packs will be handed in to the Q.M. Stores by 7.45 a.m. Officers' messes will be handed in to Field Kitchens by 7.30 a.m. Officers' valises will also be handed in to Q.M. Stores by 7.30 am

4. The Battalion will march in the following order
    Scouts & Snipers and Signallers.
    D. Coy
    2 Lewis Gun detachments
    C Coy
    Headquarter details
    B Coy
    2 Lewis Gun detachments
    A Coy
    A Coy will provide a rear party.

5. D Coy will pass Batt. Orderly Room at 9.0 a.m. moving South West.

6. B Coy will be formed up in neighbourhood of their billets at 8.45 am for presentation of medals.

7. Billets will be kept in a clean and sanitary condition

(Sgn) P.E. Williams, Captain
Adjutant 19th Bn R.W. Fus.

SECRET. COPY NO...1....

119TH BRIGADE ORDER NO. 38

Reference Map. LENS. 11. 1/100,000.

1. The Brigade Group will march from Area "A" to Area "E" on Thursday, November 2nd.

   Route via LIGNY ST FLOCHEL - TERNAS.

   Starting point - Road junction at S. end of MARQUAY Village.

2. **March table**.

UNIT.	Pass Starting Point.	Route to Starting Point.	Billets in Area "E"	Route to Billet
Brigade H.Q.	9-15 a.m.	ORLENCOURT - L of HOSTREL	MAISNIL ST POL.	-
12th Yorks.	9-18 a.m.	"	MONCHEAUX	BUNEVILLE
19th R.W.F.	9-28 a.m.	L of HOSTREL	BUNEVILLE	-
119th M.G.C	9-37 a.m.	do	PT HOUVIN	BUNEVILLE
119th T.M.B.	9-40 a.m.	do	MONTS ENTERNOIS	-
12th S.W.B.	9-41 a.m.	MONCHY BRETON - L of HOSTREL.	do	-
17th Welsh.	10-0 a.m.	do	TERNAS	-
18th Welsh.	10-9 a.m.	do	FOUFFLIN	-
231st Coy RE	10-18 a.m.		MAISNIL ST POL	-
136th Field Ambulance.	10-23 a.m.	OSTREVILLE	NEUVILLE	-
No. 2 Coy. Divl.Train	10-28 a.m.	MONCHY BRETON - L of HOSTREL	PT HOUVIN	BUNEVILLE.

3. Baggage wagons will accompany units.

4. Billeting Officers will meet units on the outskirts of their respective areas.

5. O's.C. 19th Bn Royal Welsh Fusiliers and 17th Bn Welsh Regiment will arrange to clear the roads in their respective areas to allow other troops to pass through.

                                   Captain.
                                   Brigade Major.
                                   119th Infantry Brigade.

1st November 1916.

Copy No. 1. O.C. 19th R.W.F.
         2. O.C. 12th S.W.B.
         3. O.C. 17th Welsh.
         4. O.C. 18th Welsh.
         5. O.C. 119th M.G.Coy.
         6. O.C. 119th T.M.B.
         7. O.C. 231st Field Coy. R.E.
         8. O.C. 136th Field Ambulance

Copy No. 9. O.C. No.2. Coy. Divl Train.
         10. O.C. 12th Yorkshire Rgt.
         11. War Diary.
         12. Brigade Major.
         13. Staff Captain.
         14. Camp Commandant.
         15. 40th Division. (G)

From Lieut. Col. B. Jones DSO
Commdg 9th Bn. R.W. Fus.

The 9th Bn R.W.F. will move out of billets at OSTREVILLE on the 2nd inst. The Battalion will march to BUNEVILLE.

Breakfast will be at 6.30 a.m. Personnel of all details except Q.M. Stores will parade with their own companies. Packs will be handed in by 7.30 a.m.

Companies will move in the following order:
    C Coy.
    2 Lewis Gun Detachments
    D Coy
    A Coy
    2 Lewis Gun Detachments
    B Coy

B Coy will provide a rear party.
Packs valises must be at Q.M. Stores by 7.30 a.m.
Messes must be handed in to Field Kitchens by 7.30 a.m.
C Coy, leading Sn. will pass Cross Roads OSTREVILLE at 7.30 a.m.

(Signed) P.B. Williams Capt.
Adjt. 9th Bn. R.W. Fus.

2nd 1916

SECRET.   COPY NO....... 1

119TH BRIGADE ORDER NO 39.

Reference Map. LENS 11. 1/100,000

1. The Brigade Group will march to billets in Area "H" on Saturday November 4th, in two columns in accordance with the following march table.

2. March table.:-

   Column A. Commander, Lt.Col. B.J.Jones. D.S.O: 19th Bn Royal Welsh Fusiliers.

   Starting point :- Road junction N. of P in PT HOUVIN.

   Route : NUNCQ - LIGNY SUR CAUCHE - VACQUERIE LE BOUCQ

Units in order of March	Pass Starting Point	Route to Starting Point	Destination
119th M.G.Coy	10.0a.m.	-	ROUGEFAY
19th R.W.F.	10.3a.m.	PT HOUVIN STA	BUIRE-AU-BOIS
231st Field Coy R.E	10.9a.m.	SAINS	ROUGEFAY
Brigade H.Q.	10.14a.m.	do	FORTEL
18th Welsh.	10.15a.m.	do	do
No.2.Coy.Div.Train	10.21a.m.	-	PT FORTEL

Column B. Commander, Lt. Col. H.W.Becher, 12th Yorkshire Regt.

   Starting Point: Road junction S of X in MONCHEAUX.

   Route: SIBIVILLE - FREVENT - Road junction 1000 yds N.W. of FM LEROY - BONNIERES.

Units in order of March.	Pass Starting Point	Route to Starting Point.	Destination
12th Bn Yorks.	9. 0 a.m.	-	BONNIERES (E) and BEAUVOIR
12th S.W.B.	9. 9 a.m.	-	BONNIERES (S)
17th Welsh.	9.15 a.m.	BUNEVILLE	do (W)
119th T.M.B.	9.21 a.m.	V of NEUVILLE	BOFFLES
136th Field Amb.	9.22 a.m.	do	do

3. O.C. 136th Field Ambulance will detail one horsed ambulance wagon to follow the rear of the 18th Bn Welsh Regiment from MAISNIL ST POL, under arrangements to be made between O.C. Units direct.

4. Billeting Officers will meet Units on the outskirts of their respective areas.

   Billeting parties of 12th Bn South Wales Borderers and 17th Bn Welsh Regiment will report to their respective Billeting Officers at the Cross Roads East of S in BONNIERES at 9 a.m.

5. O's C. Columns or their representatives, will march at the head of their respective Columns throughout the march.

                                              Captain
                                              Brigade Major.
3rd November 1916.   119th Infantry Brigade

Copy No. 1. O.C. 19th R.W.F.   Copy No. 9. O.C. 138th Field Ambulance
         2. O.C. 12th S.W.B.   10. O.C. No. 2. Coy. Divl Train
         3. O.C. 17th Welsh.   11. War Diary
         4. O.C. 18th Welsh   12. Brigade Major.
         5. O.C. 119th M.G.Coy.   13. Staff Captain
         6. O.C. 119th T.M.B.   14. Camp Commandant.
         7. O.C. 12th Yorks.   15. Signals.
         8. O.C. 231st Field Coy.R.E.   16. 40th Division (G)

OPERATION ORDERS BY
Lt. Colonel B.J. Jones D.S.O. Commdg.
19th Batn. Royal Welsh Fus.

Oct 3 1916.

1. The 19th Batt R.W.F. will move out of billets at BUNEVILLE on the 4th inst.

2. Companies will move in the following order
   B Coy.
   2 Lewis Gun Detachments
   C Coy
   D Coy
   2 Lewis Gun Detachments
   A Coy.

   A Coy will provide a rear party
   B Coy will pass Batt. Orderly Room at 8.30 a.m.

3. Breakfast will be at 6.30 a.m. Iron rations will be carried in haversack. Packs will be handed in by 7.30 a.m.

4. Officers' valises will be handed in by 7.30 a.m. Officers' messes will be handed in by 8.0 a.m.

F.E. Williams. Captain
Adjutant 19th Bn R.W.F.

SECRET.   COPY NO. 1

119TH BRIGADE ORDER NO. 40

Reference Map. LENS 11. 1/100,000

1. The Brigade Group will march to billets in Area M on Sunday, November 5th, in 3 Columns in accordance with the following march table.

2. <u>March Table</u>

   Column A. Commander, Lt. Col. B.J.Jones, D.S.O. 19th Bn Royal Welsh Fusiliers.

   Starting Point: Road junction at S. end of BUIRE-AU-BOIS.

   Route: NOEUX – BEAUVOIR RIVIERE – ST ACHEUL

Units in order of March	Pass Starting Point	Destination
19th Bn R.W.Fusiliers.	9.0 a.m.	HEUZECOURT
119th M.G.Company.	9.6 a.m.	MONTIGNY
231st Field Coy. R.E.	9.9 a.m.	do

   Column B. Commander, Lt. Col. R.S.Grant Thorold, 18th Welsh Regt.

   Starting Point: Road junction 500 yds S. of <u>O</u> in BOFFLES.

   Route: VILLERS L'HOPITAL – FROHEN LE PETIT.

Units in order of March	Pass Starting Point.	Destination	Route to Billets.
18th Welsh Regt.	9.0 a.m.	LE MEILLARD.	–
119th T.M.Battery	9.6 a.m.	LE QUESNEL FM	–
136th Field Amb.	9.7 a.m.	FROHEN LE PETIT	–
No. 2 Coy. Div. Train	9.10 a.m.	do	–

   Column C. Commander, Lt.Col. H.W.Becher, 12th Yorkshire Regt.

   Starting Point: Road junction 700 yds S.E. of <u>S</u> in BONNIÈRES.

   Route: BARLY.

Units in order of March	Pass Starting Point.	Destination	Route to Billets.
12th S.W.Borderers.	10.0 a.m.	AUTHEUX	OUTREBOIS
119th Brigade H.Q.	10.6 a.m.	do	do
17th Welsh Regt.	10.7 a.m.	BOISBERGUES	–
12th Yorkshire Regt	10.13 a.m.	OUTREBOIS	–

3. O.C. 136th Field Ambulance will detail 1 horse ambulance wagon to follow in rear of each Column, and to report to O's C. A, B, and C Columns at their respective starting points at 9 a.m., 9 a.m., and 10 a.m. respectively.

4. O's. C. Columns, or their representatives, will march at the head of their respective Columns throughout the march.

5. Billeting Officers will meet Units on the outskirts of their respective areas.

6. Brigade Headquarters will close at FORTEL at 8.30 a.m., and will open at AUTHEUX at 1.30. p.m.

4th November 1916.

Captain.
Brigade Major.
119th Infantry Brigade.

Copy No. 1. O.C. 19th R.W.F.
2. O.C. 12th S.W.B.
3. O.C. 17th Welsh.
4. O.C. 18th Welsh.
5. O.C. 119th M.G.Coy.
6. O.C. 119th T.M.B.
7. O.C. 12th Yorks.
8. O.C. 231st Field Coy. R.E.

Copy No. 9 O.C. 136th Field Ambulance.
10. O.C. No. 2. Coy. Divl Train.
11. War Diary
12. Brigade Major.
13. Staff Captain
14. Camp Commandant.
15. Signals.
16. 40th Division (G)
17. 40th Division (Q)

S E C R E T   COPY NO..1....

K

119TH BRIGADE ORDER : 41

Reference Map. LENS 11. 1/100,000

1. The Brigade Group will march to billets in Area "O" on Wednesday, November 15th in accordance with the following march table.

2. March Table.

    Column A.   Commander Lt. Col. E.A.Pope. 12th Bn South Wales Borderers.

    Starting Point.   LE QUESNEL FM

    Route.   OUTREBOIS - MEZEROLLES - FROHEN LE GRAND - VILLERS L'HOPITAL. Thence to be reconnoitred by each Unit.

Units in order of March	Pass Starting Point.	Destination	Remarks.
12th S.W.B.	11.30 a.m.	FORTEL.	
119th T.M.B.	11.36 a.m.	PETIT FORTEL	
17th Welsh.	11.37 a.m.	NOEUX	
136th F. Amb.	..	BOFFLES	Follows rear of 17th Bn Welsh Regt from FROHEN LE GRAND Church at about 1.15 p.m.

    Column B.   Commander Lt. Col. B.J.Jones. D.S.O. 19th Bn Royal Welsh Fusiliers.

    Starting Point.   Fork road 1000 yards N. of H in HEUZECOURT.

    Route.   H of ST ACHEUL - BEAUCOURT/VILLAGE - Bridge S of H in CHAU DE BEAUVOIN. - 1st A in WAVANS - NOEUX.

Units in order of March.	Pass Starting Point.	Destination	Route to Billet
19th R.W.F.	11.15 a.m.	BUIRE AU BOIS	
18th Welsh (less carrying party already detailed)	11.21 a.m.	ROUGEFAY & MONT HUBERT	S in BUIRE AU BOIS.
No 2 Coy. Train.	11.26 a.m.	MAMUR FM	
119th M.G.Coy.	11.31 a.m.	WAVANS.	
119th Bde H.Q.	11.34 a.m.	do	

3. Billeting parties of all Units will proceed under Regimental arrangements in advance to the Areas specified above, and will meet their Units on the outskirts of their respective areas.

4. Brigade Headquarters will close at AUTHEUX at 9 a.m. and will open at WAVANS at 12.30 p.m.   Reports to LE MEILLARD Church at 10.30 a.m; starting point of Column B at 11.15 a.m.; and Bridge S of H in CHAU DE BEAUVOIN at 12 noon.

5. One Motor Lorry per Battalion will report to Units as follows :-

19th Bn R.W.F.	8 a.m.	HEUZECOURT
12th Bn S.W.B.	7.15 a.m.	AUTHEUX
17th Welsh.	7.30 a.m.	BOISBERGUES
18th Welsh.	7.45 a.m.	LE MEILLARD.

These lorries are for the conveyance of packs only - Blankets and waterproof sheets will be carried on the man.

The packs of the 119th Machine Gun Company will be taken on Brigade Headquarters Lorry.

The packs of the 119th Trench Mortar Battery will be taken on 12th Bn South Wales Borderers.

6. Refilling point will be MAMUR FM.

                                              Captain.
                                            Brigade Major.

14th Novr 1916.   119th Infantry Brigade.

Copy No. 1. 19th R.W.F.
       2. 12th S.W.B.
       3. 17th Welsh.
       4. 18th Welsh.
       5. 119th M.G.Coy.
       6. 119th T.M.B.
       7. 136th Field Ambulance.
       8. No. 2. Coy. Train.
       9. Signals.
     10. War Diary
     11. Brigade Major.
     12. 40th Div. G.
     13. 40th Div. Q
     14. O.C. 40th Div. Train.

Operation Orders by Lt. Col. B. I. Jones DSO
Commdg. 19th Batt. R.W.F.

1. The 19th Batt. R.W.F. will move out of billets in HEUZECOURT on the 15th inst. & will march to BUIRE-au-BOIS.

2. Companies will march in the following order:-
    D Coy.
    2 Lewis Gun Detachments
    A Coy
    B Coy
    2 Lewis Gun Detachments
    C Coy.
   D Coy. will pass the CHURCH at 11.10 a.m.

3. Packs will be handed in by 10 a.m.
   Officers' valises "   "   " 10 a.m.
   Men will carry their blankets, neatly rolled inside the ground sheet & fastened to the back of the belt.

4. Each Coy. will detail 1 N.C.O. + 3 men to clear up all billets & these parties will report to the Lt. C.H. Jones at the Batt. Orderly Room as soon as their billets are in a clean condition.

15.11.16

J. E. Williams, Capt.
A & S. 19th R.W.F.

COPY NO. 1

SECRET

119TH BRIGADE ORDER NO 42.

Reference Map. LENS 11. 1/100,000.

1. Units of the Brigade Group will march from present billets to Area P on Friday, November 17th, in separate columns as follows :-

Unit.	Leave present billets.	Destination	Route via
Brigade H.Q.	10.0 a.m.	REMAISNIL CHATEAU	-
19th R.W.F.	9.0 a.m.	VILLERS L'HOPITAL	NOEUX
12th S.W.B.	10.0 a.m.	BONNIERES	-
119th T.M.B.	To follow 12th S.W.B.	do	-
17th Welsh.	9.0 a.m.	BARLY	TAVANS and FROHEN LE GRAND
18th Welsh.	9.0 a.m.	BONNIERES	FORTEL
119th M.G.Coy.	10.0 a.m.	VILLERS L'HOPITAL	
136th F.Amb.	9.0 a.m.	OCCOCHES	VILLERS L'HOPITAL
No 2 Coy Train	9.0 a.m.	MEZEROLLES	NOEUX

2. Brigade Headquarters will close at CHAU DE BEAUVOIN at 10 a.m. and will open at REMAISNIL CHAU at 11 a.m.

3. One motor lorry per Battalion will report to Units at 8 a.m. The lorry allotted to 19th Bn Royal Welsh Fusiliers will also carry for 119th Machine Gun Company.
That allotted to the 12th Bn South Wales Borderers will also carry for the 119th Trench Mortar Battery.

These lorries will carry packs, and will make two trips. Blankets will be carried on the man.

4. The 19th Bn Royal Welsh Fusiliers will detail a guard, on arrival at VILLERS L'HOPITAL, to relieve the guard at present found by the 121st Infantry Brigade, over the Coal Dump situated there.

5. Billeting parties will proceed in advance under regimental arrangements.

6. Billeting sub-areas are allotted as follows:-

BONNIERES. 12th Bn S.W.Borderers will occupy their old billets S of Cross Roads at S in BONNIERES.

18th Bn Welsh Regt will be N of the same Cross Roads.

119th T.M.Battery. East of road fork 600 yards S.E. of the same Cross Roads.

VILLERS L'HOPITAL 119th M.G.Company will be N of TAVANS - BONNIERES Road.

19th Bn R.W.Fusiliers will be S of that road.

7. O.C. 12th Bn S.W.Borderers will detail 24 men to assist the 119th T.M.Battery in pulling handcarts.

8. The march will be resumed on the 18th.

   The Brigade will probably halt on the 19th, 20th and 21st.

[signature]
Captain.
Brigade Major.
119th Infantry Brigade.

16th November 1916.

Copy No. 1. 19th R.W.F.
2. 12th S.W.B.
3. 17th Welsh.
4. 18th Welsh.
5. 119th M.G.Coy.
6. 119th T.M.B.
7. 40th Div. "G"
8. 40th Div. "Q"

Copy No. 9. Brig.Genl.C.Cunliffe Owen. C.B.
10. War Diary.
11. Brigade Major.
12. O.C. 40th Div. Train.
13. O.C. No. 2 Coy. A.S.C.
14. 136th Field Ambulance.
15. A.D.M.S. 40th Div.

N.

Operation Orders by Lt. Col. B. J. Jones D.S.O.
Commanding 19th Batt. R.W.F.

1. The 19th Batt. R.W.F. will move out of present billets in BUIRE-au-BOIS & will proceed by Route march to VILLERS l'HOPITAL

2. Battalion will move in the following order.
   C Coy.
   Lewis Gun Det.
   D Coy.
   A Coy.
   Lewis Gun Det.
   B Coy.
   Transport.
   C Coy. will pass the Church at 9.0 a.m.

3. Packs will be handed in at 7.30 a.m. Officers' valises will be handed in at 8.0 a.m. & Officers' messes by 8.15 a.m.

4. 1 N.C.O. & 3 men per Coy. will report at Q.M. Stores at 10.0 a.m. & report to an officer detailed by O.C. C Coy. that billets are clean.

16. XI. 16.

P. E. Williams. Capt.
Adjt. 19th R.W.F.

S E C R E T. COPY NO...1......

119TH BRIGADE ORDER No 43.

Reference Map. LENS. 11. 1/100,000.

1. The 119th Brigade Group will march from its present billets to Area "Q" tomorrow, Saturday, November 18th in accordance with the March Table overleaf.

2. No troops of the Brigade Group will be on or East of the FREVENT - DOULLENS Road before 1 p.m.

3. Brigade Headquarters will close at REMAISNIL at 10.30 a.m. and will open at LE SOUICH at 1.45 p.m.

4. Reports to starting point till 12.45 p.m. After that hour to head of column.

                                                            Captain.
                                            Brigade Major.
17th November 1916.   119th Infantry Brigade.

Copy No 1. O.C. 19th R.W.F.   Copy No 9. Brig. Genl. C.Cunliffe
      2. O.C. 12th S.W.B.   Owen. C.B
      3. O.C. 17th Welsh.   10. War Diary
      4. O.C. 18th Welsh.   11. Brigade Major.
      5. O.C. 119th M.G.Coy.   12. O.C. 40th Divl Train
      6. O.C. 119th T.M.B.   13. O.C. No. 2 Coy A.S.C.
      7. 40th Division. "G"   14. 136th Field Ambulance.
      8. 40th Division. "Q"   15. A.D.M.S. 40th Division,

U N I T	Situation	Pass Starting Point.	Route to Starting Point.	Destination.	Remarks
Brigade Headquarters	REMAISNIL	12.15 p.m.	BARLY	LE SOUICH	
17th Welsh Regiment.	BARLY.	12.16 p.m.	-	BREVILLERS	
18th Welsh Regiment.	BONNIERS	12.23 p.m.	BEAUVOIR	LE SOUICH	
12th S.W.Borders.	do	12.30 p.m.	do	BOUQUEMAISON	
119th T.M.Battery	do	12.37 p.m.	do	do	
19th R.W.Fusiliers.	VILLERS L'HOPITAL	12.38 p.m.	do	NEUVILLETTE	
119th M.G.Company	do	12.45 p.m.	do	do	
136th Field Amb.	OCCOCHES	-	-	BOUQUEMAISON	These two units will proceed independently via RISQUETOUT and LE COLLEGE.
No. 2. Coy. Train.	METEROLLES	-	-	do	

Starting Point (for all units except R.A.M.C. and A.S.C):- Road junction N. of AN of CANTELEUX, on BEAUVOIR - NEUVILLETTE Road.

Route :-

NEUVILLETTE - B of BOUQUEMAISON - LE SOUICH.

Operation Orders by Lt. Col. B.J. Jones. D.S.O.
Commdg. 19th Batt. R.W.F.   17.11.16.

1. The 19th Batt. R.W.F. will move out of billets at VILLERS l'HOPITAL on the 18th inst. & will route march to NEUVILLETTE.

2. Order of march.   B. Coy.
                     Lewis Gun Detachments.
                     C Coy.
                     D Coy.
                     Lewis Gun Detachments
                     A Coy.
   B Coy. will pass CHURCH   at. 10.30 a.m.

3. Order of dress already detailed will be strictly adhered to.

4. Billeting Officer & N.C.O.'s will report at Q.M's Stores at 7.30 a.m.

5. Men's packs will be handed in to Q.M. Stores by 7.15 a.m.
   Officer's valises will be handed in to Q.M. Stores by 7.45 a.m.; Messes will be ready by 8 a.m.

6. 1 N.C.O. & 3 men per Coy. will report to an officer, detailed by O.C. B Coy., at the Q.M Stores when their Coy. area is clean.

                                    P.E. Williams Capt.
                                    Adj. 19th R.W.F.

Army Form B. 2069.

Offence Report (*Field Service only*).

Corps _____

Squadron, Troop, Batty. or Company	Regt. No.	Rank	Name	Place and Date of offence	Offence	By whom reported and Names of Witnesses	Initials of Officer Comdg. Company, &c.	Punishment awarded	Signature of Officer by whom ordered and date of award	Date of entry in Conduct Sheet	Remarks

N.B.—A horizontal line should be drawn the whole length of the Return after each day's offences are entered.

(2670) Wt. W 3034—1692 600,000 5/15 H. G. & S., Ld. Forms B. 2069/7

```
O.C. 19th R.W.F.      119th T.M.B.                    119th Bde No. 9/223/G.L.
     12th S.W.B.      No. 2. Coy. A.S.C.
     17th Welsh       136th Field Ambulance.
     18th Welsh.      H.Q. 40th Division (Q)   (For information)
     119th M.G.Coy.
```

The following internal moves will take place within the Brigade Area "Q" tomorrow, Sunday, November 19th, in accordance with March Table below.

UNIT	Situation	Leave present Billets	Destination.
119th T.M.B.	BOUQUEMAISON	9.45 a.m.	LE SOUICH
No 2. Coy A.S.C	do	10. 0 a.m.	HTE VISEE. South of HTE VISEE to GROUCHES Road inclusive.
136th F.Ambulance	do	10.10 a.m.	HTE VISEE. North of above exclusive.
119th M.G.Coy.	NEUVILLETTE	10.30 a.m.	LE SOUICH
19th R.W.F.	do	10.35 a.m.	BOUQUEMAISON. East of FREVENT - DOULLENS Road.

With reference to the above :-

(1) No additional Transport will be provided for Units.

(2) The Northern Boundary of the Area of the 12th S.W.B. are billets Nos 41A - 72 exlusive.

(3) The following officers billets in the Areas of the 19th R.W.F. and 12th S.W.B. are allotted to 40th Divisional Headquarters and cannot be occupied without the consent of Divisional Headquarters. Nos. 31, 14, 10, 63, 64, 65, 98, 95, 86, 83, 82, 56, 57, 130, 121A, 114, 112, 117.

(4) If sufficient accommodation cannot be found by the 19th R.W.F. arrangements will be made with the 12th S.W.B. direct for taking over further accommodation in the 12th S.W.B. Area.

(5) Billeting areas for the 119th T.M.B. and 119th M.G.Coy, will be allotted by the O.C. 18th Welsh Regiment.

[signature]

Captain.
Staff Captain.
119th Infantry Brigade.

18th November 1916.

War Diary

Operation Orders by Lt Colonel B.J. Jones D.S.O.
Commdg. 19th Bn Royal Welsh Fusiliers

Nov 12 1916.

1. The 19th Battn. R.W.F. will move out of present billets at NIEUVILETTE and will proceed by route march to BOUQEMAISON.

2. Order of march.
    A Coy
    Lewis Gun Detachments
    B Coy
    C Coy
    Lewis Gun Detachments
    D Coy
   A Coy will form across roads 300° East of CHURCH at 10.35 a.m.

3. Billeting Officer and Billeting N.C.O's will report at QM Stores at 7.30 a.m.

4. Packs and Blankets will be carried on the wagon. Blankets on top of the valise, waterproof sheet under flap of valise, haversack on back.

5. Officers' valises will be handed in to QM Stores at 9 am. Officers' messes will be cleared by 9.30 am.

6. 1 NCO and 3 men from each Coy will report to QM Stores to an Officer detailed by O.C. A Coy last night and ammunition to draw and distribute.

J.C.Williams. Major
Adjutant 19th Bn RWF

S E C R E T   COPY NO...... 1 S

119TH BRIGADE ORDER NO.44

Reference Map. LENS. 11.   1/100,000.

1. The Brigade Group will move from its present billets to Area "T" tomorrow, November 22nd, in accordance with March Table overleaf.

2. Owing to the number of troops on the move some crossings will be inevitable. The following intervals will therefore be observed from the Starting Point onwards in the case of Battalions :-

    Battalion Headquarters, No 1 Company and Lewis Guns

    200 yards interval

    No 2 Company

    200 yards interval

    No. 3 Company and Lewis Guns

    200 yards interval

    No 4 Company

    200 yards interval

    1st Line Transport

    500 yards interval will be left in rear of each Battalion after passing the Starting Point.

    200 yards interval will be left in rear of the Field Ambulance A.S.C.Company, Machine Gun Company, Brigade Headquarters and Trench Mortar Battery after passing the Starting Point.

3. Brigade time will be obtained from the Brigade Major at the Starting point by representatives of Units at 9 a.m. All Units and Detachments will observe the usual halts simultaneously and independently - i.e. at 10 minutes before each clock hour, for 10 minutes.

4. O.C. 136th Field Ambulance will detail 3 Horse Ambulances to be North East of the Starting Point facing S.W. at 8.45 a.m. One of these Ambulances will follow the rear of the 1st Line Transport of each of the following Battalions under the orders of the respective Medical Officers:-

    12th Bn South Wales Borderers.
    17th Welsh Regiment.
    18th Welsh Regiment.

5. One lorry per Battalion will report to Battalions at 7.30 a.m. for the conveyance of packs. Blankets will be carried on the man.

    The lorry of the 18th Welsh Regt will carry for Brigade H.Q.

    The lorry of the 12th S.W.Borderers will carry for 119th M.G.Coy.

    Packs of 119th T.M.B. will be carried in the handcarts

6. Brigade Headquarters will close at LE SOUICH at 8.30 a.m. and will open at GEZAINCOURT at 12 noon.

   Reports to Starting Point from 9 a.m. to 10.30 a.m. From that hour to noon to the head of the column.

7. O.C. 12th Bn South Wales Borderers will detail 24 men to report to O.C. 119th T.M.Battery at the Starting Point at 9.40 a.m. to assist in pulling handcarts. These men will rejoin their Unit on completion of the move.

   The carts will be conveyed to the Starting Point by men of the Trench Mortar Battery without assistance.

8. O.C. 19th Bn Royal Welsh Fusiliers will arrange to have the route A reconnoitred, and will post regimental police at cross roads and doubtful points. These police will remain posted until the 1st Line Transport of the 17th Bn Welsh Regiment has passed, and will then follow in rear of that Unit to rejoin their Unit in GEZAINCOURT.

   O.C. 12th Bn South Wales Borderers will make similar arrangements for Route B. Police will join the tail of the 119th M.G.Company when it has passed.

9. Billeting Officers of Units will report to the Staff Captain at the road junction S.W. of 1st L of LE COLLEGE at 9 a.m.

21st November 1916.

Captain.
Brigade Major.
119th Infantry Brigade.

Copy No. 1. O.C. 19th R.W.F.   Copy No. 8. O.C. 136th F.Ambulance.
         2. O.C. 12th S.W.B.   9. 40th Division. "G"
         3. O.C. 17th Welsh.   10. 40th Division. "Q"
         4. O.C. 18th Welsh.   11. War Diary.
         5. O.C. 119th M.G.Coy   12. Brigade Major
         6. O.C. 119th T.M.B.   13. Staff Captain.
         7. O.C. No. 2. Coy. A.S.C.   14. O.C. Signals.

MARCH TABLE

U N I T	Situation.	Tail to be clear of road junction 800 yards N. of 1st R in BREVILLERS by.	Starting Point Pass Head	Starting Point Pass Tail	Destination	Remarks.
19th R.W.Fusiliers	BOUQUEMAISON	-	9 a.m.	9.15 a.m.	GEZAINCOURT	Route A
12th S.W.Borderers	do	-	9.20 a.m.	9.35 a.m.	BEAUVAL	Route B
119th T.M.Battery.	LE SOUICH	9.6 a.m.	9.40 a.m.	9.41 a.m.	do	Route B
119th M.G.Company.	do	9.10. a.m.	9.43 a.m.	9.46 a.m.	do	Route B
Bde. Headquarters	do	9.12 a.m.	9.48 a.m.	9.49 a.m.	GEZAINCOURT	Route A
18th Welsh Regt.	do	9.21 a.m.	10.1 a.m.	10.16 a.m.	do	Route A.
17th Welsh Regt.	do	9.30 a.m.	10.21 a.m.	10.36 a.m.	do	Route A
136th F.Ambulance.	HTE VISEE	-	-	-	BEAUVAL	Less 3 Horse Ambulances. To proceed independently via Route B, and to be clear of HTE VISEE by 9.30 a.m.
No.2 Coy. Train.	do	-	-	-	do	To proceed independently via Route B, and to be clear of HTE VISEE by 9.20 a.m.

Route A.   1st L of LE COLLEGE - L of BRETEL - D of CITADELLE - GEZAINCOURT.

ROUTE B.   DOULLENS - BEAUVAL.

Starting Point.   Cross Roads 200 yards W. of BOUQUEMAISON Church.

SECRET. 119th Bde. No. 9/274/G.L.

O.C. 19th R.W.F.   136th Field Ambulance.
      12th S.W.B.   H.Q. 40th Division. "G"
      17th Welsh.   H.Q. 40th Division. "Q"
      18th Welsh.   War Diary.
      119th M.G.Coy.   Brigade Major.
      119th T.M.B.   Staff Captain.
      No. 2. Coy. A.S.C.   O.C. Signals.

      Para. 9. of 119th Brigade Order No. 44. is cancelled.

      Billeting Officers of the 12th South Wales Borderers, 119th M.G.Company, 119th T.M.Battery, 136th Field Ambulance and No. 2. Coy. A.S.C. will report at 9.30 a.m. to the Town Major, BEAUVAL, at Town Major's Office 50 yards South of BEAUVAL CHURCH.

      Billeting Officers of 119th Infantry Brigade, 19th Royal Welsh Fusiliers, 17th Welsh Regiment and 18th Welsh Regiment will report at 9.30 a.m. to the Town Major, GEZAINCOURT at Billet No. 42 opposite Officer's Hospital, BAGNEUX.

                                            Captain.
                                     Staff Captain.
21st November 1916.   119th Infantry Brigade.

Operation Orders by Lt Colonel B.J. Jones D.S.O.
Commdg 19th Battn Royal Welsh Fus

Nov 21 1916.

1. The Battalion will move out of billets in BOUQUEMAISON and will proceed by march route to GEZAINCOURT

2. Order of march   D Coy and Lewis Guns
   200 yards interval
   A Coy
   200 yards interval
   B Coy and Lewis Guns
   200 yards interval
   C Coy
   200 yards interval
   1st Line Transport

   D Coy will pass BOUQUEMAISON CHURCH at 9.57 am.

3. Breakfast will be at 6.30 am.
   Packs will be handed in to Q.M. Stores by 7.20 am.
   Officers valises by 8 am.
   Officers messes will be collected at 8 am.

4. Dress:- Blankets will be carried on the man, fastened under the haversack, waterproof sheets under the flap of the haversack.

5. Billeting officer and billeting N.C.O's will report at Q.M. Stores at 7.45 am

6. Police Controls will be posted according to instructions issued.

P.E.Williams. Captain
Adjutant 19th R.W. Fus

S E C R E T. COPY NO. 1

119TH BRIGADE ORDER NO.45

Reference Map. LENS 11. 1/100,000.

1. The Brigade Group will march from its present billets to Area "V" tomorrow, November 23rd, in accordance with the March Table overleaf.

2. Each unit will march independently.

3. The same intervals will be observed as those ordered for today's march - i.e. 500 yds in rear of each Battalion, 200 yds in rear of each Company or other Unit.

4. O.C. 136th Field Ambulance will detail Horsed Ambulance Wagons as follows :-

   1 to follow rear of Brigade Headquarters.
   1   "   "   "   " 119th T.M.Battery.
   1   "   "   "   " 17th Bn. Welsh Regiment.

5. O.C. 12th Bn South Wales Borderers will detail the usual party to report to O.C. 119th T.M.Battery in BEAUVAL at 8.15 a.m., and to rejoin their unit at their destination.

6. Brigade Headquarters will close at GEZAINCOURT at 9 a.m. and will open at ST OUEN at 2 p.m. Reports to FIEFFES from 10.30 a.m. to 11.30 a.m.

                                            Captain.
                                            Brigade Major.
22nd November 1916.   119th Infantry Brigade.

Copy No. 1. O.C. 19th R.W.F.   Copy No. 9. O.C. 231st Field Coy. R.E.
         2. O.C. 12th S.W.B.   10. 40th Division. "G"
         3. O.C. 17th Welsh.   11. 40th Division. "Q"
         4. O.C. 18th Welsh.   12. War Diary.
         5. O.C. 119th M.G.Coy.   13. Brigade Major.
         6. O.C. 119th T.M.B.   14. Staff Captain
         7. O.C. No. 2. Coy. A.S.C.   15. O.C. Signals.
         8. O.C. 136th F.Ambulance.

MARCH TABLE.

UNIT	Situation	To be clear of present billets at	Destination	Route
119th Brigade Headquarters	GEZAINCOURT	9.0 a.m.	ST. OUEN	A
19th Royal Welsh Fusiliers	do	8.30 a.m.	do	A
12th South Wales Borderers	BEAUVAL	8.45 a.m.	ST. LEGER LES DOMART	B
17th Welsh Regiment.	GEZAINCOURT	9.0 a.m.	FRANQUEVILLE	C
18th Welsh Regiment.	do	8.45 a.m.	ST OUEN	A
119th M.G. Company.	BEAUVAL	8.30 a.m.	BARLETTE (N.)	D
118th T.M. Battery.	do	9.0 a.m.	ST LEGER LES DOMART	B
No. 2 Coy. A.S.C.	do	8.45 a.m.	BARLETTE (S.) and GENCOURT	D
136th Field Ambulance.	do	9.0 a.m.	HOUDENCOURT	D

Route A. S. end of GEZAINCOURT - CANDAS - FIEFFES - CANAPLES STA. - HALLOY LES PERNOIS - LE SOUDET.

Route B. BONNEVILLE - FIEFFES. Thence Route A.

Route C. LONGUEVILLETTE - FIENVILLERS - BERNEUIL - cross roads W of L in LANCHES.

Route D. CANDAS - FIENVILLERS. Thence Route C.

BILLETING

1. The billeting Officers of the 119th Infantry Brigade, 19th R.W. Fusiliers and 18th Welsh Regiment will report to the Town Major ST OUEN at 10 a.m. tomorrow, November 23rd.

2. The billeting Officer of the 12th S.W.Borderers and the billeting officer of the 119th T.M.Battery will proceed together to ST. LEGER to arrange allotment of billets for their respective Units.

3. The boundary between the area of No. 2. Coy. A.S.C. and 119th M.G.Company will be mutually arranged between the two units.

4. All billeting Officers will proceed to "V" Area under arrangements to be made by their respective units.

BAGGAGE

5. One lorry will report at 7 a.m. at BEAUVAL Church for the carriage of packs for the 12th S.W.Borderers and 3 lorries at GEZAINCOURT Church at the same hour for the carriage of packs for the 19th R.W.Fusiliers, 17th Welsh Regt, and 18th Welsh Regt. The lorry for the 18th Welsh Regiment will first load up packs of Brigade Headquarters and then proceed to Headquarters of 18th Welsh Regiment.

6. Units will send guide to meet lorries at BEAUVAL and GEZAINCOURT Church.

7. The 119th M.G.Company and 119th T.M.Battery will carry their packs on their own wagons.

Captain.
Staff Captain.
119th Infantry Brigade.

22nd November 1916.

1. The 1/5 Bn. R.W.F. will move out of present billets at
   CROIX COURT on 23rd inst. and will proceed to Route
   march to B OUEN.

2. Order of march.

   C Coy. Advance Guard
   200 yards delay
   D Coy
   200 yards interval
   A Coy
   200 yards interval
   B Coy
   200 yards interval
   Transport

3. Coy will pass Battalion rendezvous at 8.0 a.m.

4. Transport will move off at 7.50 a.m. There will be halts
   of 10 minutes. Officers will be 2.30 and Officers must
   report to officer on the spot.

5. Smoking, Talking and being out of rank are strictly
   forbidden.

6. Cleaning parties will be left behind. O.C.
   every Coy. will be held responsible that they
   are thoroughly carried out also.

7. There will be a billeting and quartering O.C.
   detailed on arrival.

                    (Sgd) E.T. Williams, Captain

                    Adjutant 1/5 Bn R.W.F.

SECRET.   COPY NO........

119TH BRIGADE ORDER NO. 46

Reference Maps. LENS. 11.   ) 1/100,000.
                 ABBEVILLE. 14.)

1. The Brigade Group will march from its present billets into a
   new Brigade Area on Friday, November 24th, in accordance with
   the March Table overleaf.

   Starting Point :-   5 cross roads S. of 1st A in LA HAIE FM

   Route :-   BRUCAMPS - cross roads 1000 yds
                       N. of VILLERS - AILLY - cross roads S. of
                       O in BELLANCOURT.

2. O.C. 12th Bn South Wales Borderers will detail the usual party
   to report to O.C. 119th T.M.Battery at an hour to be named by
   the latter.

3. Brigade Headquarters will close at ST OUEN at 8.30 a.m. and
   will open at BELLANCOURT at 12.30 p.m. Reports to Starting
   Point from 9.15 a.m. to 10.10 a.m. From that hour, to head
   of the column.

                                                Captain.
                                             Brigade Major.
23rd November 1916.   119th Infantry Brigade.

Copy No 1. O.C. 19th R.W.F.   Copy No. 9. O.C. 231st Field Coy. R.E.
        2 O.C. 12th S.W.B.   10. 40th Division. "G"
        3. O.C. 17th Welsh.   11. 40th Division. "Q"
        4. O.C. 18th Welsh.   12. War Diary.
        5. O.C. 119th M.G.Coy.   13. Brigade Major.
        6. O.C. 119th T.M.B.   14. Staff Captain
        7. O.C. No.2.Coy. A.S.C.   15. Signals.
        8. O.C. 136th F.Ambulance.

W.

ALLOTMENT OF BILLETS IN 119TH BRIGADE AREA.

H.Q. 119th Infantry Brigade.	The Chateau. BELLANCOURT.
19th Royal Welsh Fusiliers.	BELLANCOURT. Less 119th Brigade H.Q.
119th T. M. Battery.	MONFLIERS. North.
No. 2. Coy. A.S.C.	do South.
12th South Wales Borderers	BUIGNY L'ABBE
17th Welsh Regiment.	VAUCHELLES. South of ABBEVILLE - BUIGNY L'ABBE Road.
136th Field Ambulance.	VAUCHELLES. VAUCHELLES - CAOURS Road.
231st Field Coy. R.E.	VAUCHELLES. ABBEVILLE - BUIGNY Road
18th Welsh Regiment.	EAUCOURT and EPAGNE East of BRAY - MONFLIERS Cross Roads.
119th M.G.Company.	EPAGNE. West of BRAY - MONFLIERS Cross Roads.

1. The above areas are only approximate and where more than one Unit is billeted in the same village the boundaries for men must be adjusted between Units. If there is insufficient accommodation for officers a similar adjustment must be made.

2. Billeting Officers of the 17th Welsh Regt, 136th Field Ambulance and 231st Field Coy. R.E. will report to the MAIRE VAUCHELLES not later than 10 a.m. tomorrow November 24th.

3. Billeting Officers of the 119th Infy. Brigade, 19th R.W.Fusiliers No. 2. Coy. A.S.C. and 119th T. M. Battery will report to the MAIRE of BELLANCOURT.

4. The 119th T.M.Battery will be attached for rations to the 19th Royal Welsh Fusiliers from November 25th inclusive.

5. All billeting Officers will proceed to their Areas under arrangements to be made by their respective Units.

BAGGAGE

Lorries will report to Units as follows to morrows.

1 lorry 17th Welsh Regt. 8 a.m. at FRANQUEVILLE Church.

2 lorries 12th S.W.Borderers. 8 a.m. at ST OUEN Church.
(The 12th S.W.B. will carry the packs of the 119th T.M.B)

2 lorries 18th Welsh Regiment 8 a.m. at ST OUEN Church.

1 lorry 19th R.W.Fusiliers   do   do

1 lorry 119th Bde. Headquarters 8 a.m. at ST OUEN Church.
(The lorry after loading up packs of 119th Brigade H.Q.
will proceed to H.Q. 19th R.W.F. who will immediately
load up the remainder of lorry with packs.)

Guides will be sent by Units to meet the above lorries.

The 119th M.G.Company will carry their packs in their own wagons

                                                                    Captain.

                                           Staff Captain.

23rd November 1916.   119th Infantry Brigade.

MARCH TABLE

UNIT	Situation	Pass Starting Point.	Route to Starting Point.	Destination	Route to Billets	Remarks.
119th Bde.H.Q.	ST OUEN	9.17 a.m.	-	BELLANCOURT	-	
12th S.W.B.	ST LEGER LES DOMARTS	9.18 a.m.	DOMART EN PONTHIEU	BUIGNY L'ABBEE	-	
17th Welsh.	FRANQUEVILLE	9.25 a.m.	do	VAUCHELLES-LES-Q.	MONFLIERS	
18th Welsh.	ST OUEN	9.32 a.m.	-	EAUCOURT	PONT REMY	Will move to FRANCIERES on Nov.26th
19th R.W.F.	ST OUEN.	9.39 a.m.	-	BELLANCOURT	-	
119th M.G.Coy.	BARLETTE	9.46 a.m.	DOMART EN PONTHIEU	EPAGNE	PONT-REMY	
119th T.M.B.	ST LEGER LES DOMARTS	9.49 a.m.	do	MONFLIERS	-	
231st Coy. R.E.	DOMART EN PONTHIEU	10.0 a.m.	-	VAUCHELLES-LES-Q.	MONFLIERS	Will move to EAUCOURT on November 26th.
136th F.Ambulance	HOUDENCOURT	10.5 a.m.	DOMART EN PONTHIEU	do	do	
No.2 Coy. Train.	GENCOURT	10.8 a.m.	do	MONFLIERS	-	

War Diary

Marching Orders by Lt Col. L.J. Evans D.S.O.
Commdg. 19th Bn. Royal Welsh Fus.

Nov 13 1916

1. The 19th Bn. R.W.F. will move out of BIDEL to ST OUEN and will proceed by route march to BELLANCOURT.

2. Order of march
   B Coy
   Lewis Gun detachment
   C Coy
   D Coy
   Lewis Gun detachment
   A Coy
   First line Transport.

   B Coy will pass Q.M. Stores at 8.55 am

3. Breakfast will be at 6.30 am. Packs will be handed in by 7.30 am. Officers' valises by 8.. Officers' messes by 8.15 am

4. Blocking Officer and Blocking N.C.O's will report at Q.M. Stores at 8 am

5. No blocking parties will be left behind.

6. Dress as detailed in previous orders.

W. Williams Captain
Adjutant 19th RWF

SECRET.   COPY NO: 1

119TH BRIGADE ORDER NO. 50.

Reference Maps.   1/100,000.   ABBEVILLE.   Sheet 14
                               AMIENS.   Sheet 17.
                               LENS.   Sheet 11.

1. The 119th Brigade Group will move forward as follows :-

    December 8th. Transport of 19th R.W.F. and 17th Welsh to L'ETOILE.
                      "   " 136th Field Ambulance to AILLY LE HAUT
    CLOCHER.

        Billeting representatives of 136th Field Ambulance
        will report to the Town Major at AILLY at 11 a.m.

        Transport officer of the 17th Welsh Regt, will
        arrange billets in L'ETOILE.

    December 9th. Transport of all Units (except hand-carts of 119th
        T.M.B) will proceed independently to ST.SAUVEUR (N.W.
        of AMIENS).

        Transport of Brigade Headquarters and Brigade Signal
        Section, and the G.S.Wagon of the 119th T.M.B. will
        march under the orders of O.C. No. 2 Coy. A.S.C.

    December 10th. Personnel of all units and handcarts of 119th T.M.B.
        will proceed by rail to XV Corps Middle Area (West
        of BRAY) under arrangements to be notified later.

        Transport of all units (except handcarts of 119th
        T.M.B) will proceed to that area by road.

2. The following will proceed with the transport :-

        All transport personnel.
        1 brakesman per vehicle fitted with a brake.
        Pack animals.
        Lewis Gun Hand Carts, and 3 men per cart.
        All riding horses.
        All bicycles.

3. A minimum distance of 100 yards will be observed between
   transport of units.

4. Further instructions will be issued later.

                                                    Captain.
                                                    Brigade Major.
7th December 1916.   119th Infantry Brigade.

Copy No. 1. O.C. 19th R.W.F.   Copy No. 8. O.C. No. 2 Coy. A.S.C.
         2. O.C. 12th S.W.B.   9. Signals.
         3. O.C. 17th Welsh.   10. 40th Division (G)
         4. O.C. 18th Welsh.   11. 40th Division (Q)
         5. O.C. 119th M.G.Coy.   12. War Diary.
         6. O.C. 119th T.M.B.   13. Brigade Major.
         7. O.C. 136th Field Amb.   14. Staff Captain.

S E C R E T.

O.C. 19th R.W.F.	O.C. No. 2 Coy. A.S.C.
O.C. 12th S.W.B.	Signals.
O.C. 17th Welsh.	H.Q. 40th Division (G)
O.C. 18th Welsh.	H.Q. 40th Division (Q)
O.C. 119th M.G.Coy.	War Diary.
O.C. 119th T.M.B.	Brigade Major.
O.C. 136th Field Amb.	Staff Captain.

SUPPLEMENT TO 119TH BRIGADE ORDER NO. 50.

1. On December 9th and 10th the Transport of the Brigade Group will move under the orders of Major J. Downes-Powell, 19th R.W. Fusiliers.

    Transport of Units will cross the railway at FLIXECOURT as under :-

19th Bn. Royal Welsh Fusiliers.	11.30 a.m.
17th Bn Welsh Regiment.	11.35 a.m.
12th Bn South Wales Borderers.	11.40 a.m.
18th Bn Welsh Regiment.	11.45 a.m.
119th Machine Gun Company.	12. noon.
136th Field Ambulance.	12. 5 p.m.
No. 2 Coy. A.S.C.	12.10 p.m.
Brigade Headquarters.)	
Signal Section.)	12.15 p.m.
119th Trench Mortar Battery.)	

2. A minimum interval of 200 yards will be maintained between the Transport of each Unit.

    The Transport of Brigade Headquarters, Signal Section and 119th Trench Mortar Battery (1 G.S. Wagon) will march together.

3. The packs and rifles of brakesmen will be carried on the wagons which they accompany.

4. Routes for Transport will be as follows :-

    December 9th.   FLIXECOURT - ST SAUVEUR, N. of R. SOMME.

    do 10th.   AMIENS - VECQUEMONT - CORBIE to Camp 13 and half Camp 12, situated about the B of B. GROSSAIRE in Square H.1 (AMIENS. Sheet 17).

5. On December 10th, all Transport will be clear of AMIENS by 2 p.m.

[signature]
Captain.
Brigade Major
119th Infantry Brigade.

7th December 1916.

SECRET.   COPY NO. 1.

119TH BRIGADE ORDER NO. 51

Reference Maps.   1/100,000.   ABBEVILLE
                                 LENS
                                 AMIENS

                   1/40,000.   ALBERT

1. Personnel of the 119th Infantry Brigade Group will move into XV Corps Middle Area, by road and rail, on the 10th December, in accordance with the attached schedule.

2. Intervals will be maintained during movements by road as under :-

    Between Companies or   )
    Equivalent Bodies.   )   200 yards

    Between Battalions.   400 yards.

3. Each Unit will detail one Officer to report to the Brigade Entraining Officer, 20 minutes before Unit arrives at the Station, for instructions.

4. Lorries to convey blankets etc, to the Station will arrive at BELLANCOURT CHURCH at 4.45 a.m.

    O.C. each Battalion will detail 2 guides to meet lorries at this point, to guide them to their destination.

    O.C. 119th M. G. Company will detail one guide, and will issue instructions that the lorry allotted to him will return to 119th Brigade Headquarters as soon as possible after unloading at the Station.

    One lorry is allotted to the 136th Field Ambulance and 119th T. M. Battery. This lorry will load first at 136th Field Ambulance Headquarters, and will then be instructed to proceed to 119th T. M. Battery Headquarters to complete loading.

5. Working Parties for loading and unloading blankets etc., will be detailed as under :-

    12th S.W.B.   1 Officer and 12 O.R.)   To report to Brigade
)   Entraining Officer, PONT
    18th Welsh.   -   13 O.R.)   REMY Station at 6.15 a.m.

    19th R.W.F.   1 Officer and 12 O.R.)   To report to Brigade
)   Entraining Officer, PONT
    17th Welsh.   -   13 O.R.)   REMY Station at 8.15 a.m.

    These parties will also load blankets etc., into the lorries at the Detraining Station.

6. O.C. 17th Welsh Regt. will detail 1 Officer and 30 Other Ranks to be left at Detraining Station to clean up the trains.

7. On arrival at Detraining Station Units will move off independently in the same order as for entraining.

8. Brigade Headquarters will close at BELLENCOURT at 9.15 a.m. Locality of new Brigade Headquarters will be notified when ascertained.

9. Acknowledge.

[signature]
Captain,
A/Brigade Major,
119th Infantry Brigade.

9th December 1916.

Copy No. 1.	O.C. 119th R.W.F.	Copy No. 8.	O.C. No. 2 Coy. A.S.C.
2.	O.C. 12th S.W.B.	9.	Signals.
3.	O.C. 17th Welsh.	10.	40th Division (G)
4.	O.C. 18th Welsh.	11.	40th Division (Q)
5.	O.C. 119th M.G.Coy.	12.	War Diary.
6.	O.C. 119th T.M.B.	13.	Brigade Major.
7.	O.C. 136th Field Ambulance.	14.	Staff Captain.

SCHEDULE TO ACCOMPANY 119TH BRIGADE ORDER NO. 51.

U N I T	To arrive at PONT REMY Station	Lorries to arrive at PONT REMY Station	Time of Departure of Train.	Detraining Station	DESTINATION	REMARKS.
12th S.W.Borderers (Less working party of 200 men).	7 a.m.	6.30 a.m.	3 a.m.	EDGEHILL	Camp. 13. (K.22.c)	TRAIN NO. 1 Lt. Col. E.A. Pope, 12th Bn. South Wales Borderers in command of train.
18th Welsh Regiment.	7.15 a.m.	6.30 a.m.	8 a.m.	do	Camp. 12. (K.33.b)	
119th M. G. Company.	7.30 a.m.	6.30 a.m.	8 a.m.	do	Camp. 12. (K.33.b)	
19th R.W. Fusiliers	9 a.m.	8.30 a.m.	10 a.m.	EDGEHILL	Camp. 13 (K.22.c)	TRAIN NO. 2 Lt. Col. B.J. Jones, 19th Bn Royal Welsh Fusiliers in command of train.
17th Welsh Regt.	9.15 a.m.	8.30 a.m.	10 a.m.	do	Camp. 13 (K.22.c)	
136th Field Ambulance 119th T.M.Battery.	9.30 a.m.	8.30 a.m.	10 a.m.	do	Camp. 12 (K.33.b)	
119th Brigade H.Q.	9.30 a.m.	8.30 a.m.	10 a.m.	do	(Camp.12. (K.33.b)	

SECRET.   COPY NO. 1

119TH INFANTRY BRIGADE ORDER NO.52

Reference Map. 1/40,000 ALBERT.

1. The 119th Infantry Brigade Group will move into the XV Corps Forward Area on the 26th December, in accordance with the attached March Table.

   The 136th Field Ambulance will move independently, under orders direct from A.D.M.S. 40th Division.

   The Works Company of the 120th Infantry Brigade now in Camp 13, is attached to this Brigade and will move with it. Transport will be arranged by 40th Division "Q".

2. The Brigade will form Divisional Reserve to the 33rd Division for the night 26th/27th instant.

3. Distances on the march will be maintained as follows :-

   | Between Companies or Equivalent Bodies | 200 yds. |
   | Between Battalions. | 400 yds. |

4. First Line Transport will accompany Units on the march; usual Train Baggage Wagons will be re-allotted to Units for the move and will join them on the evening of the 25th instant. 32 men will be detailed by the 19th Bn Royal Welsh Fusiliers to assist in pushing the Trench Mortar Battery handcarts.

4. Motor lorries will be provided for the transport of baggage, blankets and '   ' jerkins. Baggage, etc., of the 119th Trench Mortar Battery will be carried on the lorries allotted to the 12th Bn South Wales Borderers, under arrangements direct between C.O's concerned.

   Allotment of Lorries and times at which they will report to units will be notified when received.

6. Packs will be carried on the man.

7. Four Huts will be allotted in Camp 21 as accommodation for Rear Parties of the Brigade, and Storage of baggage, blankets, etc, while Units are in the Line.

8. Each Unit will detail 1 Officer and 2 N.C.O's as billeting representatives, who will report to the Camp Commandant, Camp 21, at least two hours before the arrival of their Unit.

9. Rations for 27th December will be delivered by Supply Section No. 2 Coy, 40th Divisional Train, to Camps 17 and 21 on the evening of the 26th December.

10. 119th Infantry Brigade Headquarters will close at SAILLY LAURETTE at 12 noon, and will re-open at HOSPICE, BRAY, at the same hour.

11. Acknowledge.

[signature]
Captain.
A/Brigade Major.
119th Infantry Brigade.

24th December 1916.

Copy No.	1. 19th R.W.F.	Copy No.	11. 40th Division (G)
	2. 12th S.W.B.		12. 40th Division (Q)
	3. 17th Welsh.		13. 33rd Division (G)
	4. 18th Welsh.		14. 33rd Division (Q)
	5. 119th M.G.Coy.		15. A.D.M.S. 40th Division.
	6. 119th T.M.B.		16. War Diary.
	7. 136th Field Ambulance.		17. Brigade Major.
	8. No. 2 Coy. A.S.C.		18. Staff Captain.
	9. 119th Signals.		19. Commandant, CHIPILLY Area.
	10. 120th Brigade.		20. Commandant, Camp 21.

MARCH TABLE TO ACCOMPANY 119TH INFANTRY BRIGADE ORDER NO. 52

UNIT	Starting Point.	Time.	Route to be followed.	DESTINATION.	REMARKS.
119th Brigade H.Q. and Signal Section.	Cross Roads K.21.b.7.8.	9.30 a.m.	BRAY ROAD	HOSPICE, BRAY	
12th S.W.Borderers.	do	9.35 a.m.	BRAY - G.30.a.20.95 - SUZANNE	CAMP 21 (A.27.d.5.1)	Not to Halt in BRAY or SUZANNE.
17th Welsh Regiment.	do	9.55 a.m.	do	CAMP 21	
19th R. Fusiliers.	do	10.15 a.m.	do	CAMP 17. (G.9.a.2.9)	
18th Welsh Regiment.	do	10.35 a.m.	do	CAMP 17.	
120th Inf.Bde.Works Coy.	do	10.55 a.m.	do	CAMP 17.	
119th T.M. Battery.	do	11. 0 a.m.	do	CAMP 17.	
119th M.G.Company.	do	11. 5 a.m.	do	CAMP 17.	
No. 2 Coy. A.S.C. Train.	do	11.15 a.m.	BRAY ROAD.	BRAY.	

119th Bde. No. 12/192/G.L.

AMMENDMENT TO 119th

AMMENDMENT TO 119TH BRIGADE ORDER NO. 52

With reference to 119th Infantry Brigade Order No. 52, dated 24th December 1916, please make the following ammendments.

Para. 1. line 6.   For "The Works Company of the 120th Infantry Brigade".

Read "The 40th Divisional Works Battalion".

Last Line, page 2.

Add. "Copy No. 21. 40th Divisional Works Battalion"

MARCH TABLE. Column 4.

For "BRAY - G.30.a.20.95 - SUZANNE"

Read "BRAY - L.30.a.20.95 - SUZANNE"

                                                          Captain.
                                                    Staff Captain.
25th December 196   119th Infantry Brigade.

Copy No. 1. 19th R.W.F   Copy No. 11. 40th Division (G)
       2. 12th S.W.B.   12. 40th Division (Q)
       3. 17th Welsh.   13. 33rd Division (G)
       4. 18th Welsh.   14. 33rd Division (Q)
       5. 119th M.G.Coy.   15. A.D.M.S. 40th Division.
       6. 119th T.M.B.   16. War Diary.
       7. 136th Field Ambulance 17. Brigade Major.
       8. No. 2 Coy. A.S.C.   18. Staff Captain.
       9. 119th Signals.   19. Commandant, CHIPILLY Area.
     10. 120th Brigade.   20. Commandant, Camp 21.
                                       21. 40th Divisional Works Battalion.

SECRET.   COPY NO../......

119TH BRIGADE ORDER NO.53

Reference Maps.   ALBERT.   Combined Sheet 1/40,000
                    COMBLES.   1/10,000
                    BOUCHAVESNES 1/10,000

1. The 40th Division is to relieve the 33rd Division in the Right Sector of the Corps Front.

2. The 119th Infantry Brigade Group will relieve the Left Brigade Group on the night 27th/28th in accordance with attached Table of Reliefs.

3. The strength at which Battalions will move into the Line will be :-

    20 Officers   )   Right Battalion
    600 Other Ranks.)   Left Battalion.
)   Support Battalion.

   Remainder of personnel from these Units, and personnel of 119th Machine Gun Company who are not going into the Line, will stay behind in Camp 21.

4. 119th Trench Mortar Battery will remain in Camp 21 pending further orders.

5. The O.C. Battalion going into Support will send 1 Company/to Left Brigade Headquarters at 6.30 p.m.   to report

   Also 2 N.C.O's and 20 men to report at 4 p.m. to representative of 180th Tunnelling Company R.E. at B.6.b.5.0 (This party to be detailed daily by Battalion in Support).

6. Lorries will be provided to convey relieving personnel to MAUREPAS, whence they will march to the trenches. These Lorries will report to Units in Camps 17 and 21 at 11 a.m. Each Unit will detail an Officer to superintend the loading up of the lorries.

   O.C. 19th Royal Welsh Fusiliers will detail one Officer to superintend the distribution of lorries to Units.

7. Transport of Units will move up to MAUREPAS RAVINE (B.14.c.6.6) under Regimental arrangements.

8. Signal Officers of Battalions will meet the Brigade Signal Officer at Brigade Headquarters at 3 p.m. on the 27th instant.

   Two good telephone operators per Battalion will be detailed for permanent duty with Brigade Headquarters while the Brigade is in the Line. These will also report at the same hour.

9. Completion of reliefs to be wired to Brigade Headquarters.

        Code Word for   )
        "Relief Complete")   FENDER.

10. Brigade Headquarters will close at HOSPICE, BRAY, at 12 noon.

11. Acknowledge.

25th December 1916.

S.Y. Montgomery.
Captain.
A/Brigade Major.
119th Infantry Brigade.

Copy No. 1. O.C. 19th R.W.F.
      2. O.C. 12th S.W.B.
      3. O.C. 17th Welsh.
      4. O.C. 18th Welsh.
      5. O.C. 119th M.G.Coy.
      6. O.C. 119th T.M.B.
      7. O.C. 136th Field Ambulance.
      8. O.C. 119th Signals.
      9. O.C. No. 2 Coy. A.S.C.
   10. H.Q. 98th Brigade.
   11. H.Q. 120th Brigade.

Copy No. 12. 40th Division (G)
      13. 40th Division (Q)
      14. 33rd Division (G)
      15. 33rd Division (Q)
      16. A.D.M.S. 40th Division.
      17. War Diary.
      18. Brigade Major.
      19. Staff Captain
      20. Commandant, Camp 21.

TABLE OF RELIEF TO ACCOMPANY 119TH BRIGADE ORDER NO.53

U N I T	FROM	TO	TO RELIEVE	GUIDES	TIME	REMARKS
17th Welsh Regiment.	Camp 21.	Right Subsection	1st Middlesex	1 for C.O. 1 for each Coy. and Platoon Commander at PRIEZ FARM.	4.30 p.m.	
12th S.W. Borderers	Camp 21.	Left Subsection.	4th Suffolks.	do	5.30 p.m.	
18th Welsh Regiment.	Camp 17.	SUPPORT	2nd A. & S. H.	do	6.30 p.m.	
19th R.W. Fusiliers.	Camp 17.	RESERVE	4th King's Liverpool			To be at MAUREPAS RAVINE at 12.30 p.m. Arrangements direct.
119th M. G. Company.	Camp 17.		98th M. G. Company.	By arrangements between C.O's. concerned.		
119th T. M. Battery.	Camp 17.	Camp 21.	98th T. M. Battery.			To be at Camp 21 at 12 noon

The hour of relief between Works Battalions 40th Division and 33rd Division will be arranged between O's. C. concerned and time notified to this Office.

SECRET.   COPY NO. 1.

119TH BRIGADE ORDER NO. 54.

Reference Maps.   ALBERT   Combined Sheet. 1/40,000
                   BOUCHAVESNES. 1/10,000
                   COMBLES. 1/10,000

1. The following Brigade internal reliefs will take place on the night 31st Dec/1st January :-

   19th Bn Royal Welsh Fusiliers from Brigade Reserve in MAUREPAS RAVINE (B.14.c. central) to relieve the 17th Bn Welsh Regiment in the Right Subsection.

   18th Bn Welsh Regiment from Brigade Support in B.6.d. central to relieve the 12th S.W.Borderers in the Left Subsection.

2. On completion of these reliefs :-

   The 17th Bn Welsh Regiment will become Brigade Support.
   The 12th S.W.Borderers will become Brigade Reserve.

3. As the 121st Infantry Brigade is relieving the 120th Infantry Brigade in the Right Brigade Sector on the same night, the Duckboard TRACK will not be available for the 119th Infantry Brigade internal relief.

4. The O.C. 18th Bn Welsh Regiment will therefore arrange to have his leading Company on the road between ADELPHI DUMP and the end of the DUCKBOARD TRACK at 4 p.m. where guides from the 12th Bn South Wales Borderers will meet them. They must be clear of this road by 4.30 p.m.

   The 19th Bn Royal Welsh Fusiliers will march via COMBLES to PRIEZ FARM, to arrive at 4.30 p.m., where they will be met by guides from the 17th Bn Welsh Regiment.

5. Guides will be supplied on the scale of

             1 per Commanding Officer
             1 per Company Commander.
             1 per Platoon.

   Guides for the Company coming into Support near Brigade Headquarters will be arranged for between Commanding Officers concerned. The DUCKBOARD TRACK may be used for this relief after 7.30 p.m.

6. O.C. Support Battalion will arrange with the O.C. 17th Bn Welsh Regiment to have the Dug-out Parties engaged on GUM Boot Drying Rooms relieved at an earlier hour, in order that the work will not be interrupted.

7. Completion of reliefs will be wired to these Headquarters.

             Code Word   -   MARGOT.

8. Acknowledge.

                                              S.Montgomery.
                                              Captain.
                                              A/Brigade Major.
29/12/1916.   119th Infantry Brigade.

Copy No. 1. 19th R.W.F.
2. 12th S.W.B.
3. 17th Welsh.
4. 18th Welsh.
5. 119th M. G. Coy.
6. 119th T.M.B.
7. 119th Signals.
8. No. 2 Coy. A.S.C.
9. 11th Brigade.
10. 120th Brigade.

Copy No. 11. 121st Brigade.
12. 40th Division (G)
13. 40th Division (Q)
14. War Diary.
15. Brigade Major.
16. Staff Captain.
17. Commandant, Camp 21.

1.25 HR

Operation Order by Lt Colonel O.S. Flower D.S.O.
Commdg 19th Bn Royal Welsh Fus.

December 9 1916.

1. The 19th Bn R.W.F. will move out of billets at BELLANCOURT on the 10th inst, and will proceed to PONT REMY to entrain.

2. Breakfast will be at 6.30 a.m. Blankets of A,B and D Coys will be dumped at Shoemakers' shop by 6 a.m. OC C Coy will arrange for a dump for C Coys blankets near Cross Roads. Smoke jerkins and goat skins coats will be carried on the man. Great care must be taken that blankets are tightly rolled. All officers' kit and messes must be in by 7.0 a.m.

3. O.C. C Coy will detail one officer and 12 men to report to Brigade Entraining Officer PONT REMY Station at 8.15 a.m. This party will unload blankets and will also load blankets at detraining station. The party will proceed by march route.

4. O.C. B Coy will detail an officer to report to Brigade entraining officer PONT REMY at 8.30 a.m. from whom he will receive instructions. This officer will proceed by the first lorry leaving Shoemakers' shop at 7.30 a.m.

5. Companies will proceed in following order

   A Coy   C Coy
   200 yards interval   200 yards interval
   B Coy Lewis Gunners   D Coy
   200 yards interval

A Coy will pass cross roads 300 yards SW of B in BELLANCOURT at 7.45 a.m.

6. O's Commdg Coys will be responsible for the cleanliness and sanitary condition of their areas.

P.E.Williams Captain
Adjutant 19th Bn R.W.F.

C

Operation Orders by Lt Colonel B.J. Jones D.S.O.
Commdg 19th Bn Royal Welsh Fusiliers

December 20. 1915.

1. The 19th Bn R.W.F. will move out of Hq 12 Camp Bois de CELESTIN on the 26th inst and will proceed to XV Corps Forward Area - Camp 17 [Sq.a.2.9] Route to be followed - BRAY - L20.a.27.96 - SUZANNE [Refer Ref 1/40.000 Master]

2. Breakfast will be at 6.30 am. Blankets will be rolled in bundles of 10 and dumped at the junction of road leading through training ground with main road by 7.30 am.
Officers Valises will be dumped at Recreation Hut by 7.30 am
Officers Mess Kits   "   "   "   "   "   "   8.0 am

3. Companies will parade in full marching order at 9.15 am on training ground and will proceed by march route in the following order at 200 yards interval :- A.B.C.D. Two sections of Lewis Gunners will march between A & B and two sections between C & D. Packs will be carried on the man and jackets will be worn.

4. Lieut A.C. Morris & Sergeants Hall and Westwood will parade at 7.45 am and will report to the Camp Commandant, Camp 21 [R27.d.5.1.] at least 2 hours before arrival ofunit. They will proceed by first lorry from Blanket dump.

5. Officers Commdg Companies will be responsible that their huts and areas are left in a clean condition. They will detail a N.C.O and 6 men who will report that this has been done to Lieut A.C. Morris "B"Coy

6. O.C "C" Company will detail 2 NCO's and 32 men to assist in pushing R.M.B handcarts. They will report to Adjutant 119th R.M.B [S.W.B lines] at 9 am.

[Sgd]. E. Beynon Davies Lieut
A/Adjutant 19th Bn R.W. Fusiliers

Orders by Lt Colonel B.J. Jones D.S.O.
Commandg 19th Bn Royal Welsh Fus

December 30 1916

1. 19th Batt. R.W.F. will relieve 17th Welsh in Right subsector Left Brigade on night 31st December / 1st June

2. Movement will be by platoons at 50 yards interval. Lewis Gunners of each Coy will march at the head of the first platoon of each Coy.

3. Packs will be stacked and blankets rolled and stacked near Q.M. Stores by 9.30 am.
   Care will be taken that socks are withdrawn from packs before stacking.

4. Two limbers for the Lewis Guns and magazines will march at the head of "A" Coy.

5. First platoon of A Coy will leave Camp at 2.30 pm. Headquarters will follow "B" Coy.

6. Completion of relief will be notified to Batt Hqrs.

[Sgd.] P.E. Williams   Captain
Adjutant 19th Bn R.W.F.

17th R.W.F.

December 1916

WAR DIARY
-or-
INTELLIGENCE SUMMARY
(Erase heading not required.)

Army Form C. 2118

Place	Date	Hour	Summary of Events and Information	Remarks and references to Appendices
BELLANCOURT	1-9		In billets, no incident	
	10th		Entrained at SAINT REMY, detrained near MORLANCOURT and marched to billets in BOIS DES CELESTINS. Transport proceeded all the way by road.	A, B
	26th		Marched to camp 17 near SUZANNE	C.
	27th		Marched to MAUREPAS and became brigade reserve	
	31st		Took over right battalion section near RANCOURT from 7th Welsh Regt.	

Jeffreys Lt Colonel
Comdg 19 R.W.F.

WAR DIARY or INTELLIGENCE SUMMARY

Army Form C. 2118

19th Divl Infy Wksh Trn Bns

January 1st to 31st 1917

Place	Date	Hour	Summary of Events and Information	Remarks and references to Appendices
RANCOURT	1/1/17		Line Pt Sebaster RANCOURT. Usual artillery activity on both sides.	
	2/1/17		Intra Regimental Relief. Field artillery put up a barrage 7/mins, 1.25", 5.9's at about 10.10 pm today for ½ an hour on the platoon in taking place. No casualties.	
	3/1/17		Usual activities. No machine gun, rifle or T.M. fire.	
night 4/1/17 & 5th		Batts Relieved by the 11th NORL Rgt (120th Inf Brigade). On completion of Relief moved by motor Lorries to Camp 17 aft Divisional Reserve.	
	6 – 8		Divisional Reserve.	
	9/1/17		Moved by motor transport to Camp 28 into Brigade Reserve. Relieving the 12th Suffolk Regiment.	
	10/1/17		Relieved 17th Welsh Regiment in Pt de Regt – BOUCHAVESNES NORTH. Supplying carrying parties & the Front on own Right.	
BOUCHAVESNES NORTH	13,14,15		Trench Front. Line MAUREPAS RAVINE & CRANIERS. Intra regimental Relief & every night owing to bad condition of trenches. Owing to these too long the trenches men small parts had carried tops shrapnel. The only way trench could	
	16/1/17		be contained with over the strain the conditions – mud & water. Batts Relieved by the 17th Welsh Regiment and moved into Brigade Reserve at Agusta Sub. Remained at Camp 28	
	19th		Batts Relieved by the 4/5th A.&S. H. followed by Comers by motor Lorries to Camp 17 (Divisional Reserve)	
RANCOURT – per	22/23		Battn relieved 19th Suffolk Regt in right Subrn to RANCOURT. The Commanding Officer Lt Col BN am DSO wounded knee and ruptured enemy pat. On relieving the Second Reliefs & Batn Major J.R. Lewis RWF assumes Command.	
	24/1/17		2nd Regimental Relief.	
night 24/1/25			During this time also 48 casualties are brought including 14 & 4 R (2 by machine buttet + 12 shell, 1 sick + 2 accident 1 pattern shell buttet tops by shrapnel the ground was very hard, the Communication tracks supplying army 6 sick.	
night 25/26			Relieved by 17th Welsh Regiment return into Support at ALBANY.	

Army Form C. 2118

WAR DIARY
or
INTELLIGENCE SUMMARY

(Erase heading not required.)

19th Dy Infct Anstn

January 1st to 31st 1917

Instructions regarding War Diaries and Intelligence Summaries are contained in F. S. Regs., Part II. and the Staff Manual respectively. Title Pages will be prepared in manuscript.

Place	Date	Hour	Summary of Events and Information	Remarks and references to Appendices
ALBANY. CAMP P2.	27/1		Relieved by 2nd Bn K. Lives (25th Inf Brig) proceeded to huzelle Area by motor lorries. Arriving in Camp P2, BOIS CELESTINES that night	
	29		Commence training	
	31.1.17.			

J. Monckton
Major
Commanding 19th Battn R. W.

1875 Wt. W593/826 1,000,000 4/15 J.B.C. & A. A.D.S.S./Forms/C. 2118.

WAR DIARY or INTELLIGENCE SUMMARY

Army Form C. 2118

19th Service Batn. D.L.I. February 1917   Vol 9

Place	Date February	Hour	Summary of Events and Information	Remarks and references to Appendices
BOIS CELESTINES	1/2/17 to 9th		Camp 12 BOIS CELESTINES. — Exercises in the following carried out daily. Bath formations & fly day platoons.	
	10th		March route to Camp 17 Suzanne.	
	11th		Proceed to MAUREPAS by Motor Lorries & from there by march Route to 9th Battn Lines Regiment RIGHT SUBSECTOR RANCOURT when the Battalion relieved the 9th Battn Lines Regiment. Quiet Relief which was complete about 9p.m.	
	12th		Heavy frost & ground still hard. Our Heavies bombarded Hostile positions in Lt. of ST PIERRE VAAST WOOD — South from 9.30 a.m. kept up though the afternoon. At 7 p.m. the Bombardment became more intense employing 6 eight pltn platoons by the enemy. His hostile pltn platoon commenced at 6.30 p.m. with a large quantity of H.E.'s but no damage was done. Shelling ceased about 7.45 p.m.	
	13th		At 5.30 a.m. our Field Guns opened fire on enemy & wire & kept it up till 7 a.m. Enemy hostile platoons which caused no damage.	9

2. Army Form C. 2118

WAR DIARY
or
INTELLIGENCE SUMMARY
(Erase heading not required.)

1/5 Bn R.W. Fus. February 1917.

Instructions regarding War Diaries and Intelligence Summaries are contained in F.S. Regs., Part II. and the Staff Manual respectively. Title Pages will be prepared in manuscript.

Place	Date February	Hour	Summary of Events and Information	Remarks and references to Appendices
RANCOURT	13th	(night)	Interregimental Relief. Battn relieved Kings Regt on Rancourt sector.	
	14th		Done. Fairly quiet. Intermittent shelling as usual.	
	15th		About 7am Enemy bombarded our trenches on Coy front causing 3 casualties. Our artillery retaliated with abundant good effect. So many wounded were seen being taken out of the trenches. Again at 3.30pm our artillery opened fire on enemy's trenches for ½ an hour. Enemy retaliated causing 6 casualties. (1NCO killed, 5 wounded) and our trenches front about 3am. Battn was relieved by the 17th Welsh Regiment which was complete.	
	15/16	(night)	Battn set in and again proceeding to ground in a very bad condition. Battn in Reserve at MAUREPAS CAMP.	
MAUREPAS	16, 17, 18th		Very quiet.	
RANCOURT	19th	(night)	Relieved 17th Welsh Regiment in same sector. still was in a C.O.B.4. RANCOURT SECTOR extended SOUTH as far as C.O.B.4.	
	20/21.	"	___ H.Q. Rocks korack over to the left Battn (18th W.L. R.) about 9pm.	

WAR DIARY
or
INTELLIGENCE SUMMARY

(Erase heading not required.)

Army Form C. 2118

19th R.W.Frs   February 1917

Place	Date	Hour	Summary of Events and Information	Remarks and references to Appendices
	21.		Still hold Posts 1,2 + 3. Take over Batn Front & Right from the 13th/Yorks, Relief complete about 1am. Heavy mist during the day. ST PIERRE VAAST WOOD SOUTH of BOUCHAVESNES RIDGE shelled from 10am to 4pm with field guns & howitzers with excellent effect. Enemy retaliated at 4.45pm causing no damage.	
	22.		Usual artillery activity otherwise quiet. Heavy mist.	
	22/23 (night)		Batn Relieved by the 13th/Yorks Regiment completed about midnight. March route from trenches to Camp 91, last Coy arriving about 10am	
Camp 91.	23.			
BRAY.	24-25.		At 10am left Camp 91. for BRAY TOURBIERE Camp. Batn supplies working parties to Railhead.	
	26.		Colonel proceeds to Commanding Officers' Conference at His record. Major Cox-Morgan assumes command of Battn.	
	25-28.		Batn supplies working parties to Railhead.	

28/2/17.

Ey Wyn? Major.
Commanding 19th Battn. R.W.Frs

Headquarters
119th Inf Bde.

2/4/17

Herewith War Diary.

Downes-Powell
Lieut Col.
Commdg. 19th RWF

WAR DIARY or INTELLIGENCE SUMMARY

Army Form C. 2118

19th R.W.F.   MARCH 1917

Place	Date	Hour	Summary of Events and Information	Remarks and references to Appendices
BRAY.	1-6		Working parties supplied by Battn at BRAY TOURBIERE DUMP & MILLS.	
	7.		Commanding Officer returns relieving Major G.W. Morgan of command. Working parties finish the work to handed over to the 18th Divisional Works Battn.	
			BATTN moves into billets at BRAY.	
CAMP 19	8.		BATTN moves into CAMP 19.	
CLERY	9.		BATTN moves from CAMP 19 into Brigade Support (MERTON) of 1st CLERY SECTOR relieving the 20th BATTN. R.F. (33rd Divn)	
			1 Coy Buzy in immediate support of the Left BATTN in MERLIN TRENCH	
			2 Platoons buzy in immediate support of the Rt BATTN at CLERY CHATEAU.	
CLERY	9-11.		SUPPORT VALLEY intermittently shelled daily both with howitzers also long range shells. No damage was done however.	
"	12.		Relieved the 17th WELSH in Rt Subsector. CLERY SECTOR. Hostile M.G's active also many M/R grenades.	
	13.		1 N.C.O. & 2 men slightly wounded. Slight intermittent shelling but no damage. Notification & orders received of probable retirement of hostile forces on our front. Patrols were sent out during the usual night's Routes borders were normally held. Much machine Gun & M/R fire took place the hours no others at 10.30 p.m. the Caspian line were machined. When patrols renewed report & 1 magazine per Lewis gun in order to observe the effect. Retaliation was very slight but little ditto was dealer coming out later. M/G opened heavy fire on them. Normally one of our patrols fired at by an attacking enemy to the apparently a hundred hand hostile were held. In addition to field machine gun fire of intense ability a good many cattle. Large clouds of smoke were seen rising from HALLE	
	14.			

Army Form C. 2118

WAR DIARY
or
INTELLIGENCE SUMMARY
(Erase heading not required.)

19th R.W.F.

MARCH 1917

Place	Date	Hour	Summary of Events and Information	Remarks and references to Appendices
CLERY	14		A number of mobile charges were put into enemy's wire & gaps to barrier effect. Slight retaliation only. Our Lewis Gunners & Trench guns kept up an intermittent fire along the enemy's front line parapet throughout the night. Hostile machine gunners were active & more active & on several occasions induced uneasiness by sweeping the area over. Patrols report that he held his line very much	
	15		stronger than previous nights. Scottish artillery very quiet. Hostile M.G's active & also snipers, but rifle & musketry damage. Patrols went out & report that his line was held quite normally. The Both were relieved on the night by the 19th Brigade 13th Yorks R. Relay being completed about 1.30 a.m. (16/3/17)	
CURLU	16		During the blow only 3 casualties occurred. Our snipers claim about hits. Busy the enemy. The front line & communication trenches were in a very bad condition owing to present rain & the cake/mud travels. Working parties & reps on these lines. talked / were improved in the horse line program were also. Bn. were very good.	
	15/16	(night)	Bn. marched to LINGER CAMP (CURLU)	
SUZANNE (CURLU)	16		2 Coys proceed to Billets in SUZANNE	
	17		Batt. HQ proceeded to CAMP 17. SUZANNE	
			2 Coys at LINGER CAMP	
			2 Coys at LINGER CAMP employed on ECLUSIER — CURLU Road. (North side of River.)	
	17—24		2 Coys at SUZANNE employed on Quarry & BRAY TOURBIERE — SUZANNE Road.	

Army Form C. 2118

WAR DIARY
or
INTELLIGENCE SUMMARY
(Erase heading not required.)

19th RWF   MARCH 1917

Place	Date	Hour	Summary of Events and Information	Remarks and references to Appendices
SUZANNE	20.		Commanding Officer proceeds on leave. Major O. Morgan assumes command.	
	25.		BATTN moves by march route from SUZANNE to P.C. MADAME (ROAD WOOD)	
			Reconnoitred to MARRIERE WOOD & Boys & ROAD WOOD.	
	26-31		BATTN employed on Roads RANCOURT – BOUCHAVESNES – MOISLAINS – NURLU. Commanding Officer returns from leave.	

31.3.17.

For Owen Frost
Roger H. Col.
Commanding 19th R.W.F.

Army Form C. 2118

MAP 57C. SE.

April 1917.

19th Batt. R.W.F.

WAR DIARY
or
INTELLIGENCE SUMMARY
(Erase heading not required.)

Place	Date	Hour	Summary of Events and Information	Remarks and references to Appendices
ROAD WOOD.	1–6.		Batn on Road construction in neighbourhood of BOUCHAVESNES.	
ETRICOURT	7–16		Batn moves to ETRICOURT where they repaired Roads & demolished Billets in broken down houses.	
GOUZEAUCOURT.	17.		Batn. moved into outpost position in front of GOUZEAUCOURT where we relieved the 1st SUFFOLK REGIMENT also relieving the 8th DIVISION of a post. Our "A" Coy was on the right, "D" Coy on the left. The remaining two Coys were in reserve & in support. — at Q34.D.3.7 (MAP 57.C.SE).	
	19.		8th DIVISION attacked GONNELIEU but failed to take it. To assist in this operation it was necessary for our RF Coy (A Coy) to push forward a little, but owing to failure on our Rt (8th Div) we retired on to our former posts R.25.C. without casualties.	
	20.		Our "A" Coy (RF) under Capt. P.E. Williams advanced their posts to the QUARRY (R25.D) without opposition at the same time the (8th Div) moved their left flank forward in order to gain a better advantage on GONNELIEU.	
	21.		The batn were ordered to take part in an attack in conjunction with the 8th DIV on our Rt whose objective was GONNELIEU, and the 12th S.W.B. on our Left whose objective was FIFTEEN RAVINE. (our objective was R26.B.33. — R19.d.3.8. fifteen minutes prior to the Zero hour (4.20 am) the Batn was lined up parallel to the objective. At zero hour the Barrage opened and our troops advanced. At 5.15 a.m. all our objectives had been gained and consolidation by the support Coys begun, having in front covering parties & patrols of the assaulting Coys. The assaulting Coys were A & Rt "D" on Left under the commands of Lt. V.H. PERRY & Capt. Williams respectively.	2 sheets

1875 Wt. W593/826 1,000,000 4/15 J.B.C. & A. A.D.S.S./Form/C. 2118.

Army Form C. 2118

WAR DIARY
or
INTELLIGENCE SUMMARY
(Erase heading not required.)

April 1917. Map 57c S.E.
19th Battn. Royal Welsh Fusiliers

Instructions regarding War Diaries and Intelligence Summaries are contained in F.S. Regs, Part II. and the Staff Manual respectively. Title Pages will be prepared in manuscript.

Place	Date	Hour	Summary of Events and Information	Remarks and references to Appendices
			While the Supporting Coys were B (R.A.) & C (R.A.) under the commands of Capt O. LLOYD ROBERTS & CAPT R. LEWIS respectively. At 5.15 am. the 2nd Rifle Brigade staked [***] a successful raid on enemy lines from our A Coy (A Coy). 2nd Lt J. DUNN immediately carried out a successful raid on many strong point at R20.C.5.4. and at the same time our Lewis gunners & Snipers engaged effectively trench Machine Guns situated at R27.a.0. At the same time the Coy were deployed to bring enemy fire to bear on EAST of GONNELIEU. No 33307 Pte E. Ponsford did excellent work enemy off both Machine Gunners, also L/Cpl F.C. NUNN 45304 who accounted for several of enemy casualties during the raid on R20.C.5.4. LT V.H. PIERCY & CAPT R. LEWIS both led their Coys with great skill setting a fine example. The casualties in attaining objectives were negligible but the R. Coy suffered badly during consolidation. Total Casualties 2 Officers (LT V.H.PIERCY & 2nd LT GOOD) & 30 O.R. Pte George Ellis No 28784, Stretcher Bearer with great courage under heavy shell fire attended a wounded going backwards authorwards [?] from front line to Aid Post at least a dozen times.	
	21/22 (night)		Battn went into Support in Sunken Road Q30 D.S.E. Being relieved by the 18th W.L. R	
	24.		Battn in Support of 17th & 18th W.L.R. in a joint Brigade attack on VILLERS PLOUICH. Days being in FIFTEEN RAVINE & 2 Coys moving in SUNKEN ROAD Q30 D.98. The attack proved successful and all objectives were taken.	
	29/30.		Battn relieves 17th W.L.R. Regiment at R.4 central. Strength about 800 very little casualties.	
	30/1 May (night)		Battn relieved by the 13th Suffolks. Few casualties during the tour.	
P.3	19th on 20th April		LT V.H. PIERCY on these two occasions carried out a successful day/night reconnaissance patrols when a [*****] obtained information which proved to be of the greatest value and essential in the attack which followed.	

19th March [signed] Lt Col.
Commanding 19th Battn.
Royal Welch Fusiliers

WAR DIARY or INTELLIGENCE SUMMARY

Army Form C. 2118

19th R.W. Fus.   MAP SHEET 57c S.E.   MAY 1917

Place	Date MAY	Hour	Summary of Events and Information	Remarks and references to Appendices
R14.Central GOUZEAUCOURT	April 30/May 1	(night)	(AMENDED WD) Battn. was relieved in R.14 central by the 12th Bn Suffolk Regiment & the 126th Bde. The Relief was completed about 1 am. The Battn. then moved into Close Support in GOUZEAUCOURT. BHQ in QUARRY R.23.d & A'Coy in old outpost line R.25.c. B Coy in QUARRY R.23.d. Company being in by 7 am. Daylight.	
	1–4		Both supplied working parties on harass and Rets. Camps. Daily employed day & night. On line of M.G. at R.26.b central. Coy. reports also employed.	
	5/6	(night)	Battn. moved out & acted as "Mopping-up" on 21 August raid on LEVACQUERIE – R.15 central – & BONNET FARM. Le 17 th held R.7 to R.21.B & 31s. This line formed the defensive loops in conjunction with the 121st Bde under C/O of the 8th Division on our right. Battn. B & C coys Hand Bomb and Rifle up ready to advance but the 110th Bde. managed to enter LE VACQUERIE too successfully Leverage 60. Enemy to the village was not held by our A. In the village the moppers up passed thro'. Line of B.Coy. reached A.5758 to B.5 culvert 2390.6.5. this Battn. to left flank. Coy. 8's mopping up complete to cover such point with Lewis guns. Both story point acted only as escorts and where possible assist with ammunition to enemy line heavy. Battn. was reserved a holding mortar. He mounted to hand by the Battn. over B.108 & N.68 & N.68c. 21 wounded & 2 Sgt. missing. After he went the mopping up period was blocked hostility owing emerged which had been two by no means in any one make from's heavy shellfire.	
	6/7	(night)	Bn. was reserved by the 17th Bde. & L.B. in Close support & marched up to DESSART WOOD under command Coy. of the BROWN LINE (Second Line) G.S. & A. Battn. supplied working parties take 3 daily from D. BROWNLINE – FIFTY CHATEAU & Watched & Turned to BN AF too next week FIFTEEN RAVINE. 7/5 & 3 Cdt. of 8 assisted. Supplies for removal of RET8. & an Emy counter GES. reek. Major Finlayson assumed command.	
	8			

WAR DIARY or INTELLIGENCE SUMMARY

Army Form C. 2118

19th R.W.Fus

May 1917

Place	Date May	Hour	Summary of Events and Information	Remarks and references to Appendices
DESSART WOOD	8-14		Working parties to R.E.'s	
	12		Major J.T. Edwards M.C. 2nd in Command. Reconnoitres Tournament.	
GOUZEAUCOURT	14/15	(night)	Battn. moves into close support to GOUZEAUCOURT 3 Coys. in A.C.D's in Sunken Road. Q.30 Cent.	
			One Coy (C) in Road Q.30 D.1.	
	14		Major R.C. Coker 3.S.O. 7th R.W. 41 assumes command of Battn.	
	15		Battn. supplies working parties to Front line, Batt. H.Q. D Coy & B Coy Front Line & B Coy Left Support Road Q.39.a. (C Coy) moves up to Road Q.29.d. R.9 D.1.	
	15-22		Working parties D.R.E.'s. on trenches in Front Line systems. Daily reconnaissance in close support of the Battn. sector. Road and trees between new Battn. Sector & Road Q.30.a. receiving completion.	
	22/23	(night)	Battn. Relieves 17th R. in Front Line. 2 Coys in Front Line (A) Coys (KNIGHT) Road. B Coy (C) in Ravine R.30.a. 2 Coys in support (B & D Coys) 18 Kings on Right. 6 Divn. on Left.	
	23		26 R.A.F on Right 20 R.W. Rt Coy Left. Battn. Sends up for Equipment	
	24		R reserve & sees whether items could be seen of an advance by covered routes.	
			S etc.	
	26/27		Battn. relieved by the 11th R. in F.Rd H.Q. moves into DESSART WOOD hutment camp.	
	28-31		Battn. rearmament and reorganises & training.	

[signature]
Commanding 19th R.W.F.

WAR DIARY
INTELLIGENCE SUMMARY

Army Form C. 2118

19th R.W.F.
June 1917

Place	Date	Hour	Summary of Events and Information	Remarks and references to Appendices
DESSART WOOD	1/2	Night	Battn in Div. Reserve DESSART WOOD.	
	2/3	Night	Battn moved to Battn Reserve. 1 Coy + B.H.Qrs. SUNKEN RD. Q29.c.7.a. 1 Coy Q29.a.1 + 2 Coys Q30.B. Relief the 20th Middlesex Regt. Col. A.J. Mc. Neal D.S.O. returns to take command of the Battn.	
	3/11		Battn Supplies working parties for trench repair + Wilmot tramway and evacuation of R.E.	
	11/12	Night	Battn relieves the 12th R.W.B. the 18th Welsh, left. Battn (VILLERS PLOUICH). Strength of Battn, including H.Q. 21 ms. (?) 800 all Ranks. Relief was completed about 1.30am. During the day patrols was pushed out during the relief + night the enemy's lines were hotly reconnoitred by Lt. King-Parks. From Dawn + not dark occupied hostile patrols in working parties. The our of sight day was very quiet on the whole, with the exception of intermittent shelling. Chiefly on support lines, by shrapnel + Back areas. The last two days of tour Battn. Hd. commenced using signal-rockets but without effect. Our Artillery active during day, concentrating shells + also on targets and working parties, etc. During the night a ... enemy Recce Patrol, under the leadership of 2nd Lt. Hooke unknowingly walked in to enemy post, they were at once brought in withdrawing from shelling range, the patrol was unfortunately split up. Both parties however returned safely to our own lines about Dawn.	
	12			
	14		Relieved 3.30 p.m. 11th J. Shankland carried out a daylight reconnaissance proceeding from our lines he made his way crawling in the long grass towards R15.c.5.5. which he managed to do until within 50 yds of his objective, when at this point he was spotted by a sentry at the far end of the sap, who immediately proceeded to Say Lance + shot a very cartridge	

Army Form C. 2118

Instructions regarding War Diaries and Intelligence Summaries are contained in F. S. Regs., Part II. and the Staff Manual respectively. Title Pages will be prepared in manuscript.

WAR DIARY
or
INTELLIGENCE SUMMARY
(Erase heading not required.)

19th R.W.F.
2
June 1917

Place	Date	Hour	Summary of Events and Information	Remarks and references to Appendices
	14		but did not fire. The wire around the left, to extraordinarily thick, long made up of concertina interlaced with thick Barbed Wire fastened round iron Wooden Stakes. It was at least 4 yds deep, & no gap was visible. The Officer then returned to our lines.	
	19/20	Night	Batt'n relieved by the 11th King's Own on the Right Sub-sector. Relief was complete about 11.30p. & then moved into Div: Reserve at SORE L/erdel:Canvas	
	20/27		Batt'n carries out a Programme of training	
	27/28	Night	Batt'n relieves 20th Middlesex in Brigade Support.	
	28/30		Batt'n supplies Working Parties for the front line consolidating & wiring under supervision of R.E.	

George L. Morgan
Major
Commanding 19th R.W.F.

Army Form C. 2118

WAR DIARY
or
INTELLIGENCE SUMMARY
(Erase heading not required.)

19th R.W.F.

July 1917

119/40

Place	Date	Hour	Summary of Events and Information	Remarks and references to Appendices
Bde SUPPORT W9d87	1-4		Batt'n supplied working parties for the front line & digging & consolidating under supervision of the R.E.	
	5-6	Night	Batt'n relieved the 12th S.W.B. in the left sub sector. Relief completed about 1 a.m. During the two of eight days, strong fighting patrols were sent out nightly from dusk till dawn occupied the one occupied outposts, encountered a strong enemy patrol & a few casualties were inflicted on both parties. One of our M[achine] G[un] gunners in some mysterious manner, was cut off from our patrol, failed to return to our lines that night, however after concealing his gun & lying in No Man's Land for three days & nights, he returned to our lines on the afternoon of the fourth day & both the sick lieu of two or three slight wounds, he was little the worse for his experience. Our own & enemy Artillery normal. Batt'n moved into Bde Reserve being relieved by the 12th S.W.B.	
			DISTRIBUTION Two Coy's at GOUZEAUCOURT VILLERS-GUISLAIN ROAD R31d one Coy in trenches behind QUENTIN MILL R31 one Coy in the SUNKEN ROAD W.6.d Batt'n H.Q at W.6.a.	
Bde RESERVE	14-20		Batt'n supplies working parties nightly for constructional work of Bde H.Q & working parties for the front line & supports under supervision of the R.E.s from 9 P.M. until 5 P. Batt'n carried out a daily programme of training in Musketry.	
	21-22	Night	Batt'n relieved the 12th S.W.B.'s in the left sub sector. Relief completed about	

1875. Wt. W593/826 1,000,000 4/15 J.B.C. & A. A.D.S.S./Forms/C. 2118.

Army Form C. 2118

WAR DIARY
or
INTELLIGENCE SUMMARY
(Erase heading not required.)

19th R.W.F.

July 1917.

Place	Date	Hour	Summary of Events and Information	Remarks and references to Appendices
	21.22	Night	Mid-night. The tour of eight days, was on the whole, quiet. Strong fighting patrols were sent out nightly from dusk till dawn & not once did they molest any hostile patrols or working parties. Hostile Artillery fairly active on the CAMBRIA ROAD & GONNELIEU damage was slight with the exception of the morning of the 27th when between 9 & 10 a.m. about 30 rounds of 4.2 were fired over our left. Over our right evening 2 few casualties.	
	29.30	Night	Batt'n moved to Bde Support being relieved by the 12th S.W.B's relief complete about mid-night. <u>DISTRIBUTION</u>. One Coy in dug-outs, Bellet at GONNELIEU R.26.d.4.4, one Coy in GREENSWITCH R.31.d. two Coys in INTERMEDIATE LINE R.31.d. & R.26.a. Bn H.Q. R.31.a.0.0.	
	30.31		Batt's working on front line & support lines, one Coy working by day, three by night under supervision of R.E.s	

(signed) Lieut-Colonel
Commanding 19th R.W.F.

War Diary

19th (S) Bn: Royal Welsh Fusiliers.

August 1917.

Army Form C. 2118

REF. MAP GOUZEAUCOURT.
Ed 1A Special Sheet,

WAR DIARY

INTELLIGENCE SUMMARY

(Erase heading not required.)

Instructions regarding War Diaries and Intelligence Summaries are contained in F. S. Regs., Part II. and the Staff Manual respectively. Title Pages will be prepared in manuscript.

19th R.W.Fus.

ORDERLY ROOM
2 SEP. 1917
No.
19TH BATT. ROYAL WELSH FUSILIERS

Place	Date AUGUST	Hour	Summary of Events and Information	Remarks and references to Appendices
GONNELIEU	1-6		Battn in Bgde. Support with HQ in Q.31.c.00.95.. Dispositions of Coys. as follows:- A Coy in FIFTEEN RAVINE - C Coy in Railway Embankment. R.19.d. B Coy:- in GREEN SWITCH R.31.b.0.2. - D Coy in GREEN LINE. R.26.b.0.2. astride the MAIN CAMBRAI ROAD. A & C Coys in SUPPORT of the LEFT BATTN. & B. & D Coys in SUPPORT of RIGHT BATTN. Battn. at work under supervision of RE's on FRONT LINE SYSTEM. WEATHER, a number of warm and fine. No unusual occurrence.	
VILLERS PLOUICH SECTOR	6		LT. COL B.T. JONES. D.S.O. relinquishes command of Battn. & hands over to MAJOR J.F. PLUNKETT. M.C. The Roy. Irish Batts. Regt.	
	6 evening		Battn. relieves the 12th Bn. S.W. Borderers of the Bgde. in the LA VACQUERIE SECTOR (Rt SUBSECTOR of BDE) Relief complete about 7.30 p.m. Strength of Battn. going in was 452 all ranks. No unusual occurrence. Hostile artillery quiet. Strong fighting patrols sent out nightly, but no hostile patrols or working parties encountered.	
	6-12		A raid planned with the object of penetrating enemy trench at R.21.d.95.90 protected by 2 strong double belts of wire. Raiding party to consist of 33 all ranks, officers in charge of operation Capt. L.H. Morgan. with 2nd Lieut. G.E. Phillips, leader of left half party and 2nd Lieut E.T. Roch, leader of right half party. It was decided to cut away through the outer belt of wire and to blow a path through the second belt using bangalore torpedoes, patrolling carried out in pursuance of the plan.	
	12/13		Zero hour was 1 a.m. and, following a above- Barrage concentrated up on BARRIER TRENCH for five minutes, the party rushed the trench, which was found to be heavily manned. On entering the trench the melee	

WAR DIARY
INTELLIGENCE SUMMARY

(Erase heading not required.)

19th RWF (2) **AUGUST 1917**

Army Form C. 2118

Place	Date	Hour	Summary of Events and Information	Remarks and references to Appendices
	14		led by 2nd Lieut. Mullend worked to the left, and the section led by 2nd Lieut. Pock worked to the right, inflicting heavy casualties upon the enemy garrison, destroying his shelters & dugouts, and bringing back with them 2 unwounded prisoners of the 6th Bavr. Res. Infr. Regt. Communication between O/c Operations and Coy. H.Q. was by telephone. Our casualties were:- 1 Off. [2nd/Lieut Mullend] and 7.O.R. slightly wounded. 1 N.C.O. [24473 Sgt. C.J. Barker "B" Coy.] died of wounds. The following decorations have since been awarded for these minor operations:- 2nd Lieut. G.G. MULLENS. - M.C. 45781 Sgt. E. LARWOOD. - M.M 26192 L/c E. RANDLES. - M.M. 15910 Pte J. VALENTINE - M.M. 45790 Pte R. FURNEY. - M.M. 29241 Pte W. MARSHALL - M.M.	
	21 22		The Battn. relieved by 12th Bn. S.W.B. moves into Bgde. Support. Relief complete at 7.30 p.m. Total casualties, whilst in the line:- 1 Off. 417. O.R. wounded, + 2 O.R. Killed. Preparations of Coys. and work as before. Battn. relieves the 12th Bn. S.W.B in Right Subsector. Relief complete at 7 p.m. Trench strength 434 all ranks.	

Army Form C. 2118

WAR DIARY / INTELLIGENCE SUMMARY
(Erase heading not required.)

19th RWF   (3)   AUGUST 1917

Place	Date	Hour	Summary of Events and Information	Remarks and references to Appendices
	22-27		Strong fighting patrols sent out as before. No enemy patrols reported and situation normal.	
	28/29		A silent raid was carried out on enemy trench at R.22.c.05.60, with the object of obtaining identification and inflicting casualties. O.C. operations, Capt. P.E. Williams. Officers in charge of raiding sections Lt. E.O. Mill and 2nd Lieut. J. Dunn M.C. Total strength of raiding party, all ranks, 2/Lt. Dunn became a casualty, and was replaced by 2nd Lieut. W.F. Cooke. A gap was blown in the enemy wire with a Bangalore, and the party succeeded in entering the trench, where they met with strong resistance. 14 of the enemy were killed, and a dugout blown up with a mobile charge, after which the party withdrew, bringing back with them 1 prisoner of the 6th Res. R.I.R. Our casualties were, 1 Off. & 4 O.R. wounded, and 1 O.R. missing, believed killed. 1 Off. & 1 O.R. of the R.E., who assisted in the operation, were also wounded. Total casualties during tour in the line. 1 Off. 9 O.R. wounded, & 1 N.C.O. missing, believed killed.	
	30		Battn. relieved by the 12th Bn. S.W.B. moved into Bde. Support. H.Q. & Coys. as before.	
	31.		Relief complete about 6.45 p.m. Disposition of Battn. finds working parties for FRONT LINE SYSTEM as before.	

Army Form C. 2118

WAR DIARY
INTELLIGENCE SUMMARY
(Erase heading not required.)

Place: 19th R.W.F. (4)   AUGUST 1917.

Date	Hour	Summary of Events and Information	Remarks and references to Appendices
11.		Officers reporting for duty to the Battn. during the month of August.	
23.		Capt. C.T. Ellis.	
29.		Sec/Lt. E.J. Jones.	
		Sec/Lt. C. Harland.	
		Lieut. V. de S. Perks.	
8.		Officers leaving the Battn. and struck off the strength during the month of August	
14.		Lieut. H.A. Parry. [Transferred to R.F.C.]	
22.		Sec.Lieut. G.G. Mullens M.C. [Wounded]	
29.		Capt. E.C. Powell. [Transferred to R.F.C.]	
31.		Sec/Lieut. J Dunn M.C. [Wounded]	
		Lieut. A.C. Morris. [Transferred to R.F.C.]	

Lieut-Colonel
Commanding 19th R.W.Fus.

Vol 16

War Diary

19th (S) Bn. Royal Welch Fusiliers

September 1917

WAR DIARY or INTELLIGENCE SUMMARY

Army Form C. 2118

(Erase heading not required.)

GOUZEAUCOURT

September 1917

Place	Date	Hour	Summary of Events and Information	Remarks and references to Appendices
GONNELIEU SECTOR — CENTRE BRIGADE (R-SUBSECTOR)	Sept 1st to 7th		Bn in Rly Support. Dispositions as follows:- B.H.Q. & R.E.C.30. 75 HQ:- FIFTEEN RAVINE. D. Coy:- RAILWAY EMBANKMENT. C. Coy:- GREEN SWITCH & D. Coy GREEN LINE. A & B Coy:- in support of Left Bn. C & D Coy in support of Rt Bn. Bn works upon 2nd line system under R.E. Supervision. Weather Dry but dull. Health good throughout. The following decorations were awarded as result of our minor operation of the night 28/29 August:—	
			Lieut. E.O. HILL — M.C.	
			No. 28488 Sgt H.M. HOLLIDAY — M.M.	
			No. 37168. Pte C.E. BAYSON — M.M.	
			" 39302 " J. CURRAN — M.M.	
			"A" Coy gallant conduct and skilful handling of his men during successful raid on enemy trenches on morning of 29 August 1917. No fatal casualties being suffered, chiefly from 3" T.M. Enemy retiring to Gouzeaucourt & having on…	
	7th		(Evening) Relieved 2nd V.W.B. of this Bde in R. Subsector and gone into line with strength of A.3.4. OD ranks. Relief on the G about 6.30 p.m.	
	8		Bn received a draft of 88 O.R.	

Army Form C. 2118

WAR DIARY
or
INTELLIGENCE SUMMARY

(Erase heading not required.)

Place	Date	Hour	Summary of Events and Information	Remarks and references to Appendices
	9/4/17		[Handwritten entry - largely illegible. Contains references to: Objectives - (A) to obtain identification (B) to destroy enemy dug-in shelters... Bangalore Torpedoes... about 100 yds N. of CANAL RD. E side, about 100 x 3 ap... R.E. Slings of Ruding force - 6 off + 100 O.R. (including 1 off + 16 O.R. R.E.) Distribution... whole divided into two lots of working parties, Advance Party... of CANAL RD. W. PARA... escorted by R.E. (Lieutenant Ley had Marshall's + C.S.M. Underwood, No 1st section. Lieutenant Reading Party under L.H.Q.T. Morgan assisted by 2nd 3/0 M.G. Mc... Signal Roche of 1st Section... Lieutenant Sinclair with attd. party of complement of... Artillery F.O.O. Barrage. Capt. Miller M.C. of Signal had (Wireless to M.ACHORAL Rd about 50 from enemy line) took 20 O.R. acting as repairer... a crew allotted under command. TElephone communication between O.P.s of Operation & division B.H.Q. & RE section being at 2nd line Regt. Cos. H.Q.)...	
	9-12 (Night)		O tickling and shooting going to enemy lines, hell of our machine guns & trench Mortars...	
	13/14 (Night)		Great operation anticipated eventually N. of RD... 7 P.M. O.J.'s also left our lines proceeded searching to plans. Enemy's much heard of some...	

1875 Wt. W593/826 1,000,000 4/15 J.B.C. & A.   A.D.S.S./Forms/C. 2118.

WAR DIARY or INTELLIGENCE SUMMARY

Army Form C. 2118

(Erase heading not required.)

September 1917

Place	Date	Hour	Summary of Events and Information	Remarks and references to Appendices
	Sept 13/14	Night	...in which at times opened fire but through by means of Verey lights and bangalores etc... observed towards the hill which consisted of a belt of wire unaffected by our continued attack of set fact. 1.40 am the bangalores were fused and successfully reached the gap had. After pounding about 15 yards in our left wire we continued... to the further front line very softly through. Very lights to throw ones on completed. Casualties after suffering counted were through back. (R.E.) wounds d all of which counted were through back. The following message was received from the Bde Commander concerning this one Shipton. "I am directed by the G.O.C Hq Bd Bde to inform you had luck was pushed with the gallantry and perseverance displayed by all ranks who took part in last night's raid." Signed Bde Major. The following decorations awarded in respect of above described... CAPT. P.E. WILLIAMS – M.C. 16319497 Sjt. (A.L.Cpl)(A/M) C.H. UNDERWOOD – M.M. No. 28771 Pte. A.T. SIMMONS – M.M.	
	15th		Men returned to 12 N.W. B. ...Bde lighter deposition and took up line.	
	23rd (evening)		Bn relieved by 1/1 B in R. Lubecker and goes into line 530 all ranks strong.	

WAR DIARY
INTELLIGENCE SUMMARY
(Erase heading not required.)

Army Form C. 2118

Place	Date	Hour	Summary of Events and Information	Remarks and references to Appendices
	Sept 24th to 26th		Weather good. No unusual occurrence. Strong fighting patrols kept out to secure comfort nightly. Kept "No Man's Land" clear of enemy parties. Considerably increased artillery activity on part of enemy due to minor operation of Bthn. on our R. & left.	
	Sept 27/28		A Bangalore Party of 2nd D.R's led by 2nd Lt to [illegible] attempted to blow gap in enemy wire S. of CAMBRAI Rd. Party forced through heavy front trench & tried in vain [illegible] to do so; at same time Lewis M.G. & T.M. were opened upon our party. After repeated efforts to lay bangalore during which bangalore suffered casualties 2.OR. (1 O.R.) killed & 3 O.R. wounded our party was forced to withdraw.	
	29/4 to [illegible]		Losses incurred in Raids if O.R. – O.R. [illegible]	
			During the week the following N.C.Os proceeded to England as candidates for Commissions: [illegible] No.15050 C.S.M. R. Jenkins, No.28560 Sgt. H. Smith, No.50882 C.H. J. Leonard and to followed between later the Snr. Lents. wounded and Bns. patrols back [illegible], all wounded of.	

30 September 1917 [signature] Lt. Col. [illegible] Commanding 10th R.W.F.

Army Form C. 2118

WAR DIARY
or
INTELLIGENCE SUMMARY

(Erase heading not required.)

WAR DIARY

10th (S) Bn. Royal Welch Fusiliers

October 1917

Copy No. 1

WAR DIARY
or
INTELLIGENCE SUMMARY

(Erase heading not required.)

Army Form C. 2118

October 1917.

Place	Date	Hour	Summary of Events and Information	Remarks and references to Appendices
Brigade Reserve.	Oct. 1.		The Battalion was relieved in the front line by the 12th K.R.R.S. and went into Brigade Support.	
	6.		The following officers joined the Batt. for duty, and were posted to Coubands as shown against their names.	
			2/Lieut. N. Williams. H. Coy.	
			" J. S. King. "	
			" H. M. Pulham. B "	
			" G. J. Board. C "	
			" J. Crabtree. D "	
			" V. E. James. "	
	7.		The following officer joined for duty, and was posted to "H" Coy. Capt. J. N. Fletcher.	
HEUDECOURT.	7.8.	Night.	The Battalion was relieved in Brigade Support by the 10th Batt. K.R.R. and proceeded to HEUDECOURT, where it was accommodated in huts.	
DOINGT.	8.		Battalion entrained at HEUDECOURT and proceeded to DOINGT, where it was accommodated in huts.	
	9.		Promulgation of Honours to the 119th Brigade in the GRANDE PLACE, PERONNE, by Lieut. Gen. Sir. W. P. Pulteney. K.C.B., K.C.M.G., D.S.O., commanding the 3rd Corps, where the following officers and O.R. were presented with ribbons of Honours awarded to them.	
			Capt. Pte. Pulham M.C.	
			Lieut. E.O. Hill "	
			21291. Sgt. A.C.S.M. Underwood M.M.	
			29130. Pte. Curran J. "	
			28441. " Simmonds H.G. "	
			Capt. & Adjt. Hill proceeded to England for duty.	

WAR DIARY

INTELLIGENCE SUMMARY

(Erase heading not required.)

October 1917.

Instructions regarding War Diaries and Intelligence Summaries are contained in F. S. Regs., Part II. and the Staff Manual respectively. Title Pages will be prepared in manuscript.

Place	Date	Hour	Summary of Events and Information	Remarks reference Appen
DOINGT.	Oct. 9.		The following officers joined the Battalion for duty, and were posted to Companies as shown against their names. 2/Lieut. D.J. Jones. "B" Coy. " R. Vaughan. "C" "	
SIMENCOURT.	10.		Battalion proceeded to FLAMICOURT-PERONNE Station where it entrained for BEAUMETZ-LES-LOGES, arriving 12 midnight. Marched to SIMENCOURT, and accommodated in huts.	
	12.		Battalion commence training. The following officer joined for duty and was posted to "D" Coy. 2/Lieut. S. Phillips.	
	16.		First match of Brigade football competition, between this Battalion and the 19th Welch Regiment. Result. 19th Batt. 2 goals. 17th Welch Regt. 2 goals. Replay between 17th Welch Regt. & 19th Bn.F. which resulted in a win for this Battalion by 3 goals to 1.	
	17.			
	18.		Second game in Brigade championship, between 19th Bn.F. and 119th M.G.C. Result. 19th Bn.F. 2 goals. 119th M.G.C. nil.	
	20.		Final of Brigade championship between this Battalion and the 116. F.A., which resulted in a win for the latter team by two goals to one.	
	21.		Battalion sports held on training ground Results. "D" Coy. 21½ points (winners) "C" " 21 " "B" " 15½ " "A" " 8½ "	
	22.		Practice attack by Battalion.	

WAR DIARY

INTELLIGENCE SUMMARY

Army Form C. 2118

October 1917

Place	Date	Hour	Summary of Events and Information	Remarks and references to Appendices
SIMENCOURT.	Oct. 23.		Practice attack by Brigade.	
	24.		119 Inf. Brigade inspected by G.O.C. 40th Division. The following officer joined the Battalion and assumed the duties of Second in command. Major H.P. Eyles.	
	25.		Capt. P.E. Hilliard, M.C. resumed command of "A" Coy., and Capt. J.N. Fletcher assumed command of "C" Coy.	
	26.		Practice attack repeated by 119 Brigade. Message received from H.Q. 40th Div. H.Qrs. that the French had advanced to a depth of two miles on a six mile front in the Soisson sector. Over 80 guns and 1000 prisoners captured.	
	27.		Letter from 119 Brigade H.Q. as follows:- "The G.O.C. 119th Inf. Brigade desires all ranks to be informed that the Major-General commanding 40th Division was very satisfied with the "appearance and steadiness of all ranks of the 119th Infantry Brigade "on the 24th October 1917, and noted the manner in which they marched past."	
COUTURELLE.	29.		Battalion proceeded by route march to COUTURELLE, via ARRAS-DOULENS road, arriving at 12 noon. G.O.C. 119th Inf. Brigade expressed himself as very satisfied with the turnout and appearance of the 19th Bn., whilst on the march.	
	30.		Army Act. Sec 44-41, read out to all ranks on Parade. Platoon marching competition, open to one platoon from each company.	

Army Form C. 2118

WAR DIARY
or
INTELLIGENCE SUMMARY
(Erase heading not required.)

October 1914.

Place	Date	Hour	Summary of Events and Information	Remarks and references to Appendices
COUTURELLE.	Oct. 30		Course, 3 miles. Points were awarded for the following:- (a). Time taken to complete course. (b). March discipline. (c). Dress. Points to be deducted for men failing to complete the course with remainder. The prize of 50 fcs. was awarded to No 8 Platoon, B. Company.	
	31.		Cross-country run, open to all subaltern officers, and 40 O.R. per company. First 8 of each company to count. Distance 3 miles. Prizes were awarded as follows:- Team prize (20 Francs) "D" Company. 1st man home (9 fcs.) "C" Coy. 2nd do do (5 fcs.) " " 3rd. do do (3 fcs.) " "	

October 31st 1914.

[signature] Lieut. Col.
Commanding 1st Batt. Royal Welsh Fusiliers.

WAR DIARY
or
INTELLIGENCE SUMMARY.

(Erase heading not required.)

Army Form C. 2118.

Place	Date	Hour	Summary of Events and Information	Remarks and references to Appendices

Instructions regarding War Diaries and Intelligence Summaries are contained in F. S. Regs., Part II. and the Staff Manual respectively. Title pages will be prepared in manuscript.

Army Form C. 2118

WAR DIARY
INTELLIGENCE SUMMARY

November 1917.

(Erase heading not required.)

Place	Date	Hour	Summary of Events and Information	Remarks and references to Appendices
COUTURELLE.	1-15.		Brigade and Battalion training.	
SIMENCOURT.	16.		Battalion moved by route-march to SIMENCOURT, via BAVINCOURT.	
GOMMIECOURT.	17.		Move by route march (night) to GOMMIECOURT where Battalion was accommodated in huts.	
BARASTRE.	19.		Night march to BARASTRE, where the Battalion was accommodated in huts.	
DOIGNIES.	21.		Battalion moved by route-march to DOIGNIES	
ANNEUX.	22.		Move by route march to ANNEUX, where the Battalion relieved the 12th Bn. Yorks and Lancs Bn. in the front line.	
	23.		Battalion took part in attack on BOURLON WOOD. Ref. Sht. NIERGNIES Ed. 1. 20000. The attack. At 10.30 a.m. our own artillery opened intense fire on S. edge of wood, and the 19th R.F. and the 13th S.F. & B. advanced, this battalion being on the right, and entered the wood at 10.45 a.m. A few enemy machine guns opened fire on the advancing infantry but did not check them. When the Batt. was about 100 yards inside the	

WAR DIARY or INTELLIGENCE SUMMARY

November 1917.

Army Form C. 2118

Place	Date	Hour	Summary of Events and Information	Remarks and references to Appendices
BOURLON.	23.		Bosch U. reorganised and moved forward again about 11 a.m. From this line an Bosches were being sent back in batches. The enemy had a series of posts with L.G's, but these were overcome by bounding and getting in with the bayonet, and at 11-40 a.m. the Batt. had reached the line L.3.a.8.7 to L.m.a.6.4. Bosch M.G's were then moved to L.3.a.2.4. Batches of prisoners were still coming in. At 12.20 p.m. the Batt. had reached N. edge of wood. The L.O. then went forward to see how the situation stood. He collected about 60 of the Batt., and placed them in Lewis holes about L.Y.d.3.9. to L.S.c.6.4. These were later reinforced by men of the Batt. and continued the line across E. edge of wood to L.m.a.9.1., a base of the M.G's that captured by Lewis'es sent from there. The enemy was reported running of in couries of parties retreating N.E. the Batt. was keeping touch with the 51st B'n on the right. Several messages sent back from consolidation	

WAR DIARY
or
INTELLIGENCE SUMMARY

Army Form C. 2118

November 1917.

(Erase heading not required.)

Instructions regarding War Diaries and Intelligence Summaries are contained in F.S. Regs., Part II. and the Staff Manual respectively. Title Pages will be prepared in manuscript.

Place	Date	Hour	Summary of Events and Information	Remarks and references to Appendices
BOURLON.	23		a post defensive line. A general stir was going on by the S.O.S. Rockets being sent up & heavy Flank and the 19th BDE returning their sig Stack. The bosh were now seen approaching I.12.a.2.2. — I.7.a.3.6. — I.8.c.9.4. — I.14.central, & every burst being established at I.8 onwards I.7.a.3.4. This line was to be that of the post the 19th Field Regt. coming up & behind the 8th Div with two Companies, one Company in reserve to the 19th BDE on the ridge running from I.8.c.5.7.3.a.8. — I.7.a.3.4. to I.9.t.a.13, the front boundary being in rear at I.13.a.4.6. The Commanding Officer of the Bat. had once Capt N Gordon but not Lieut Pearce at command of the whole line. During the morning two Columns of the 19th L & N.H. came up, & there were seen to stiffen the line at but which had evident heavy from S.O.S. fire. Apt 11-115 from the enemy attempted to break through but	

Add Y L.F. Div.

1875 Wt. W593/826 1,000,000 4/15 J.B.C. & A. A.D.S.S./Forms/C. 2118.

Army Form C. 2118

WAR DIARY
OF
INTELLIGENCE SUMMARY November 1917.
(Erase heading not required.)

Place	Date	Hour	Summary of Events and Information	Remarks and references to Appendices
BOURLON.	23.		was quiet. Situation unchanged and Bourlon during the night.	
	24.		Two companies of the L.N.L. reinforced. At 9 am the situation was & heavy shell fire on the outskirts of BOURLON VILLAGE and there was hostile heavy shell fire along the outskirts N.E. of the wood. The unfortunate object on a line approximately S.18 b.61 to SUNKEN ROAD near 2 pm. the G.O. was reorganised, and the whole of the 19th I.B. thickness of G.H.Q. men taking the section number which are garrisons of parts of the wood. At 6.C. laying the section number which were these the sector became the original and kept up men to etc. the Battn. was again reorganised. One working had observed on the N. edge of the wood, enabling the sector being assembled. The enemy attacked several times driving our men out the line held firmly until about H. Johns, when it was broken. One Coy. was attached and

Army Form C. 2118

WAR DIARY
or
INTELLIGENCE SUMMARY
November 1917

(Erase heading not required.)

Instructions regarding War Diaries and Intelligence Summaries are contained in F.S. Regs., Part II. and the Staff Manual respectively. Title Pages will be prepared in manuscript.

Place	Date	Hour	Summary of Events and Information	Remarks and references to Appendices
BOURLON WOOD.	24.		reached the high ground. The line was held until relieved by a Battalion of the 62nd Guards, and two counter-attacks of the King's Own.	
	25.		During the night our wire had been front line, was moved to attack. At 2hrs an attack was launched. The Guards being on the right of the sunken road running N. & S. though the wood and moved units on the left. Having gained the high ground, the line was consolidated and lowered down on the right of the 25th. The line now was to B.18.b.11 — 2.f. a.34 — along the 20 contour to SUNKEN ROAD about Z.14.a.8.3. The enemy's losses on N.E. of wood during the 23rd & 24th were enormous, so he repeatedly attacked "A" and "C" Companies but could make no headway. This were eventually withdrawn slightly S. eastern to the sunken line. H.Q. advanced during the attack. 12. Prisoners taken — 250 officers & men	

1875   Wt. W593/826   1,000,000   4/15   J.B.C. & A.   A.D.S.S./Forms/C. 2118.

WAR DIARY
or
INTELLIGENCE SUMMARY

November 1914.

(Erase heading not required.)

Army Form C. 2118

Place	Date	Hour	Summary of Events and Information	Remarks and references to Appendices
BOURLON WOOD	25		Casualties of the Battalion, including those absent & who were since ...	
			Killed. Wounded. Pct & missing. Died of Wounds. Prisoners. Total.	
			Officers (none attacked) 4. 1. 1. B.C.	
			O.R. 30. 234. 53. 1. 23. 342.	
	25/26	night	Batt. relieved in BOURLON WOOD by a Bn. of the 62nd Division and bivouac ...	
			6 mg. arr. at Ruyaulcourt at K.6.	
LECHELLE	26		Batt. moved by route march to LECHELLE where it was accommodated in huts.	
BIENVILLERS	27		Batt. entrained at YTRES station for BIHUCOURT thence by route march to BIENVILLERS	
			Special Order of the Day by the 40 & 119th Inf. Brigades as follows:—	
			"The G.O.C. 119th Infantry Brigade wishes to congratulate all ranks of the Brigade on the results of their efforts in action on 23rd & 24th – 25th Novr. 1914"	
			"Hurriedly and under weather displayed our Brigade Bn. behaved all ranks"	
			"at most important point position in BOURLON WOOD and exhibited not only an"	
			"23rd, and held against heavy attacks but actually but continued to Bourlon Wood under, recaptured a wood by 26th Inf. Brigade on the night of 23rd/24th November"	
			"The flanks were fully secure & this absence of ... attacks"	
Note reverse see note.			"the enemy attacked up to the last moment of relief" (contd.)	

1875 Wt. W593/826 1,000,000 4/15 J.B.C. & A. A.D.S.S./Forms/C.2118.

Army Form C. 2118

WAR DIARY
of
INTELLIGENCE SUMMARY
(Erase heading not required.)

November 1917.

Instructions regarding War Diaries and Intelligence Summaries are contained in F. S. Regs., Part II. and the Staff Manual respectively. Title Pages will be prepared in manuscript.

Place	Date	Hour	Summary of Events and Information	Remarks and references to Appendices
BIENVILLERS	27.		"The official duties of maintenance of communications and supply of S.A.A. and rations" "were carried out by all concerned in a very efficient manner despite very heavy shelling," "and replies and such an 19th Bn. Signal Station. Battalion organised such runners, and Brigade & Battalion Runners offices and personnel. "The evacuation & tending of wounded was carried out in a most trying circumstances" "by all concerned in the most self-sacrificing manner." "Over 500 prisoners were taken by the Brigade from 2nd and 3rd Guard Division," "which in view of the strength of the enemy facing the Brigade, and the "inferiority in numbers to the foot position." "That results should not have been achieved can not all more than relieved for" "the common cause – holding the Boche."	
	28.		Battalion clean up.	
	29.		Commence training.	
	30.		Training.	

F. Hunter
Lieut. Col.
Commanding 19th Bn. N.F. Fus.

Army Form C. 2118.

WAR DIARY
or
INTELLIGENCE SUMMARY.

(Erase heading not required.)

Vol 19

War Diary

19th (S.) Bn. Royal Welsh Fusiliers.

Dec. 1917.

Army Form C. 2118.

WAR DIARY
or
INTELLIGENCE SUMMARY.
(Erase heading not required.)

Month: December 1917.

Instructions regarding War Diaries and Intelligence Summaries are contained in F.S. Regs., Part II. and the Staff Manual respectively. Title pages will be prepared in manuscript.

Place	Date	Hour	Summary of Events and Information	Remarks and references to Appendices
BIENVILLERS.	Dec 1.		Battalion proceeded by route march & rail to form to ERVILLERS, & Batt relieved the 1st Batt Yorks & Lancs in front line BULLECOURT sector. Dispositions as follows: 'D' Coy, Right front line, 'C' Coy, Left front line, 'B' Coy in support, 'A' Coy – two platoons in close support & 2 platoons in reserve.	(A)
BULLECOURT.	2-6.		Batt in front line. Work of reorganising line and after recent operations carried on.	(B)
RIGHT SUB-SECTOR.	7/8.		Batt relieved in front line by 12th D.L.I. B. and billeted by route march to DURHAM CAMP where it was accommodated in huts.	(C)
	8-13.		Training. The following officers having joined the Batt for duty were posted to Coys. as shown against their names:	
			Lieut W.B. Shipham B. Coy. Lieut & adj D Bulman D. Coy.	
			" W.B. Hall	
			" C.R.C. Thomas	
			" C.D. Griffith	
			" H Grant	
			" S.T. Collyer D. Coy	
			" K.D. Rush "	
			2 Lieut B.L. Dawbarn	
	14.		Batt relieved the 12 SW.B. in front line.	
	15.		Wire obstacle carried out by Batt. Est. Asst. HENDECOURT SPECIAL SHEET 10 p.m.	(D)
			Objective (a). To clear enemy out of NEPTUNE TRENCH, U.10.d.64 to U.11.9.3, & to obtain prisoners.	
			(b). To destroy dug outs & tunnels.	
			(c). To establish blocks in TRIDENT and VIRGIN TRENCHES, install permanent look out	(E)

WAR DIARY or INTELLIGENCE SUMMARY

Army Form C. 2118.

(Erase heading not required.)

December 1917.

Place	Date	Hour	Summary of Events and Information	Remarks and references to Appendices
RIGHT SUB-SECTOR	15.		Established at the junction of these trenches with NEPTUNE trench. Wires laid down the whole length to the enemy. (A). To connect up the Lieutenant Knox's report to no. (C) to COLLINS TRENCH. The right party consisted of Capt Estill M.C., 2/Lieut. L.P. Mathias and 2/Lt B.P. Lee Daly, Capt Evans, 2/Lieut Horlaux, and 26 O.R. Right party. Distribution. (1) bombing party of 1 O.R., under 2/Lt Crabtree went in not under Lewis lead, accompanied by 2 men working along Bangs V.2 along Bangs. (II) N.C.O + 3 men to deal with enemy dug up about 13'x P3. (III) Bomb. borrowing party of 1 N.C.O + 3 men to follow first bomb party at about 20x distance. (IV) 1 N.C.O+ 3 men to accompany R.E. parties about 20 yd of TRIDENT VLEY. (V) 2 men to accompany R.E. party working to proceed advance to dug out 3. (VI) Sapboming party of 1 N.C.O + 3 men to follow advance party at about 20x distance. 16 men carry along TRIDENT's extension of NEPTUNE UBY to reel + if so 3 to assist with the R.E. lowering party. Left Data. Distribution. 5 more and twe save line. (I) + bombing party under 2/Lt Mullock no. 2. (I) (II) Bomb Carrying party no. 2. (I) (III) 1 N.C.O + 3 men to reconstruct a trench about 20 x up TRIDENT VLEY (X) Bot bombing party no. 2 (I) (XI) do. no. (II). (XII) Right 3rd off laying half extractor after 2 minutes, at other extract on right off off Boring thus out the front of Junction TRIDENT VLEY and NEPTUNE TRENCH. The night party crossed enemy fort, about 3' x 3'm of Junction TRIDENT VLEY and a bombing light across. The Sup was unhindered. They took possession of a MC and being used a bombing lightly formed. The dug out party worked. This body grouping up, and being knocked into a position. English were seen at this point in an area now both handed the munitions dug out and bombing men so seem as they were seen out gathering the enemy to moved on. The R.E. officers with their steam laid wins out up gathering the enemy to	

Army Form C. 2118.

WAR DIARY
OF
INTELLIGENCE SUMMARY. December 1917.
(Erase heading not required.)

Instructions regarding War Diaries and Intelligence Summaries are contained in F. S. Regs., Part II. and the Staff Manual respectively. Title pages will be prepared in manuscript.

Place	Date	Hour	Summary of Events and Information	Remarks and references to Appendices
RIGHT SUB-SECTOR	18.		To come out. Had the Aug. out blown up. A small party of the enemy was afterwards seen and disposed of, our wounded were being taken prisoner. Brought off but 15 others not in Aug. and about 10. The left party encountered little opposition, worked down of the enemy cab. It was killed. The Bodies and Lewis Pistol and NEPTUNE at 3.30 p.m. R.S. destroyed 3 dug-outs. It was a bit that 2 him exploded in mens kit-bags observed by Lieut Lt. About 11.45 p.m. a normal relief was blown out along NEPTUNE TRENCH & a couple of bombs for consolidation of our trenches was carried out. People went under gunfire & it seemed to outwatch enemy. billet 20. Our casualties killed A.Cpl Howard 19 D.C. Wounded of remaining [illegible] with. Pnt. [illegible] to bow. His by P.O.&S. & previous to supply ten. The following L.Cos & men are awarded the Honours shown against their names for gallant conduct in the operations of Dec 23, 24th & 26th.	
	No 19. 20.		31005. Sergt. A. B. Jail M.M. 13182. " J. Hartley " 263444. " A. B. Dobson " 29626. L/Cpl. L.B. Pitt " 445651. Pte. J. E. Lauder " 36700 " H. Warren " 29230 " H. Richardson " 29294 L/Cpl H. Woodward "	

Army Form C. 2118.

WAR DIARY
at
INTELLIGENCE SUMMARY. December 1917.
(Erase heading not required.)

Instructions regarding War Diaries and Intelligence Summaries are contained in F.S. Regs., Part II. and the Staff Manual respectively. Title pages will be prepared in manuscript.

Place	Date	Hour	Summary of Events and Information	Remarks and references to Appendices
RIGHT SUB-SECTOR	20-25.		Batt. in support. Moved into front line.	
	26.		Batt. relieved the 12th H.L.I. in front line. Right Sub-Sector.	
	26-31.		Batt. in front line. Bombardment of our front line continued.	
			The following honours were awarded to officers of this Battalion for gallant conduct during the operations in BOURLON WOOD on Jan. 23, 24 & 25. 1917.	
			Lieut. Col. J.G. Plunkett. L.C. D.S.O.	
			Capt. P. M. Neilcome (died) M.C. Bar to M.C.	
			Capt. J.R. Harvie. M.C.	
			Lieut. A.H. Mgils. M.C.	
			2/Lieut. J.S. Keily. M.C.	
			2/Lieut. C.S. Prekhand. M.C.	
			Honours to N.C.Os and L.Cos as follows:—	
			2/294 Sgt. (A/CSM) E.H. Underwood. D.C.M.	
			28938 Cpl. H.E. Berger. D.C.M.	
			28481 L.Cpl. A.E. Fox. D.C.M.	
			6316 (A/RSM) J. Watson. D.C.M.	
			The following officers joined for duty on dates shown against their names.	
			Lieut. M. Bown. 10.12.17.	
			" J.G. Gough. 8.12.17.	
			2/Lieut. L.R.M Cameron. 11.12.17.	
			" D.A.L. Geige. 15.12.17.	
			Major. L. Scott. 17.12.17. (absorbed second in command)	

J.C. Colquhoun
Lt Col
Commanding 9th Batt. R.S. Fus.

Army Form C. 2118.

WAR DIARY
or
INTELLIGENCE SUMMARY.
(Erase heading not required.)

War Diary
19th R W Fusiliers
January 1918

Army Form C. 2118.

WAR DIARY
or
INTELLIGENCE SUMMARY.
(Erase heading not required.)

Instructions regarding War Diaries and Intelligence Summaries are contained in F. S. Regs., Part II. and the Staff Manual respectively. Title pages will be prepared in manuscript.

January 1918.

Place	Date	Hour	Summary of Events and Information	Remarks and references to Appendices
BULLECOURT SECTOR. Right Sub-Sector Bn. Hd.	1/2		Bn relieved in front line by 12th A.I.B. and proceeded by route march to NORTH CAMP MORY in buses.	
	2nd 3rd		Training	
	4th/5 5/6		Bn in reserve. One Coy each day in front line.	
	6/7/8 9/10		Every night during tour Rifling parties were sent up to cut enemy wire.	
	9/10		Bn relieved up to Right of 46th Bn and to SUPPORT LINE	
	10th/11 13th		Bn in support. Coys finding working parties.	
	13/14		Bn relieved 13th AIB in front line.	
	14–15		Patrols sent out on two two nights	
	16–17		Right sub-sector not having supports all companies being in front line became a battalion sector and the Bns on flanks extended their fronts	

Army Form C. 2118.

WAR DIARY
or
INTELLIGENCE SUMMARY.
(Erase heading not required.)

Instructions regarding War Diaries and Intelligence Summaries are contained in F. S. Regs., Part II. and the Staff Manual respectively. Title pages will be prepared in manuscript.

Place	Date	Hour	Summary of Events and Information	Remarks and references to Appendices
	16.7.		Extracts from O.R.O. No 287. G.O. Commanding the Brigade wishes to express his appreciation of the gallant conduct of parties who were by re-enforced Infantry of 10 gained ground the operations on BOURLON WOOD on 23rd, 24th and 25th Nov. 1917 :- T/Capt O R Roberts T/Capt J. G. Kemp Sgt It & Cpl U 45 milne 17381 Sgt Dunn W Rehuld 20446 Sgt J Price 28366 Sgt 2/Lt Wilson 34963 L/Sgt Bello 45648 Sgt Jones 25649 Cpl Rodgers 29128 Cpl Perry 28310 L/Cpl C Plank 28383 L/Cpl Mahone 246760 Pte L Barclay 29227 " R Bradbury 45648 " J E Hay 201138 " Sh Jones 54377 " W A Morgan 28936 " E Mills 23289 " D Grough 28147 " J Weatherell	

Army Form C. 2118.

WAR DIARY
or
INTELLIGENCE SUMMARY.
(Erase heading not required.)

January 1918

Instructions regarding War Diaries and Intelligence Summaries are contained in F. S. Regs., Part II. and the Staff Manual respectively. Title pages will be prepared in manuscript.

Place	Date	Hour	Summary of Events and Information	Remarks and references to Appendices
RIGHT SUB-SECTOR	17/18		Batt. relieved 4th Bn 12th F.S.B. in front of sub sector	R
	18-21		to NORTH CAMP, RORY.	R
			Training. Turks pushed for work on underground camps	
	21/22		Batt. relieved 1/10 H.H.B. in the left sub-section	R
	22-25		Strong fighting patrols sent out at night.	R
	23/26		Bath. relieved by [illegible] Inf. to SUPPORT LINE	R
	26-29		Batt. in support. Working parties supplied daily to work on	R
	29/30		trenches under R.E. supervision.	R
			Batt. relieved 1/10 H.H.B. in front line	
			Casualties from 1st Jan. to 30th April 1918	
			Lt-Col J.S. Luckett M.C. M. DSc
			Capt. L.A. Morgan K
			Capt. A.M.C. A. Green Lieut. Brown
			23067 Lce. Cpl. A. Jones D.C.M.

Army Form C. 2118.

WAR DIARY
or
INTELLIGENCE SUMMARY.
(Erase heading not required.)

Instructions regarding War Diaries and Intelligence Summaries are contained in F. S. Regs., Part II. and the Staff Manual respectively. Title pages will be prepared in manuscript.

Place	Date	Hour	Summary of Events and Information	Remarks and references to Appendices
			The following officers joined for duty on dates shown against their names:— 2nd Lieut. W.T. Huntley 16-1-18 2nd Lieut. B. Legge 17-1-18	

Army Form C. 2118.

WAR DIARY
or
INTELLIGENCE SUMMARY.
(Erase heading not required.)

War Diary

February 1918

10th Royal Welch Fusiliers

WAR DIARY or INTELLIGENCE SUMMARY.

Army Form C. 2118.

February 1918

Place	Date	Hour	Summary of Events and Information	Remarks and references to Appendices
BULLECOURT LEFT BDE RT SUB-SECTION	1st	-	Batn in front line.	
	2nd/3rd	8 p.m.	Batn relieved by 1st N.W.B. and proceeded by route march to NORTH CAMP MORY where it was accommodated in huts Batn in Gnl Reserve. Handed over to the 119th Infy Bde Troops.	
MORY	6.		Kit sale Inspection. Equipment handed in to DADOS 140 Div. Batn embussed & detraining, 8 officers & 152 OR from D Coy proceeded to join the 2nd Batn R.W.F. in reserve at R.E.C. Provided by motor lorries to BOYELLES where it entrained for BAILLEULVAL. The men were accommodated in horse tram huts & in tents.	
BAILLEULVAL	7th		Men visited bath. Lt Col J.F. Plunkett invalided to hospital for special treatment. Lt Col Ellis assumed	

Army Form C. 2118.

WAR DIARY
or
INTELLIGENCE SUMMARY.
(Erase heading not required.)

February 1918

Place	Date	Hour	Summary of Events and Information	Remarks and references to Appendices
BILLEULVAL	8		Continued with Platoon Training.	
	9-14		Training.	
	15		Batn. endeavoured with 10th R.W.Fus. forming the B.E. Entrenching Batn. orders to concentrate at Frévin Capelle	
			19th (S) Batn R.W.Fus. will Cease to exist as a unit